Schiit Happened

The Story of the World's Most Improbable Start-Up

By Jason Stoddard
Co-Founder, Schiit Audio

Dedications

To Mike, for going along with this crazy idea.

To Rina, for support, naming the company, and tolerating the whole mess.

To Eddie, for helping us really get started when we needed it most.

To Tony, for testing dang near everything we've made.

To Alex, for taking over, making things right, and running the show.

To Dave, for doing the hardest stuff.

Table of Contents

Foreword: Christmas Presents Until the End of Time? vii

CHAPTER 1: The Line is Down. Here's an Undocumented Test Rig. Fix It.... 1

CHAPTER 2: Fifteen Years On the Marketing Front Lines 11

CHAPTER 3: From Death, Rebirth: Armageddon 2009.................................23

CHAPTER 4: "You Always Say You Have Schiit to Do, Why Don't You Just
Call It That?" 29

CHAPTER 5: 800 In Screws?...38

CHAPTER 6: The First Order Is…For Something We're Not Selling 48

CHAPTER 7: Metal Debacle, Valhalla Style 55

CHAPTER 8: We Screw Up Sennheiser and Insult Some Big Guys.................60

CHAPTER 9: Powering Up: Lyr..69

CHAPTER 10: Our First Employee, Our First Board House 75

CHAPTER 11: USB Sucks! Or, Mike Joins the 21st Century............................84

CHAPTER 12: Schiit Goes Evil?...97

CHAPTER 13: "Isn't the Symbol for USB the Long Flat Rectangle?" 106

CHAPTER 14: Technical Help Via Time Warner, and The World's Most
Irritating Failure Mode 116

CHAPTER 15: DAC in a Toilet Paper Roll..125

CHAPTER 16: Growth, Garage Style..132

CHAPTER 17: Resurrecting the Circlotron and Other Mid-Centuryisms.....138

CHAPTER 18: The Pinch-Off Problem 153

CHAPTER 19: Every Road is a Dead End: Early Adventures with Magni ...164

CHAPTER 20: The HOA Problem..172

CHAPTER 21: You Catch a Cold, We Die: Bigger Products, Bigger Problems .182

CHAPTER 22: Introducing the Schiithole 192

CHAPTER 23: "I Didn't Know People In the Private Sector Were As Lazy and
Incompetent As the People In Schools".....................................201

CHAPTER 24: Getting Our Schiit Together 210

CHAPTER 25: Dead Media Ain't Dead: NYT Strikes 220

CHAPTER 26: Finally, the $99 Solution 232

CHAPTER 27: Twilight of the Gods—the Ragnarok Saga from 2009 Until Today 240

CHAPTER 28: "You'll Never Do Any Upgrades Anyway." 256

CHAPTER 29: Worst. Customer. Ever. 266

CHAPTER 30: Death of a Product 280

CHAPTER 31: R&D Sometimes Means, "Try It, See If It Works" 288

CHAPTER 32: Name Me One Non-Standard Format That's Succeeded, Ever, Or, A Trickster Cometh 296

CHAPTER 33: No Sample Left Unchanged: Digital Today 305

CHAPTER 34: Black Friday 315

CHAPTER 35: You Want to Pay How Much? Or, How We Moved Again .. 322

CHAPTER 36: A Real Company? 332

Bonus: Mike's Yggy Backstory 341

Coda: One Year Later 363

Foreword

Christmas Presents Until the End of Time?

"SO, DO YOU THINK IT'LL go? Do you think they'll sell?" Mike Moffat asked, looking at the first assembled Asgard on the engineering bench in my garage. He was being Mike-fidgety, rocking from heel to heel in the small, chilly space.

"Well, on paper it looks good," I told him. "But you know how that works. They'll either sell, or we'll have Christmas presents until the end of time."

Mike laughed, a little nervously. Because he knew how these things go. You can plan and plot, do endless market research and cost studies, run focus groups and get tons of input from key prospects, and do all the little things that companies do to procrastinate and dither and second-guess before releasing their next product…and things can still go sideways.

But this isn't a story about stuff like that. This is a story about gut feelings, good guesses, and not following the herd. And succeeding.

This is the story of Schiit Audio, the world's most improbable start-up.

Yes. Schiit. Let's start with that as an improbability factor. What company in its right mind would name itself that? I mean, if you were a marketing agency and proposed that name to a client, how would they react? You'd be picking your butt up off the pavement outside their headquarters, post-haste.

But that isn't all that made us a crap candidate for succeeding. Consider:

- We started this with no outside funds, no venture capital, no crowdfunding

- We'd both been out of audio for about fifteen-plus years—more on that later

- We went with direct sales, even though that had only really worked for one other company—Emotiva

- We started with no staff, in my garage

- We decided to make everything in the USA, even though the prevailing wisdom of the time was "China's the world's manufacturing floor, why even try to compete?"

- And, in a complete burst of insanity, we decided to start with inexpensive products

Ah, and it's now probably past time I introduce myself. I'm Jason Stoddard, Co-Founder of Schiit Audio. Mike Moffat's my business partner. Our official titles are "Head" and "Number 2" respectively. Hey, Mike asked for it. No, we don't take ourselves too seriously here.

I won't bore you with our full CVs (that's fancy-speak for wut we dun), but you may have heard of Mike Moffat. He was the founder of Theta (the first one, the analog one), in the late 1970s. You can blame him, at least in part, for resurrecting tube audio. He was the first person to use 6DJ8s in audio. He installed Philip K. Dick's stereo systems. He sold amps to L. Ron Hubbard (no, you can't make this schiit up). Then, in the 1980s, he became the Father of the DAC with Theta Digital. His DSPre was the first standalone DAC on the market, and it was a showstopper—its own digital filter algorithms running on Motorola DSPs so powerful they couldn't be exported into the Soviet Union, for a start. Theta mopped up in the DAC world for several years, then Mike founded Angstrom, the maker of the world's first upgradable surround processor. From there, Mike moved into entertainment, creating complex systems for digital movie distribution. At least until I tempted him away with Schiit.

I'm...well, I'm confused. I'm a published, award-winning science fiction author (strangeandhappy.com), a summa cum laude BS Engineering analog geek (schiit.com) and twenty-year veteran of the marketing wars at another company I founded (centric.com). I've done stuff as strange as lecture Harvard professors on virtual world marketing, and as driven as earning my way to Vice-President, Engineering at Sumo at age twenty-five, which nominally made me Ed Miller's boss—he was the founder of Soundcraftsmen, Sherwood and Great American Sound, and head of engineering for SAE, to drop some names. Not that Ed cared, he just did his own thing. He was cool.

I'm the one writing this book. You can blame it all on me. I have no illusions of this being a best-seller, or of it changing the world. But I think we have an interesting story—one that others can learn from, both in and out of audio.

"Oh yeah?" you ask, leaning back and crossing your arms. "Well, I ain't gonna read no hunnert thousand words about some small-time company just to get few phrases that belong on Suckses-sories posters."

Cool. Gotcha. So I'll cut to the chase. If you're only interested in business intelligence, you won't have to read any further than the next seven bullet points:

1. Shooting to be the next billion-dollar mass-market company is insane—you might as well buy lottery tickets.

2. Niche is where it's at—specifically a niche where people can get in fistfights over the color of a knob.

3. Pick a niche you know and love, and do something nobody else can do—"me-too" never works.

4. Be memorable—this isn't about getting *everyone* to *like* you, this is about getting *some* people to *love* you.

5. Go direct—distribution is a poisonous remnant of 19th-century economics in a disintermediated world.

6. Run from both conventional marketing wisdom and the social media mavens—both of them are geared towards the

mass market with eight-digit ad budgets and multiple decades to build a brand.

7. Don't think this'll be easy—this is hard work, but you'll also be having a whole lot of fun if you're doing it right!

Okay, now you're skeptical. You're thinking: *But I just read a book from (insert the name of some multibillion-dollar-valuation corporate CEO here), and he said it's easy to reach the masses and change the world, and it seems like anyone can do it, why would I shoot for less than that?*

That's cool. That is, if you're lucky enough to come up with something different enough to merit venture funding, if you get through all the rounds with the team and product intact, if something better doesn't come out of nowhere, if the public whims don't change, if you don't get ousted before the real money starts, if you're cool with hundred-hour weeks and lots of travel and losing touch with the real fun of creation and becoming a new salesman with his dog-and-pony show for the money guys in Silly Valley or Singapore or wherever the money is in this moment, more power to you. Go ahead and create the next Amazon, Apple, Facebook, or Google. This book isn't for you.

But I have a lot of friends who have gone down that route. Brilliant people. Hard workers. They don't have any problem with all of the above. They go even further, begging and scraping to keep the team stapled together when the money gets thin, mortgaging everything they have on the One Big Idea…

…and doing it again when the first one doesn't get past angel funding.

…and doing it again when the second one doesn't get its second round.

…and doing it again and again and again, as many times as it takes.

Bottom line, there are plenty of billion-dollar ideas out there. Making one into a real company that succeeds isn't just a lot of work. It's about money, luck, connections, money, luck, money, and luck. And more luck.

This story is for people who don't have a lot of the above. For people who are shooting to create a company that might do a million a year, or ten million, or maybe a hundred million, eventually, way out in the future. You know, the old-school Amurrican "build it from the ground up" thing.

So, if you'd like to know how start-ups really work when you haven't won the multimillion-dollar VC lottery, read on.

Oh, and about those Asgard Christmas presents?

To date, we haven't had to give a single one away. In fact, staying in stock through the holidays is one of the hardest things to do around here. Yes. Even forty-two months later.

And with that, let's flash back twenty-plus years…

CHAPTER 1

The Line is Down. Here's an Undocumented Test Rig. Fix It.

MY FIRST DAY AT SUMO in 1989 was maybe the most bizarre first-day-on-the-job ever.

I literally just walked in the door to find Ed Miller pacing the hallway, eyes darting from left to right. He'd clearly been waiting for me to show up.

"Oh good, you're here," he said, motioning for me to follow him.

I trailed him past a series of nondescript offices, out onto the factory floor, and into a cluttered, messy little room with a giant glass window that looked out onto the pc board (PCB) assembly line.

"We have a problem," Ed said. "I hope you can fix it. I took a look, but I don't have the notebooks. But if you can't fix it, maybe you can whip something up."

I wasn't really listening to Ed. I was staring at the battered blue-and-white engineering workbench. Or trying to. Because the entire top surface of the workbench was littered with about fifty pounds of discarded resistors, capacitors, output transistors, screws, wires, solder blobs, candy wrappers, scrawled Post-its, and other unidentifiable electronic and nonelectronic trash. And this was what was on top of a hunk of low-nap industrial carpet. Below it was about another inch of the same kind of junk. Below that, there was another piece of carpet, considerably more frayed, and another inch or two of junk.

Yes, this was what the previous engineer did. Instead of cleaning up, he just threw another rug over it and piled more junk on top.

"So, want to have a look?" Ed said, gesturing at a battered aluminum Bud box in the middle of the carpet-desk. It had ten red LEDs on it, a socket for a power transistor, and a pushbutton.

"What is this?" I asked, trying to come back to reality.

"It's a MOSFET matcher. But it's not working. And the line is down," Ed said, looking pointedly out the window at the PCB assembly team. Outside, ten women looked back at me, arms crossed, clearly waiting for something. "They can't get back to work until the MOSFET matcher is fixed."

Ah, crap. It finally sank in. They were waiting for this test rig. Everything was at a dead stop without it.

And the job of fixing it had just been dumped on me.

I said nothing, suddenly realizing just how much I was in over my head. I was seven months out of college. I didn't even know MOSFETs needed matching. I didn't know what they matched. And I certainly didn't expect to see some homebuilt device at my great new engineering job. Hell, I'd just come out of working on spread-spectrum communications at Magnavox APS's "black hole" lab, where $100K gate array prototypes were all over the place.

"Do you have a schematic?" I asked, feeling a little ill.

"No. That's the problem."

Great. Just great.

At that moment, I thought about asking for my old job at Magnavox back. They told me I had an open door any time. And it was easy. Real easy. Hell, they got pissed when I worked too fast, because they couldn't bill out their entire project to the government. They'd never throw me into something like this. Hell, they'd given me two weeks just to play with the layout software when I started at Magnavox.

Maybe I didn't want to be in audio after all.

But no. I wanted to be in audio. I loved audio. I had a speaker company on the side, one I'd started in college. My senior project in engineering had been a switched-capacitor adaptive noise reduction system. I had years in audio. I always dreamed about going into audio. I'd almost fallen off the chair when I'd seen the Help Wanted ad in the paper, and its enticing offer to "join the Sumo engineering team, and advance the future of audio." I'd been beside myself when I was asked to come in and interview.

And that was when I made the decision to stay. I couldn't let it all go now. *I'd figure it out. Somehow.*

"I'll take a look," I told Ed.

And then I sat there, crapping my pants. The women were still staring at me. Nobody was working. Everything was in my hands.

No pressure, no pressure at all.

Business lesson 1: Say you can do it. Then deliver—at all costs.

I can make up a story about how I brilliantly fixed the tester, but I really just got lucky. The problem was just a bad connection. I reattached it, and it worked. I was a hero.

But I still knew absolutely nothing about what I'd gotten into. Looking at the schematics of the Sumo products was like looking at an Olde English codex—massively confusing and completely incomprehensible. Why did they use so many parts? What did they all do?

Don't laugh. I was a green engineer. Very green. Sumo was only the second "real" job I'd had since graduating. And it was leagues away from the regimented, spotless, cutting-edge environment of Magnavox APS, where I'd mainly done software and PCB layout. It was messy, old-school, a union shop, and part of a larger company that owned it, at least when I started there.

I didn't believe companies like Sumo existed in the brave new world of nearly-1990. When I interviewed, Ed showed me their layout room, where they taped up all the PC board artwork, and their blueprint machine, where they ran copies of hand-drawn schematics. Those things had been done with software and pen plotters at Magnavox.

"You don't actually use those things, do you?" I asked him, looking around for the CAD workstations. But there were none in sight.

Ed just laughed, a little nervously, and shooed me off to the rest of the interview. At the time, I thought his titter meant, "Of course not." But it turned out it meant, "How else would we do it?"

And yes, the first boards I did for Sumo were taped up. It was what had to be done. And I learned a lot from doing it. In six months, I understood what made a good amplifier (or so I thought) and was designing new Sumo products as Chief Engineer. In two years, I was Vice-President, Engineering. And by the time I left, I'd gotten us into new markets with new products, and made the company much, much more efficient in terms of production and parts commonality.

But it wasn't all rosy.

This second anecdote should be a poster for *What Not To Do, Ever*, at any company.

The Mystery of the Immolating Amplifiers

My second job at Sumo after the MOSFET tester heroics was debugging their shiny new Andromeda II amplifier. It was selling briskly, because it was one of the few amps that could drive the insane load of the Infinity Kappa 9, a popular speaker at the time. The problem was, Andromeda IIs were also coming back, blown up, in scary numbers.

I dove in, went back to the books, and quickly noticed a big problem with the amp: the P-channel MOSFETS were only rated for 75% of the current as the N-channel MOSFETS. Combined with a slow breaker-based protection system, that could end with blown-up parts in a hurry.

I found an alternate part and dropped them in the amp. But the revised amps still smoked. And by smoked, I mean parts would literally catch on fire, and flames would come out of the vent holes. What's more, it did it after the protection system did its job and blew a breaker!

Digging deeper, I found that the new power supply didn't completely shut down when the breakers opened. Which meant the front end, and the drivers, could completely drive themselves to death (fire) when the breakers blew. I rigged up a circuit to shut it down, and voila—the revised Andromeda II behaved as it should.

Then I did what any idealistic young engineer would do—I told everyone in the management meeting that we had to stop shipping Andromeda 2s immediately, revise the boards for the new outputs and the more advanced protection system, and then ship new, perfect, safe amplifiers.

So what did they say? Come on, you know what's coming, don't you?

They said, "Are you crazy? We have to make numbers this month. Ship them anyway."

And what did they do? They shipped them, of course. Lots and lots of them. I think about 70% of them eventually came back, and contributed to an extreme service load that never went away in my five-year tenure.

Business lesson 2: Don't ship stuff that blows up. Ever.

Yeah, I know, it sounds like common sense. But it's amazing how common sense can go by the wayside in companies that live and die by receivables financing. When you hear "we have to make numbers for the end of the month," be scared. Very scared.

Sumo was, by and large, the company that taught me what *not* to do.

Exhibits of What Not To Do:

1. **The example above—shipping stuff that you know will break.** Come on, this isn't rocket science.

2. **Don't ever tell anyone, "I don't care that you say it can't be done at that price.** I'm VP of Marketing, I make four times what you do, and I've already sold a bunch to our dealers. That's the price, make it work."

3. **Re the above: never sell anything you haven't made yet.**
   Period. Ever. Nor tell someone about stuff that's coming up,
   or show products that aren't yet products. If they aren't on
   shelves ready to ship, they don't exist. (It took us a while to
   remember this one when we started Schiit—oops.)

4. **Don't lose customer returns. Or use them to fix other
   customer returns.** Yes, I know, more common-sense stuff.

5. **Don't try to go too broad.** In Sumo's case, this meant getting
   into speakers. The Sumo Aria was an amazing planar
   speaker. Also, it was an amazing pain, because most of them
   broke, and they were made on a contracting basis for us by
   an outside company.

6. **Don't be cheap,** especially to the point of having the checks
   be late. Especially paychecks.

But Sumo had one thing going for it. Its heart was in the right
place. We were trying to make inexpensive components that could
compete with the "best of the best." We didn't do insanely over-
wrought chassis for megabuck amps. And this taught me to be
efficient, and work with what we had. It's one of the reasons we're
good at production engineering now.

**Business lesson 3: Don't dwell on the negatives—learn from
them.**

And Sumo was where I was converted from a hardcore objectivist to subjective-objectivism.

"Ah hell," some of you are saying now. "I don't want to hear
this hoo-ha about how all amps sound different. Properly engi-
neered amps run within their limits all sound the same; anything
else is placebo / misdirection / insanity!"

Amen, brother. Or that's what I would have said in 1989. By 1990,
I wasn't so sure.

When I started at Sumo, I already had better amps than they
made. Amps rated at almost twice the power, packed with shiny

new technology and lots of marketing copy to describe it. They were small, they ran cool, and they were clearly light-years ahead of Sumo's porky Andromeda II.

Eventually, I gave in and took an Andromeda II home to try, clearly expecting to have the more powerful amps wipe the floor with it.

Until I turned it on. *Holy crap.* Not only did Sumo's "underpowered" amp wipe the ground with the Carvers in terms of higher output, it also sounded better. Way better. Everyone noticed it—audiophile and non-audiophile alike.

And that's what started me down the road to subjective-objectivism. Not pure subjectivism, of course—measurements are still very important. But it led me to dig into the reasons why the Sumo amp sounded different than the Carvers. It started with simple things, like current capability and rated power.

It continued into gain stage structure and out of band performance, and led to me dramatically changing Sumo's amplifiers—to the point of doing a zero-feedback, single-gain-stage preamp shortly before I left (Artemis—very, very rare) and several no-overall-feedback amplifiers (The Ten, The Five, Andromeda III) that measured as well as the full-loop-feedback amps that preceded them, but sounded much better.

And yeah, yeah, I know: *You're crazy. All amps sound the same!*

Business lesson 4: Don't discount personal experience.

There are a thousand other stories about Sumo, but let's cut to the part where I met Mike Moffat of Theta Digital.

At the time, Sumo just happened to be in the same business park as Theta. I knew the company, of course. They were really tearing it up in the DAC market.

But I didn't go out of my way to meet Mike Moffat, Theta's head. It was too intimidating. Plus, they made expensive stuff, and we made cheap stuff. Plus, he'd probably be a golf-playing blowhard who was too full of himself.

But Sumo and Theta shared a components sales rep, and she kept insisting I meet with them for drinks. After a while, I relented.

And I forgot all my rationalizations for avoiding the meeting. Mike was, and is, a character. Instead of being uptight and high-and-mighty, he was very casual and approachable. Hell, after he got to know us at Sumo, he'd sneak out of Theta to come over to use our bathrooms to change into a suit when he was going to the opera. He didn't want his employees to see him in a suit, but the LA Opera was the only place he could hear unamplified music.

At Theta, I found the company I wanted Sumo to be.

Mike's Theta ran on incentives. Employees were paid bonuses based on the number of units shipped, and on their individual performance, and on stepping up to do tedious things, like upgrades. Some of his techs made several times their salary in bonuses. The office was casual to the point of not even having part numbers for their parts—instead of a 05-1225, a 1K 1/2W 5% resistor was called a 1K 1/2W 5% resistor.

Yes, I know, not very exciting. But consider the results: in half the space of Sumo, Theta was selling ten times the dollar volume of products. Their net profit was easily eight times that of Sumo.

I told the president of Sumo this. His response: "That's stupid, paying people bonuses. Then you have variable salary cost; you can't predict it."

I wanted to say, "Well, it seems a whole lot more stupid to run an inefficient business like this," but for once, I said nothing.

It was becoming very clear that nothing I could do would change the way the company ran.

Business lesson 5: Be open to meeting new people, and trans-formative ideas.

And that's why I started moonlighting for Theta. Mike Moffat was really intrigued by the idea of doing an inexpensive DAC. After more dinners and more drinks, we finally hatched the idea of Cobalt. The Cobalt 307 was my design, with input from Theta—a true hybrid of Sumo's ideas and Theta's ideas.

Cobalt blew up the DAC market, selling 1000 per month for some time—which happened to be about 2.5 times the total market size according to one industry pundit. The combination of solid name and inexpensive price really set the high-end world on fire.

And—I think it's important to note here—"inexpensive" would seem pretty pricey today. The Cobalt 307 was $599. In 1993. That's about $970 today. If we'd been able to sell Cobalt direct to the customer, like we do Schiit, it would have been $349.

Yes, that's how much the dealer takes. More on that later.

But in 1993, selling direct wasn't feasible. We would have had to take out full-page ads in all the magazines to the tune of $20,000 or so a month, and we would have had to have multiple employees in a full-time call center to take orders. There was no Amazon Marketplace. No Shopify. No pay-per-click advertising. Hell, there was no viable Internet. It was a different world.

At Theta, I also designed the discrete, current-feedback output stage of the top-end Theta Gen V, mainly on a bet. Mike and Dave—Mike's lead engineer at the time—were convinced that op-amps were the way to go, but I'd learned enough about discrete design to know they were wrong.

"I can design a stage that will work better than any op-amp," I told them.

"Even on measurements?" Dave asked.

"Even on measurements."

They took the bet, and I came up with a design that was an exercise in insanity. Two hundred sixty parts on a 4" x 6" Teflon circuit board, with two PCM63 DACs in balanced configuration.

But it beat the op-amp stage, both in measurements and in the listening room. And that's how the Theta Gen 5 was the first discrete output DAC that Theta made.

Business lesson 6: Take a chance, do crazy things...a lot of times it's worth it.

Even as Theta was kicking ass, audio was getting, well, weird. Theta stuff cost a lot to make, so it was priced very high. And customers had the dealer margin to pay, of course.

But Theta's products weren't priced high because they were lookers. It was all about the technology inside.

Theta's competitors took a different tact: make it pretty and even more expensive. Theta's balanced Gen V was $5,500. Mark Levinson "outdid" Theta with a $16,000 DAC. Krell upped the ante with $32,000 amplifiers. The magazines ate it up. The race towards "gold-plated Bentley" audiophilia was on.

Mike and I didn't get it. He didn't want to put a $250 board in a $2500 chassis. He wanted to make game-changing stuff. But it seemed the magazines were only interested in the megadollar price tags. Eventually, that led Mike to start Angstrom and get into the field of surround sound.

Me? I went evil. I went into marketing...

CHAPTER 2

Fifteen Years On the Marketing Front Lines

"MARKETING?" I KNOW SOME OF you are asking. "What does that have to do with engineering?"

Well, not much. But, like I said, I'm confused. In addition to an engineering major, I also took enough English classes to be an English minor—and my GPA in English was higher than for my summa cum laude engineering degree. Yay for foreshadowing.

Also, back in the Sumo days, when I did the first brochure for our speaker company, Odeon—which is an odyssey in itself, from getting kicked out of Vasquez Rocks for the photo shoot (we didn't know about things like "permits" and "insurance" back then) to the Cretaceous-era desktop publishing software—the first dealer said, "Well, if you can't make it in speakers, you definitely have a future in advertising."

At the time, I brushed off the comment. I wanted to make audio stuffs, not brochures!

But I kept coming back to marketing. At Sumo, when the VP exited, I ended up doing the copy, layout, photo art direction, etc. for their brochures and print ads. Theta counted on me to do the brochure for the Cobalt 307 and newsletters.

Fun Fact: the Cobalt 307 had blue LEDs for one reason only: to thumb our nose at Krell. Until the Cobalt 307, blue LEDS were astoundingly expensive (about $10) but we were able to get some of the first inexpensive ones around (less than $1.)

So this is the tale of Centric (centric.com), a company I am still involved with. Centric is a company that does marketing for tech companies, food companies, and many other kinds of organizations, including some high-end audio firms. Centric just passed its twentieth anniversary in 2014.

But First, Let's Talk About the Marketing Industry

If you're expecting this to read like the boozy exploits you see on *Mad Men*, prepare to be disappointed. The top-tier, multibillion-dollar ad agencies are working with clients who are the corporate equivalent of the Rockefellers, Rothschilds, and the Sultan of Brunei—companies with so much money they could buy your town as a joke.

We didn't work in that rarefied realm. Consider this: the cost of an average thirty-second Super Bowl ad is $10 million. This counts $4 million for the airtime, and $6 million for production, logistics, pre- and post-distribution, social media, online media, etc., etc.

Consider just two facts:

- $10 million is six to ten times higher than a typical annual marketing budget for an $50-100 million tech company—and this includes marketing salaries
- $10 million is larger than the annual revenue of all but a handful (literal handful) of audio companies

So yes. Rothschilds. Rockefellers. Sultans. That's what we're talking, when we're talking Super Bowl ads. And big advertising in general.

Did you know that Toyota spends $100-150 million in advertising to launch a new car? Did you know that a single brand at P&G, such as Tide, can have a $50-100 million annual advertising budget?

Aside: When your agency starts trotting out "branding examples" from names like this and suggests you emulate them, you run. Fast. They have nothing to do with the reality of a by-the-bootstraps company.

But I'm getting ahead of myself. Let's disambiguate this whole "marketing biz" thing a bit. I'm sure some of you are sitting there, wondering:

- What the heck is the difference between marketing agencies, advertising agencies, PR, social media, etc.?
- Why the heck companies think they need marketing— shouldn't the best product win?

Okay, so let's break it down:

- **Advertising Agency.** Primarily develops and places advertising. Many agencies identify themselves as a "creative agency" (thems the dudes who drink a lot) or "media agency" (thems the guys who buy the ads and make a profit on them), or both. But today, it's more complicated. Are they primarily broadcast? Primarily online? Both? Do they do print? Outdoor? In-store? Native? Social? Ad agencies can do all of that.
- **Interactive Agency.** An ad agency, but subtract the print, broadcast, and outdoor, and add web and mobile development. Most smaller agencies these days are by default "interactive agencies," because that's where most of the action is.
- **Social Agency.** An ad agency, but one that annoys your friends where they hang out online, like a crazed cybernetic door-to-door salesman.
- **Design Agency.** An ad agency, but subtract the focus on persuasion and turn up the emphasis on great art and visual communication.
- **PR Agency.** In the past, this was your conduit to the press. They knew the editors and could help you get placements. Today, that's evolving rapidly as conventional media (like magazines, newspapers, etc.) crumble and online media / blogging / social rises.

- **Marketing Agency.** Like all the agencies above, with different strengths in different areas. Usually focused on one or more niches. May drink less. May drink more. Centric is a marketing agency.

"Well, hell," you're saying. "Do I need all those agencies to succeed?"

No. You may not need a single one of them. I'll get to that. But for the moment, let's cut back to the birth of Centric, and why marketing?

The Centric Rationale

My rationale for starting a marketing company was something like this:

1. Hey, I did this for Sumo and Theta and my own company, so I have some experience.
2. It's not a manufacturing company, where you have inventory, overhead, labor, distribution, etc.—it's a lot easier to get started.
3. The products usually don't ever catch anything on fire.

In retrospect, not the best reasoning. But hey, I was twenty-eight. Leaving a VP of Engineering job to start a business in a field I knew nothing about seemed perfectly sensible at the time. So, as audio went into exponential price expansion, I jumped ship and started Centric in January of 1994.

Now, if you're a L.A. resident, you might be thinking, "Hmm, wait, isn't that when the 1994 Northridge earthquake hit?"

Right. I started the company exactly one week before the earthquake, and I was living about ten miles away from Northridge when it hit. I was renting a house on a hill above the San Fernando Valley, and I clearly remember waking up in the early morning, sitting up in bed to look out the window at the valley, and watching them shut down the whole starry mess of it, grid by grid, as shelves toppled inside the house and the fires began outside.

And I remember thinking, *Holy crap, if this just hit downtown L.A., kiss this business goodbye. Because there ain't no downtown no more.*

In earthquakes, what matters is how far away you are from the epicenter. If the epicenter was Sylmar, where I was living, okay, that's bad, but not the end of the world. If the epicenter was downtown, and it was strong enough to knock over nearly everything in a house forty miles away, that was, like, The Big One. End story. Full stop.

And again, remember—no Internet. And I didn't have TV. Didn't believe in it. I was into audio, remember? So I had no idea where the epicenter was. I sprinted over the crap on the floor and went out to the car to listen to the radio. And the first thing they said: *L.A. It was in L.A.*

Yep. Done. Pack it up.

And that's what I did. I got in the car and went up to Valencia to see if some friends were all right. It was like driving in a zombie apocalyptic horror movie, with trailer parks burning on one side, toppled phone poles and smoldering transformers, and nobody, nobody on the road.

Later, we found out the epicenter was Northridge, and that L.A. itself was still intact. While tragic for Northridge, it turned out not to be the end of the world. Hell, two days after the quake, I was driving to see a new prospect for Centric in Rancho Cucamonga.

And, over the next few years, we added companies like Threshold, Infinity, 3D Systems, Pioneer, Veeco, Compaq Capital, HP, and a whole bunch of other tech, industrial, and consumer electronics companies to the list.

And for a while, everything was glorious. We rode the wave of the first Internet boom, doing some of the earliest web development work, earliest e-commerce, earliest web marketing…all built on the basis of personal incentives, like I'd seen at Theta.

And marketing was fun. I got to see all sorts of crazy new cutting-edge technology, and the clients loved me because I could talk to the engineers and scientists and not be dismissed as "the agency freak."

I even had a hell of a science fiction moment at one client, when they were showing off their new Pico-Force measuring system based on atomic force microscopy, where they could actually unfold individual protein strands and manipulate them at the molecular level.

"That's like the nanomanipulators in Neal Stephenson's *The Diamond Age*," I said.

At that point, two of the scientists turned around to look at me, eyes open and jaws slack in shock.

"You read that too?" one of them asked.

"Where did you think we got the idea?" the other said.

And we also got to do a lot of cool, cutting-edge stuff in marketing. In addition to some of the earliest web development and online marketing, we were able to do some of the earliest social work for Warner Brothers, and built HP's presence in the virtual world of Second Life, as well as "the largest virtual experience ever" in the words of *MIT Tech Review*, on the David Rumsey Maps project. We've constantly experimented with what's new in marketing.

And…paradoxically, that's why we're more conservative today. We haven't seen the results from social marketing, unless it's for an entertainment company.

Condensed Marketing Stuff Follows

"So what does this mean to someone who wants to start their own company?" you ask. "Or to someone who's just on the outside, thinking about it?"

Well, to summarize what we learned in the past two decades, and give you the "key takeaways" (sorry, lapsed into corp-speak there):

1. **Most companies are too terrified to be effective at marketing.**
   Show them something amazing, something catchy,
   something incredibly effective, and the first reaction (at
   most clients) is, "Wow, this is wonderful, let's do it!" Then,

two days later, an email appears. It usually goes like this: "Our CEO / lawyers / accountant / design intern / marketing director's daughter / fish / dog looked at it, and we're concerned that it may be too 'out there...'" Yep. Done. *Key takeaway: Don't be scared to stand out.*

2. **This terror can affect everything they do, so they may not be effective at *anything*.** The second-guessing of great ideas doesn't stop at marketing. It usually extends all across the organization, to product development and customer service. That's why you get so many me-too products and crap customer service. "But our competition is doing it," whines the product manager. "But the competition doesn't provide any better support," says the director of customer service. *Key takeaway: A race to the bottom helps nobody. Don't benchmark yourself into mediocrity.*

3. **Most companies have no idea what to do in marketing.** "Let's do social, I heard it's cheap and easy," or, "I'm tired of the website, let's change it," or, "Well, all of our competitors are going to that show, so we need to be there," or, "I know the magazines are getting less and less effective every year, but I think we need to be in the books," is the rule of the day. *Key takeaway: Marketing should be a portfolio strategy, with the most money going to the most effective and measurable tactics, with detailed analytics on what is working and what isn't, with a small percentage reserved for experimentation on "new" or "interesting" ideas. If marketing doesn't make money, it shouldn't be done. Period.*

Why this fear is important:

1. **Fear is the mind-killer.** Fear is the little death...no, wait, that's from *Dune*. But it's true. Second-guessing your first reaction to something you love usually doesn't result in great things. *Trust your gut. If the marketing creative work stops you, it works. Do it.*

2. **Kill the fear before it spreads.** If you start a company and instantly start worrying about if your product has every little feature that your competitors do, you might as well name it the RX-4001i-RevA and hope that someone mistakes you for Epson, or some other company that's been around since the earth cooled and can get away with crap like that. *Apple's products never have the best specs, most features, etc.— and yet, even now, they're the highest-value company in the world.*

3. **Marketing is important, but don't do it blindly.** Today, you can measure any aspect of anything you do online, down to which ad drove which specific sales of which product. Get the reports. Sit down with the agency and torture them until they bring out the one dude who really understands them, and have him explain it to you. *Do more of the stuff that works, and less of the stuff that doesn't.*

   a. **Corollary 1: Don't believe nearly everything an agency tells you.** They're going to trot out these ancient case studies about how P&G and Toyota do it, and imply that those are the right models for you. One hundred percent total bullschiit. These brands had hundreds of millions to billions of dollars to spend on a single product or model, over decades. You don't have that money or time. *Create your own can't-be-ignored product and personality.*

   b. **Corollary 2: See above, times 10,000 if it's "something new."** Agencies love "something new." It's usually confusing and not measurable, and they are more likely to win an award for it. So they'll trot out a case study about how someone got like 12 billion views on YouTube or 1 million Facebook likes, but they'll leave out the convenient fact that (a) the company also had a $150 million ad campaign running at the time, or (b) they're a celebrity, or (c) they were just damn lucky. *Forget chasing new / easy / cheap. Marketing is none of the above.*

c. **Corollary 3: Mass advertising is unmeasurable, and almost never works for smaller budgets.** This is why agencies love it. Well, at least the first part. Smaller budgets are defined as $10 million or less. They'll try to dazzle you with reach and frequency and such, but bottom line, you're not going to track a magazine ad or TV spot back to a specific purchase. *Stay online. Measure. Refine. Do better.*

d. **Corollary 4: Mass social almost never works, unless you're an entertainment company.** Entertainment properties have fans. They're natural for social. Almost every other company isn't. People are there to talk to their friends, not BUY NOW. You're entering their living room, their pub, and their coffeehouse. They don't like it. Social produces ten times the results of conventional advertising for entertainment, and one-tenth the result of conventional advertising for everyone else, in our experience. *Forget big social—it's a distraction that can eat your company.*

e. **Corollary 5: On the other hand, microsocial almost always works, unless you're a dick.** Finding the small, specific, passionate communities that are interested in your products, whether they are barbecues, espresso machines, audio gear, or high-end bicycle accessories, is almost always worth it. Going out, joining these communities, answering questions that come up, and not selling at all is a wonderful way to get the word out. But don't think you're King Salesman of the Universe out to convert the masses, or start attacking other brands, moderators, or forum members. One problem: most agencies are too lazy to do this hard work. And it is hard work. *Pay lots of attention to microsocial, and be prepared to post, respond, meet new friends, piss some people off, delight some others, and become part of your specific niche.*

So, Do I Need Marketing?

Yes. It will be critically important to the success of your company. You may not need to have a single agency to do it, but you will need to get the word out—in a memorable, compelling way.

"But that's not true!" bleats one member of the audience. "I hear that Gen Y'ers are so cynical and jaded to marketing that it doesn't work anymore. I hear we're moving into a post-advertising future."

LOLOLOROFLCOPTER. No. Sorry. In 500 years, when we've all enhanced ourselves to be perfect physical examples of the human species, immortal and all-knowing, or uploaded ourselves to the grid, there will still be marketing. There will be ads. You can bet on it. And the successful companies and organizations will know how to use it effectively.

It's true we're moving into a different ad regime, though. Gen Y doesn't like screamy, shouty, "This is the biggest bestest most amazing product in the universe, it will transform your world, and happy bunnies will follow you wherever you go." Because words like "best" and "amazing" and "super" have been overused.

Gen Y, in general, wants to know more about the nuts and bolts. Spare the superlatives. Give them the facts.

But, you know what? Whether it's an AMA on Reddit, a post on smokingmeatforum.com, or a banner ad on Gizmodo...it's still advertising—and still marketing. If you, as a company principal, can do some of the marketing basics, it might be enough to save you from having to hire an agency.

If you can't, shop very carefully, ask a lot of questions, measure everything they do, remember that you're not a Rockefeller, and remember this short advice:

1. The most important thing is your website and e-commerce system.

2. The second most important thing is how they work on mobile devices.

3. The third most important thing is press, and by press we mean mentions and articles both online and off, in and out

of the niche press.

4. Online ads are probably next, but make sure you can track all the way to a sale. You're shooting for a cost per sale that's less than the profit on the sale. Don't let them tell you anything else.

5. Everything else comes after: shows, brochures, T-shirts, lifesize figurines of your founder, skywriting, heat-activated urinal billboards (which are actually a thing), sponsoring your own events, laser-blasting your logo on the surface of the moon, etc....

Marriage and Writing

Okay, one more anecdote, and then we'll move on to the founding of Schiit. Which wasn't called that at first. Actually, it had no name. But I'm getting ahead of myself.

During my time at Centric, I built it up to a big, successful, multimillion dollar business. We did very well. Not bragging, just facts. And, one day, I sat back and wondered, What's next?

What's next turned out to be Lisa, AKA Rina, my wife of fourteen years. Would I have started Schiit ten years earlier if I hadn't met her? Probably not. But she challenged me enough to keep pushing, keep expanding what I could do, that she certainly got me into the right headspace to start something new.

It started when Rina and her writing buddy, Jen, announced they were going to write a book and get it published. This was 2002.

Now, I'd done some writing in the past, and I had even sold a couple of things. I knew how hard it was. So I muttered something vague and wished them good luck, and figured that would be the end of that.

Eight months later, they had a book contract.

I couldn't be outdone, so I pulled out the computer and started writing again. The end result is my own three novels and about thirty published stories, as well as a first place win in the Writers of the Future contest, being a finalist for a Theodore Sturgeon award, and twice a finalist for a Sidewise Award.

The point is: I had this capability all along. But I didn't do any-thing about it until someone (figuratively) kicked me in the butt.

Who's going to kick you in the can? When will you do your writ-ing, or company-building, or adventuring, or whatever you want to do?

CHAPTER 3

From Death, Rebirth: Armageddon 2009

ALL GREAT THINGS COME TO an end. And in 2009, I thought Centric might come undone.

We'd weathered the web development downturn, and we'd ridden through two business hiccups that were either our fault or just the changing winds of the marketing times, but I'd never seen anything like the complete and utter disaster that was two-double-ought-nine.

Clients slashed budgets. New management jettisoned us. Proposals sat forever or were teleported onto the world filled with single unmatched socks and pen caps. And, to top it off, one of our biggest projects ever, a near-$500k development of a kid's virtual world, went slowly and painfully—then finally turned into a major debacle when the initial traffic brought the site to its knees.

Sue, my business partner at Centric, summed it up at the end-of-the-year Centric party. "The only good thing we can say about this year is that it's over. Slam the door, nail it shut, and never look back."

But out of that disaster, we got Schiit.

Why?

- **First, let's start with the ass-kicking factor.** Like Rina, that year kicked us in the ass. And it made us think. For Centric, it led to an entirely new office (moving from the Academy of Television Arts and Sciences building in North Hollywood, with an office overlooking the Emmy statue, to an old wine shop in old-town Newhall), an entirely new way of working with our staff, with more flexibility, more freedom, less overwork…and by mid-2010, Centric was back on track, and doing better work than ever.

- **Second, the audio factor.** I'd toyed with the idea of starting another audio company from time to time, but I'd always been distracted by the "real" work of marketing, and by memories of how hard it was to work through distribution. The economic disaster of 2009 gave me more time to think about it.

- **And finally, writing—and a fortuitous gift.** In 2009, I was deep in writing mode, working on two of my own novels, planning more, submitting stories, attending writing groups. And writing takes a lot of time. And, for me, writing also means time without distractions. I'm not one of those coffee-shop word-crafters who can work with screaming children running around their chair and baristas barking names at 110dB. Hell, I can't write if there's a TV on in the other room.

The solution? Use headphones. At first, just the Apple earbuds that came with my iPhone. Yes. Don't barf. We all have to start somewhere, right? They let me drown out the distractions and write. It was all good.

Except, in the back of my mind, a little voice kept whispering: *This could be better.*

A friend gave me a pair of V-Moda earbuds. And they were better than the Apple earbuds. Which made the voice in the back of my mind louder. But it was still okay. I was focused on my writing. I could think about audio later.

Then, the fortuitous gift. A friend sent me a Chinese tube headphone amp, simply because he traveled to China a lot and knew I used to be into audio, and…and I sat there looking at this intricate thing, thinking, *How the hell can this be only $300? No wonder manufacturing is dead in the USA.*

Of course, it didn't work so great with the earbuds, being too noisy for them. My wife bought me a pair of AKG 701s, mainly because they seemed to be highly regarded and relatively inexpensive. They worked pretty well with the tube amp. Good enough that I began to understand what some of that "tube magic" was.

A sidenote: I'd never really been into tubes until Schiit. Sumo was all solid state. So was Theta. I knew Mike did something with tubes, way back when, but that was it.

I used that combo for a time, but I kept looking at it, and wondering, *Can this be even better?*

Speaker Amp Experiments

On a whim, I tried the headphones with an old Sumo prototype that never made it to production—the Sumo Antares integrated amp. Oh, Sumo never made an integrated, you say? You're almost right. We only made one of them.

But it was a speaker amp. Would it light up the headphones? What would it sound like? Was I totally insane?

Then I hooked it up and listened. And sat there listening for hours. This was it. This was what those headphones needed. So much more detail, control, and—and, well, it had a slightly nasty etched top end, and, well, it was kinda noisy, but you can't have it all, can you? And it was really, really good, this ancient, 60WPC speaker amp.

That really set my mind going. Headphones were efficient. They didn't need 60 watts. Which meant the power supplies could be regulated to kill the noise. And you could easily do Class-A. And you could play with super-simple topologies that would never work in the speaker realm. It would allow me to do things that weren't practical before—and that could be a lot of fun!

The Question of the DAC

All that thinking about amps got me wondering about DACs. I had an old Cobalt 307, and I found that my MacBook had optical outputs, and that Monoprice made funky cables that went from 1/8" Toslink to regular Toslink.

Soon, I had the Cobalt running into the Antares, and again—what a revelation! This antique DAC and geriatric amp were doing some amazing things. I didn't want to write. I wanted to sit and listen to music.

But—they had to be doing a lot more interesting stuff with DACs and such these days, right (don't laugh, I'd been out of the game a long, long time.) I started to spend a lot of time online, researching what was out there. I discovered Head-Fi. I read about ten thousand reviews.

And I sat there, stunned. All the energy that got sucked out of two-channel audio when it started going down the road to ever-bigger price tags was back, and bigger than ever.

I showed it to Mike.

"It's like high-end around 1980," Mike said. "Just getting started. Before we went insane."

Of course, Mike didn't know that I was going to start a company and drag him into it. I still didn't know for certain myself.

But thoughts kept piling on each other: What if we could do something here? What would we do? Where would we make it? How would we sell it? Dealers again? How would that ever work in a world where Chinese manufacturers were selling direct on eBay? And direct? The only company I knew selling direct was Emotiva, and I had no idea how they were doing.

Fun fact: Centric actually subleased office space from Dan Laufman in 1995-6, when he was running a PCB assembly and contract manufacturing business. Yes, the Dan Laufman who would go on to found Emotiva, after getting tired of doing OEM work (that means, in English, makin' stuff fo' other peeps.) By 2009, though, we'd fallen out of touch.

But, hmm, direct. Direct changed everything. Because it cut out the reps, the distributors / warehousers, and the dealers.

A Quick Primer on High End Economics

Let's pause for a brief look at how pricing works in the high-end world. Cue everyone in traditional high-end audio hating me now. If I die of mysterious circumstances, you know why.

Here's how it works with a traditional distribution chain:

- Reps take 8-10% (thems the guys who go out and sell your stuff to dealers)
- Warehousing can take 5% (at the dealer or third-party, if you need it)
- Dealers take 40-50%* (thems the guys who take the order)

Note: this is highly variable depending on the product, and, in some cases, is changing for the better these days—and it's different for mass consumer products, which operate on much lower margins. Best Buy doesn't make 40% on computers.

That means that 48-65% of the cost of a product can be in its distribution. So, the chain that sells, shelves, and stores the product take half to two-thirds.

That means the manufacturer—that is, the company that engineers, designs, certifies, tests, packages, ships, markets supports, warrants, and repairs the product gets one-third to half of the retail cost.

Go back and read that again. *The guys who put it on a shelf get as much, or more than, the company that creates and supports the product.*

Yes, I know. Insane.

This is why, when I was last into audio, manufacturers would set MSRP at four to six times their fully burdened production cost. Your $499 amp? Under the old rules, they paid $80-120 to make it, including labor and overhead. But the manufacturer might only see $200 of that $500, with the rest going to distribution.

Now, don't get me wrong. Dealers provide a service to customers by letting them compare a whole lot of different products. This is definitely worth something. And we are losing that as they go away.

In the past, it really was a different world. Audio companies were completely dependent on getting the connected, aggressive reps who would get them into the right dealers. If the dealer required local warehousing or co-op money for advertising or spiffs for the salespeople (aka, the mob boss visiting you for his protection money), you did it. Because there wasn't any other choice. If you didn't do it, the dealers would sell the competing products that did.

But in 2009, we didn't have those constraints. And, looking around, I saw the roster of dealers had already shrunk considerably in the last fifteen years. It seemed the pendulum was already swinging away from old-style distribution.

And we knew how easy it was to set up an e-commerce site.

And we were a marketing company, after all.

At that moment, I stopped wondering. And started thinking: *Yes. Let's do something with this.*

CHAPTER 4

"You Always Say You Have Schiit to Do, Why Don't You Just Call It That?"

IT'S A LONG ROAD FROM thinking to doing, though, especially when you've been out of the game for so long.

I was rusty, incredibly rusty. I'd forgotten a lot of what I knew about engineering, simply because I hadn't used it in so long. And a lot of stuff had changed.

Change. As a single example, let's consider a conversation I had at Semicon, the semiconductor manufacturer's trade show, about 2001 or so. I was talking to an engineer about a new product, and mentioned that I'd been an engineer and had worked with VLSI gate arrays back at Magnavox—cutting-edge prototypes that cost $100,000 each.

"How many gates?" the other engineer asked me.

"About 100k," I told him.

He laughed. "Not the price, the number of gates."

"Right, a hundred thousand."

The other engineer laughed even harder and waved a hand, as if dismissing a servant. "100k? We put stuff like that in toasters today."

Yep. Twelve years took $100k prototypes to $1 commodities. And now, twelve years later, we're all carrying smartphones. In another twelve years, we'll be wondering how we got along without Google Ambient and pervasive intelligent packaging.

But back to Schiit. There were a billion questions before we got started:

- Was everything SMD (Surface Mount Devices, very hard to work with)?

- Where had component costs gone?

- What kind of components were people using for audio these days—was discrete design even feasible anymore?

- Where should you get them? In the old days, the reps would come visit us and give us data books and quotes (yes, as in ink printed on paper), but how did it work now?

- Same for PC boards—what were the costs now?

- What PC board layout software did people use these days?

- How about schematic capture?

- How about CAD for drawing up chassis? In the old days, we just used Illustrator.

- What did it cost to make a chassis?

- Where would you get it done?

- Who'd do the transformers?

- What were transformer costs like?

- How would we assemble the products?

- What safety approvals did we need?

- What did a modern R&D setup look like?

- Where would we do it all?

A lot of the information I needed was online. Component availability and cost, PCB cost, transformer cost—that was all there. Most surprisingly, all of them were much cheaper than we'd paid twenty years ago. Thank globalization, or the downturn, or whatever, but even parts that were made in the USA were far, far less expensive than we expected. And, despite the bleating of the apocalyptic crowd about how "there ain't no more good audio parts out there," there were actually plenty—and even more new options when you got on the surface-mount side.

But then there was software. Mike used (and still uses) Altium for doing schematics and PCBs. Altium is 100% old-skool big-ticket software.

But I didn't want to stump for the Altium price, especially since I was still in the "foolin' around" phase. The company that would be Schiit had no name. Centric was deep in the tank. I didn't want to pay for anything I didn't really need.

In fact, as I thought about it, I decided on a goal: *Can we start this for $10K, including the costs of the first run of products?*

Ten thousand dollars we could gamble with. If it went nowhere, well, hell, as Mike said, Christmas presents. We'd lost more money at Centric on bankrupt companies and deadbeat buyers. $10K was doable. It wouldn't thrill me to flush it down the toilet, but it wouldn't kill me, either.

But $7200 for Altium suddenly meant that I would be looking at something more like $20K. I wasn't ready to commit to that. So I looked a bit more and discovered that software, like everything else, had changed. In addition to Altium, there were other, lower-cost alternatives like Eagle. And there was a funky little open-source program called KiCad. It was free.

Yes, free.

Interlude: Let's pause for a moment to salute open-source software. Who would have ever expected that Microsoft would have been routed by open source? Who would have predicted that open-source is what powers most of the Internet? Who would have known that there would be opportunity created all over the Internet by software like Linux, WordPress, Drupal, Joomla, and a hundred others?

Just consider Google. Google gives away things like Android, Gmail, Google Apps for Work, Google Drive, and plays with crazy stuff like self-driving cars and longevity enhancement. But Google is really an ad company. Yep. That's how they make their money. They sell ads. Their ads show up everywhere—unobtrusive text ads in search and on websites, or banners served up on millions of sites across the desktop and mobile world. And those ads drive the free software that billions of people use. Pretty amazing business model.

But, back to the free software. Sure, why not give it a try?

Most free stuff isn't very well worked out, but KiCad was pretty full-featured and stable. I decided that KiCad was good enough to use for the first layouts.

And the gamble paid off. Not only did KiCad work well enough for those first layouts, I still use it today. Now, KiCad is much more full-featured, and has a solid roadmap of updates and an active developer community.

CAD? Yeah, we looked at a number of open-source options, and eventually ended with Alibre (now Geomagic.) How'd we arrive at that decision?

1. I remembered their name from the days when we were doing marketing work for MSC Software.

2. They had a $99 special.

Yeah. We're cheap. What can I say?

But the CAD story doesn't end there. In fact, four years after start-up, we're only now getting serious about 3D CAD. The learning curve for parametric modeling was just too steep. To start, we went back to the old days—2D drafting in Illustrator.

The 01 Cometh

Okay, so how did we end up with Schiit's simple, minimalistic, elegant chassis? It's almost entirely a story of economics. To make something that would compete with Chinese prices, we needed a cheap box. Period.

That immediately threw out a couple of things:

• Lots of little pieces and fancy cosmetics, like Chinese tube amps

• Anything machined out of a solid piece of aluminum—you don't want to know what that costs when you aren't making Apple-esque quantities in China

In the past, we'd do a steel clamshell and a thin aluminum front panel, like we did on Cobalt. Three pieces. Two steel. That's good, because steel is far less expensive than aluminum—and if it's damaged in handling, it's easy to send it back to be refinished.

But we had another problem: getting rid of heat. Amps need heatsinking, especially Class-A amps like we were thinking about making. Traditionally, you use board-mounted heatsinks or hang a slice of heatsink extrusion out the back of the amp. The problem with those approaches was that they were pricey for the amount of heat we had to get rid of. In the case of the heatsink extrusion, it also meant another cosmetic part, and another chassis component, to deal with.

That's why we soon decided to use the chassis itself as a heatsink—economics. The problem with that was that it killed the old "steel clamshell and front panel" design. Steel doesn't work very well as a heatsink. The chassis would have to be aluminum. And it would have to be fairly thick aluminum, too, so it could effectively spread the heat.

At first, I thought about extrusions. Extrusions are where you take metal and squeeze it through a form, like toothpaste. Except way hotter.

In fact, originally, the 01 (our extremely imaginative name for our first product from our as-yet-unnamed company) was supposed to be a 7" x 7" x 2" sharp-cornered square, with the volume pot set exactly in the middle and slot vents on the top. The 7" x 7" square would be a custom extrusion, and the top and bottoms would be flat aluminum panels.

One catch: what do you extrude?

- **The outside perimeter, like we originally planned?** Wow, that's a BIG extrusion. Sure, you can do it. Bring $30,000 or so. No.

- **An L-shape for top and front?** Nope, not enough surface area to get rid of the heat. And it's still a big extrusion. No deal.

- **A U-shape for front, top, and bottom?** This gives you the area you need, but now you have to deal with extrusion tolerances. The open end of the "U" might be too far open—or too closed. Notgonnahappen.com.

But a U-shape…that could be bent from sheet aluminum. And it could be grained before bending. And you could precisely control the tolerances. And, combined with a steel inner "sled," you had a simple two-piece chassis.

Form Factor Adventures

Of course, the first drawings were still 7" x 7" square. In fact, the first prototype of what would become an Asgard was designed for a 7" x 7" square. At least until reality intruded, in the form of the transformer. It was simply too close to the input to be dead quiet.

So that design went in the trash, and I drew up a new chassis. That's how the 01 got its 6" x 9" form factor with an offset volume pot—to move the transformer away from the input traces and circuitry. Seems really simple, in retrospect. Like I said, I was rusty.

But that was really just the first step—figuring out what the chassis would be. Next was the big question: Would it be inexpensive enough to make us competitive? For that, we needed quotes.

Let's pause here and talk about manufacturing. When you need something made, you have two choices:

1. **Buy the machinery to make it yourself.**
   a. In the case of aluminum and steel chassis, this means $100K CNC mills, punch presses, laser cutters, a precision brake, a timesaver, an anodizing tank, powder-coating equipment and an oven, silkscreening gear or laser engraving.
   b. Plus people to run all this equipment.
   c. Plus stuff you probably just can't do—try to get a new anodizing shop approved in California. Have fun with that.
2. **Contract with someone who can supply finished parts.**
   a. Very simple!

    b. Until they screw up.

    c. More on (b) later. As Mike says, "There is nothing more certain than death or taxes than your metal supplier will screw up eventually."

Okay, so let's say you're sane and go with (2). Now you need to find a manufacturer who understands:

1. What "consumer level" finishing is

2. That your deadlines actually mean something

3. You expect them to hold close to the pricing they quoted after the first run

4. You are not an aerospace company or government contractor (translation: you are not made out of money)

This really isn't as bad as it sounds. Clear communication with any outside supplier is absolutely key. Most metal suppliers in the USA are not doing consumer products. They're making instrument panels for submarines, or screws for aircraft, or heavy frames for industrial equipment, or precision-machined stuff for scientific gear.

This means that if you expect to get consumer-level products (that is, nicely finished with a very low rate of cosmetic imperfections), you need to go in and show them. Clearly explain what has to be perfect, and what isn't cosmetic. And pay for a "first article,"—this means, sample—to see how close they can get. If they can't get it in 1, run.

The Origin of Schiit

Now, if all of the above sounds like a lot of work, it was. Between doing schematics and laying out boards and researching suppliers and screwing up the first design and having to do it all over again—while at the same time buying a new scope and other assorted test equipment, getting prototype parts, doing research online, etc., it always seemed like I was running out to the garage (where the workbench was).

"I've got schiit to do," I'd tell Rina, and disappear.

She's endlessly patient, but one day, she'd finally had enough. "Why don't you just call it schiit?" she shot back, crossing her arms.

"Call what schiit?"

"The new company. You're always saying you've got schiit to do. Why not just call it Schiit?"

At first, I laughed. *A company called Schiit? No sane company would do that.* If we proposed that name to any Centric client, I imagined what they'd say. *Way too out there. Can't believe you'd propose that. Piss off too many people. What a crazy idea.* Then they'd fire us.

But I'd had fifteen years of marketing playing it safe, second-guessing everything we did, and watering down every great idea until it was meaningless. Maybe you can blame my decision on that history. Maybe it was nothing more than that.

"Nobody would ever forget it," I replied, eventually.

"It would cut down your marketing costs," Rina agreed.

"And we could say we make some really good Schiit."

Rina laughed. "Why not? Go ape Schiit."

"And Schiit happens."

"If you don't have our stuff, you're up Schiit creek," Rina added.

I nodded and sat back. Suddenly it didn't seem so crazy. Hell, the word was meaningless for, what, 80% of the world that didn't speak English? And if you spelled it funny, it could sound vaguely German.

And a name like Schiit would be unforgettable. Nobody could ignore it.

And, fact is, great marketing polarizes. Some people hate it. Some love it. An ad that hits the middle ground of "nice" is pure crap. Which is what most companies shoot for. Might as well cash out the whole marketing budget, roll logs of $100 bills, and have a big bonfire.

But we weren't here to hit a nice middle ground. We were here to be unforgettable. (And hey, we didn't have that many hundred dollar bills, either.)

And in that moment, everything gelled. *We would be Schiit.*

CHAPTER 5

$800 In Screws?

IT'S FUNNY WHAT SETS OFF your doubtometer.

The name "Schiit" never did. From that first conversation, it stuck. Hundreds of hours building and testing prototypes, the first of which were massive failures, never fazed me. Getting into tubes for the first time and working with 200 volt rails didn't scare me, once I figured out how durable, simple, and fuss-free tubes are. Running around to a bunch of different metal vendors to get prototypes was no problem. Placing big orders for electronics components didn't even register.

But when it came time to order screws, that $800 almost brought the whole mess down.

The design work was done, and we had working prototypes that sounded good and worked well. But the huge work of getting a working inventory and production system in place wasn't done. We didn't have all the parts we needed, we didn't have a place to make the products, nor people to do the work.

And—to be clear—this is huge work. If you dismiss it as "only purchasing" or "only operations," your business is going to be headed for trouble. And, once you've grown up and have someone to handle your purchasing and ops, you'll still be in trouble if there's no oversight.

Aside: There may be one other thing more sure than death and taxes (besides "your metal vendor will screw up eventually.") That is: "If you have one critical part that you can only get from one company, an unsupervised purchasing manager will order the wrong one—or will neglect to tell you that it'll be out of stock for twenty-two weeks until the production run."

By the time I got serious about purchasing parts, it was February or March of 2010. It was also about the same time that Centric starting showing some serious signs of life. And with marketing picking up, things were actually looking better on the "ain't going out of business" front.

So, I had less incentive to work on Schiit.

I remember sitting there in front of the computer and thinking, "$800 in screws? What will we do with $800 in screws if this doesn't go somewhere? We have no use for $800 in screws."

And I sat there for a long time, wondering just what the hell we were doing. *How did we expect to just start up a new company in a field we we'd been out of for so long, and expect that it would simply work?*

In that moment, the whole thing could have come undone. I'd told Mike Moffat that we should do a new company, and we'd laughed about the name, but there were no formal documents. He might even decide just to keep working in entertainment.

The doubts piled on: *Would people really buy these things online? Would they think it was all a joke? Would our hacky-ass e-commerce system even work (more on that later.)*

It actually took a few minutes to press that button. At this point, the nascent company was still a money-drain and a time-sump. It would have been a lot easier to give into the doubts.

And that brings up an important point. *If you start a business, there will be doubts.*

Lots and lots of doubts. There will be days when you'll take $5 for the whole mess. There will be days you want to quit. These doubts, and these dark times, will be far larger than anything you can imagine if you're working for someone else, even if the company is muttering about downsizing and layoffs. Because the whole mess is on you. There's nobody else to fall back on. There's nobody else to blame.

Production, Garage Style

"When I was back at Theta, we used to have a great board house," Mike said. We were past the $800 screw order, and were talking on the phone about how we'd actually get everything made. "They're in Simi Valley."

"I was thinking we'd just hand-solder everything to start," I told him. "The stuff is simple enough."

"Ooohh-kayy," Mike said, doubtfully. "But who's going to do it?"

"I'll do it," Rina chimed in, before I could answer. She'd been listening to my side of the conversation and had figured what we were talking about. At the time, she was starting to get her own business off the ground and was looking for extra cash anywhere she could find it.

"Rina says she'll do it," I told Mike.

"Ohhhh-kayy," he said, even more doubtfully.

"Mike's skeptical," I told her.

"Has he forgotten that I solder better than him?" she shot back. "How many of those Theta amps did he make himself?"

I said nothing. It made a lot of sense. Rina knew electronics, and electrical, and had more experience soldering than any of us.

"I think we let her have a shot at it," I told Mike, thinking, We can always switch to someone else if it doesn't work, or go to a board house if we ever do a second run of these things.

"Your call," Mike said. "So who's going to put them together?"

"Me, for now."

Silence from Mike. This was his even-more-skeptical mode.

"We'll get help when we need it," I told him.

"Better start looking now." Mike said. Mike's always more of the planner. He thinks ahead. "And where are you going to make it?"

"In the garage."

"The garage?" Skeptically.

"Hey, if it's good enough for HP and Apple, it's good enough for us," I told Mike. "Remember, Christmas presents."

More silence.

Now, you gotta know that Schiit was a fundamentally different company than anything Mike had done before. In the old days, you brought out your biggest bestest baddest product first, then moved down to less expensive gear. This works well in a market where the press can be the spokesperson and the dealer can be the psychologist for a customer investing thousands of dollars. But nobody is going to throw down a credit card on a multi-thousand-dollar piece of gear from an unknown company. Schiit was always intended to work the opposite way—start with the inexpensive products, build a following, and move up.

"I'll get you the phone number to the board house," Mike told me.

Fun fact: Rina (sometimes helped by me or Jean, Centric's bookkeeper and ex-Tektronix module assembler) ended up soldering about 1000 boards for Schiit, before we caved under the pressure and went to Jaxx Manufacturing, the assembly house we still use. The first 600 or so Asgards and Valhallas were assembled by me, before Eddie came on the scene—more on that later.

Aside aside: And, actually, we didn't build them all in the garage. We stuffed boards at the kitchen table (and, in Rina's case, on a 1966 Corvette hood), bent resistors while watching movies, built in the garage in a 20' x 3' wide space (no kidding), and burned in and did listening testing in the living room.

Duct Tape and Baling Websites

In 2010, websites and e-commerce, for Centric, was easy. Add money, and we could build whatever custom site and e-commerce system you want, with whatever features and workflow you needed.

Of course, Schiit didn't have money. Or at least none I wanted to spend. But we still needed a website and an e-commerce system secure enough to handle a reasonable number of orders. And this led us to an entirely new approach, one we use to this day for start-ups with limited budgets.

- **First, we did a WordPress template to our own custom design.** Getting your own WordPress template only costs a few hundred dollars, especially when you're doing the design (you can blame me for the Schiit brand, design, aesthetics, and copy, by the way.) WordPress gives you a very versatile content management system, so you can easily maintain the site by yourself.

- **Second, we hooked up to an easy-to-integrate payment processor.** In those days, it was Google Checkout. Rina did the hack-and-paste code that allowed people to put products in a cart and check out.

- **Third, we figured out a rough shipping cost** for domestic and international shipments, and used manual shipping calculation. Of course, this was inaccurate, cumbersome, and painful. I wouldn't do it again.

But, in the end, we had what we needed: a working e-commerce website for a few hundred dollars—and a few dozen hours of time.

Update: Today, the general principles above hold true, but you have more options. You could easily use a platform like Shopify to get up and selling fast, without any code, and with much more robust shipping and payment options. You could build the whole thing in Squarespace. You can buy a commerce-friendly responsive WordPress theme from ThemeForest for $40 or so, which will have tons more features than we ever imagined. Hell, you can even just set up an Amazon store and have them fulfill (take orders and ship products) for you. Bottom line: selling online is easier and less costly than ever. Don't let it stop you from having your own business.

Okay, Let's Talk Business

Before I go further, let's talk business. Real business. As in, business plans, business structure, all that good stuff.

No, don't roll your eyes. I know, you can read about this in pretty much any "Start UR Own Biz!" book, but let's apply the sharp point of experience and turn up all the key points to eleven.

First, business plans are, in general, an incredible waste of time.

I know someone is going to blow up about this point, but I'll stand by it. I have written about a dozen serious business plans since leaving college, and every single one of them was seriously researched, complete, and sounded compelling.

Not one of those businesses ever got off the ground.

Why? At least in part because business plans are big and intimidating. A standard business plan template has dozens of sections and subsections, asks for broad knowledge across a wide range of disciplines, demands decent writing skills, and requires some serious number crunching. It's a lot easier to sit and stare at the thing, thinking, "I ain't never gonna finish this," or "I have no idea what these bozos are talking about," than to finish it.

Because of this, business plans promote paralysis by analysis. If you really want to fill in all the blanks on a business plan, you'll:

1. Eat up an incredible amount of time that could be used for getting started
2. Stir up a thousand doubts that can keep you from ever starting
3. Be so amazingly exhausted that you might not want to do a business at all

"But business plans are what you need to get capital," someone at the back says.

Uh-huh. Right. Trust me, if you don't have a working product that's making money, you're not getting capital even if your business plan was written by the clones of Hemingway and Rockefeller. Period. And no, I don't care if you're friends with one of the board members. All VCs know that business plans are fundamentally BS.

"But it helps you keep your eye on the big picture," someone else says.

Um. No. The big picture changes every day. This is not the slow, distribution-centric world of thirty years ago. Today, a new competitor can pop up on Amazon overnight—from literally anywhere in the world. Online pundits can make or break a new company with a single post.

What business plans promote isn't big-picture thinking, they promote "railroad syndrome." As in, the business plan is the rails, and you're a train. It's easy to continue driving down the same wrong path until it's too late, because:

1. It's what's in the plan, so it must be true
2. You spent so much time researching / writing, it really has to be true
3. If it's not true, you don't want to spend all that time again to figure out what is now true

So, throw away that business plan. Forget it. Pay attention to your market. Learn your market. And keep learning. Because it changes every day.

"But I don't want to just wing it," yet another audience member says. "I want some structure in my business. What can I do besides a business plan?"

Okay, fine. Let's try something new. I'll call it a Business Brief. It can be no more than a page long. It's not for getting capital. It's not for answering every question. It's about having some answers to the most important questions. To create a Business Brief, answer these questions:

1. **What will this company do that no other can do?**
2. **If others can do this, or are doing this, how are you significantly better?**

3. **Why would someone pay money for it?**

4. **How will they find out about it?**

5. **How much money do you need to start it?**

The goal isn't a dissertation—single sentence answers are ideal. Let's do this for Schiit.

1. **What will this company do that no other can do?**
   a. Make amazing-sounding, amazing-looking high-end audio products in the USA for prices similar to Chinese manufacturing.

2. **If others can do this, or are doing this, how are you significantly better?**
   a. Nobody else truly manufacturing in the USA can beat our prices; we also have unique aesthetics and compelling features.

3. **Why would someone pay money for it?**
   a. Because it's a helluva deal, and they laughed their butt off when they heard our name.

4. **How will they find out about it?**
   a. By people with no sense of humor carping about the name to their friends on forums. (No, seriously: through an unforgettable brand and direct engagement in microsocial activities.)

5. **How much money do you need to start it?**
   a. $10,000, and two years of no salary.

See? Easy. And very easy to change when the game changes. A business brief makes you answer the two key questions of what you do and why it matters.

Second, you incorporate. Full stop.

Don't even think about silly stuff like partnerships or sole owner-ship. If you are making things that plug into a wall, even with CE and FCC certifications, you need to be a corporation. Period. Yes, it's expensive ($1000 or so in California), and yes, it's a pain in the ass (as in keeping your personal and company assets completely separate, corporate minutes, resolutions, etc.), but here's why you incorporate:

Let's say someone wants to listen to your great new tube amp. While in the bathtub. What's more, they love it so much they give it a big hug in the warm, watery depths. They die. Their family does not understand that stupidity does not give someone carte blanche to free money and sues your company.

- If you are a corporation, the corporation pays for a successful defense or reaches a suitable bribe—er, settlement—to make the family go away… or it pays for an unsuccessful defense, pays the family, and may go bankrupt in the process. It will be a terrible time for you, but they can't touch your own personal investments, house, cars, etc.
- If you are anything but a corporation, they can go after everything you have, whether or not it was yours before starting the company. And by everything, this means everything.

Third, you truly understand "cash flow."

They call it cash flow for a reason. For about two years, you get to watch the cash flow from your customers, through your hands, and back out to your vendors. And that's about it. A fast-growing company eats cash like mad. You'll be reinvesting everything you make in growth. And there won't be any left over for you.

- Yes, that's right. Expect no salary for a couple of years.
- Yes, I know, that's unrealistic if you don't have the savings or an alternate form of income.
- Yes, I know that's not fair because you can't find anyone to give you free money, and it's holding you down, you could take on Elon Musk and The Reincarnation of Steve Jobs with

one hand tied behind your back.

It's not fair, but it's the way things work. If you can't afford to put in some money up front and have no salary, you'll need to start a company that requires little or no capital, and can be done in your off-time from your real job.

Wow, this is starting to sound like a business book. And it's taking far too long. So let's cut to one more aside, and then close it up for now.

The Schiit Ass Guard?

Believe it or not, we never connected "Asgard" to "Ass Guard" until people started to comment on it after launch. So no, "Schiit Asgard" isn't an inside joke for "Schiit Ass Guard." Or maybe the joke's on us.

CHAPTER 6

The First Order Is…For Something We're Not Selling

LAUNCHING A PRODUCT ISN'T LIKE live theater in one respect: at the theater, you've got a play date. The show's gonna go on, whether you're ready or not. It doesn't matter if all the costumes were lost because a drunk truck driver drove them down a ravine, or if the lead actor is sick, or if you really don't have the whole performance gelled. You need to get on stage and do *something*.

So, with a product launch, you're lucky in at least one respect: you can pick the date. And you can move it if things aren't ready. And, if you're not stupid and don't talk about the product until it launches, then nobody will be the wiser. You'll look like a company that profoundly has its Schiit together.

(Oh, how I wish I could jump in a time machine, go back four years, and yell, "Never talk about Ragnarok and Yggdrasil until they are DAMN GOOD AND READY to launch.")

But launching a new product, especially when you're also launching a new company, is like theater in at least one respect: you're baring yourself to the ruthless examination of the public. *What will they say? What did you mess up? Is it gonna be "meh" or "omg?" What could have been better about it? What if everyone laughs you out of the game? What competitor did you miss? What if you, well, just screwed up?*

Because I gotta believe that even Steve Jobs, when he got up on stage with the first iPod, had no idea how it would go. And some of the first press commentary was pretty scathing. "Too expensive, from a niche company nobody pays attention to, why would you want to put all your music on one device?" But we all know how that played out.

Look, I work with creative people every day. And not one of them can sail blithely into a client review, thinking, "They're gonna love it, no question." Because they might not love it. They might think it's stupid. They may even make some very pointed, personal remarks about how the creative director is an unoriginal hack.

And that's why creative people get so cynical. "The client won't get it. Give them something easy and obvious. I'll save my best work for myself."

Except you can't. Because then you really are a hack.

Do you think engineers are any less creative than artists? Do you think they're hurt any less by savage commentary that questions their competence?

Almost Competent

Anyway, enough with the emo stuff. When we launched Asgard and Valhalla, we had a chance to look supremely competent—and had to settle for "almost."

It was June 15 of 2010. We had about 20 Asgards built and ready to ship. It was time to make the website live, send out the press releases, and see what the public would say.

There was one little catch, though: *we had no Valhallas.* As in, we had exactly one working prototype board without a chassis. As in, the prototype wasn't even fully worked out yet.

So, yeah, we launched with half of a product line. Like I said, almost competent. We could have shut the hell up about the Valhalla and surprised everyone a couple of months later. But no, we had to go and show that we were going to have a full line.

This is what you call "ego talking." This gets you in trouble. Shut up. Perfect the product. Then launch it. Anything else isn't "product launch." It's "product escape."

And yeah, I know, everyone likes to talk about what's coming up. A lot of companies do it. But that doesn't mean it's right.

Product escape blunts the impact of the launch. By the time you've gotten it out, everyone might be tired of hearing about it.

And, wouldn't you know it...the first order we got was for a Valhalla.

Of course.

How to Launch (Not an ICBM)

Okay, let's take a little tour of that marketing niche known as PR, or public relations.

Nobody really knows why it's called this, because it would be more aptly known as *press relations.* Because thems the guys who have the relationships with the editors, writers, opinion leaders, market makers, dudes with a blog and a million unique visitors a month, guys with 40,000 forum posts, etc. And because of those relationships, your PR guys can get you "free advertising" in the form of mentions and reviews.

Please note: the scare quotes are not there just for show. To a good PR company, "free advertising" equates to "pay us $4,000 to $20,000 per month for the chance of coverage in the *WSJ*." Not exactly free.

The reality is, a brick can get free coverage. That is, if the brick can write, send emails, and follow a few simple rules.

Here's how you do it:

- **Find your press contacts and get their emails.** These are usually on the site. You're usually shooting for the Editor / Managing Editor / First Name on the Editor List. They'll make sure it gets where it needs to go.

- **Write a real press release and put it on your site, with photos (at least.)** A real press release doesn't read like marketing. If you go on about how your product makes music sound so real that it's like you dropped acid and traveled back to 1968 to tour with The Doors, or how every other product is complete crap, it's going in the trash bin. If it's more than 400 words, it's not gonna get read. If it doesn't follow the inverted-pyramid journalistic style, it's getting canned. Here's a basic formula that works:

- **Headline:** what you are introducing, in a few words
- **Subhead:** why it's important
- **First paragraph:** everything they need to know about what the product is and why it's important, in about sixty words max.
- **Second paragraph:** a quote from an important person in the company—showing personality here is fine
- **Third, 4th, 5th paragraphs:** product details
- **Final paragraph:** pricing and availability
- **About the Company** block—keep this short and nonhyped

- **Write an email addressed to each editor personally,** tell them the most important thing about the product that will get their attention, and link to the press release on your site. This is where you can have some more fun and show some personality, but remember what the real goal is here: finding something they'll consider interesting enough to write about.

This is exactly what we did when we launched Asgard and Valhalla, and it resulted in coverage on virtually every audio site, as well as breakout coverage on *Wired*, *Engadget*, Gizmodo, and TechCrunch. YMMV.

The Deluge

Before we launched, I worried that we were gonna fall flat on our face. Two days after launch, I was terrified we weren't going to be able to keep up.

It was madness. In less than two hours after the press release went out, the first online articles showed up. Then, a thread, *Cool Looking Schiit,* was posted on Head-Fi.

The emails started pouring in. They were a mix of disbelief and delight. Disbelief at the name, and delight at the looks and the price of the products. We got emails from prospective buyers, engineers, Mike's old friends, my old friends, other manufacturers, writers, bloggers, audio press, mainstream press.

Then that first Valhalla order came in. Rina called to let me know. She knew we were nowhere near to shipping any Valhallas. She wasn't thrilled.

I looked up the order online, and thought I recognized the name. I Googled it, and crazily enough, it was a reviewer—Vade Forrester, who wrote for *SoundStage*.

Ah, hell. The first order wasn't just for a product we didn't have. It was for a reviewer.

"So what do we do now?" she asked me.

"Contact him," I told her. "Make sure he saw that it was a pre-order only. And offer him an Asgard to try in the meantime."

Sidenote: don't offer preorder. Ever.

"You're the marketing guy. You do it," she told me. "I gotta go stuff some boards."

"But I've got like a million emails!"

"And whose idea was it to do those preorder Valhallas?" she shot back.

So contacting Vade fell on me. And good thing I did—he took the Asgard loaner, liked it, and wrote a nice review on it for *SoundStage*. Unfortunately, he wasn't able to get the Valhalla in there, though he ended up liking it even better.

And all the other emails fell on me. It was overwhelming. How overwhelming? I actually went home from my marketing company, claiming illness. And that wasn't far off the mark. My guts were churning as I realized, *Holy schiit, we may actually have something here. Now what?*

I called Mike.

"Hey, uh, Mike, I think we might have a winner here with

Schiit," I told him.

"Yeah? Cool," Mike replied, sounding unconcerned.

"No, I mean really. People are going crazy. I have like a hundred emails to answer."

"That's a good thing, isn't it?" Mike asked.

"But, you know, we never really did the business details," I reminded him. "You still want to be part of this, right? You still want to help?"

And that's the truth. We had no formal agreement in place when we started up. Just a couple of old engineers, playing with gear. But when it gets real, you have to get real. And Mike, I knew, was doing Hollywood work. What if he couldn't break away from that? What would I do?

What had I done, going and launching a new company?

"Of course I'll help," Mike told me.

"But this might get big."

"We'll make it work," Mike told me. "One way or another, we'll make it work."

"We're going to need that DAC now," I reminded him.

"Ah," Mike said, and fell silent. Schiit just got real for him.

As soon as I hung up, the phone rang again. It was Jude from Head-Fi. The founder himself.

Holy schiit, again. I knew who Jude was, of course, from the press research we did. But we never thought we'd hit the biggest audio forum on the planet so fast.

Jude had a lot of questions—many of which seemed to boil down to, "Are you guys insane?" How can we set the prices so low? Did it sound any good—what were we comparing it to? Were we making enough margin to be a sustainable business? What plans did we have for the future? Did the stuff look as good as the pictures?

The answers, in order, should have been, "We're good production engineers and crappy CFOs, we certainly hope it does or we won't be around for long, hell if I know, answering about a billion emails, and yes."

I don't remember all I really said, but I must have sounded confident enough to convince Jude to buy an Asgard and try it out for himself.

Which was both exciting and terrifying. Exciting, because in a couple of days the founder of the biggest headphone site was going to be listening to our Schiit, and terrifying, because if he didn't like it, we wouldn't have to worry about having a company for long.

The New Normal

Luckily for us, Jude liked the Asgard. A lot of early owners liked it too, and added their impressions. I jumped on Head-Fi with the truly awful username of SchiitHead and began answering some questions.

And, in the evening, we built. Because the orders were coming in. Rina stuffed and soldered boards, I tested and assembled them, and she shipped them the next day after burning in overnight. We could, full-out, assemble about ten Asgards a day.

The orders kept coming in, and we kept shipping. It became the "new normal." In the little time I had, I finished up the Valhalla tweaks, got Mike's blessing on the sound, and got the PCB artwork and metal drawings out for production.

For a while, things became almost sustainable. I began running numbers in my head, and decided that this could end up being a decent hobby business. Maybe I could put in an outbuilding behind the house so we'd have enough space to run it out of and not have to spend money for an office.

Yes, I know, don't laugh. But hindsight is always 20/20. I wonder what I'll be thinking, when I look back in a few years.

Then the Valhalla metal came in, and our world imploded.

CHAPTER 7

Metal Debacle, Valhalla Style

"HEY MIKE, THE NEW VALHALLA METAL just came in," I said, holding one of the outer aluminum chassis in my hand.

"Great! I want one of those—" Mike began.

"They're junk," I said, cutting him off.

Silence on the other end of the line.

"The second shipment of Asgards came in. They're junk too."

More silence. Then: "How many?"

I looked around the garage, which was now piled high with crumpled sheets of foam that had been protecting the outer chassis. Dozens of U-shaped pieces of aluminum covered every horizontal surface. I'd already gone through every box. And every chassis I pulled out was complete crap in one way or another. What had been a smooth curve on the top and bottom of the front panel was wonky and uneven, where someone had manually tried to re-grain the parts. Some still had deep cracks at the bends, indicating why they'd tried to refinish the parts.

"All of them," I told Mike.

"How bad is it?" Mike asked.

"Unsellable. Stuff cracked. They tried to fix it."

"Fudge," Mike didn't say. He said something much more offensive than that.

"And we're out of Asgards. And it's a week before we said we'd ship Valhallas. People are already asking when they're gonna ship."

Mike sighed. "And you've called the metal shop."

"Yeah. They think it's cosmetically acceptable."

Mike groaned. "I hate being right…there's nothing more certain than…"

"…your metal vendor will screw up eventually," I finished for him.

After a few weeks of shipping products, answering emails, and getting into a rhythm, I was crushed. I didn't have an alternate metal supplier. And these guys didn't want to help. They did mainly industrial control panels. They thought of us as the picky, pain-in-the-butt small client.

Aside: vendors get lots of picky, pain-in-the-butt small clients. Try to make sure they know *exactly* what you're looking for, and don't be a cheap-ass.

And for the second time, I wondered if I really wanted to get into manufacturing again. It was clear that Centric would have a good year. Mike wasn't working full-time on Schiit yet. Neither of us was going to see any money for a very long time. Maybe it was time to pack it up and go home.

But that's just fear. Fear is normal. It's okay to be scared a bit. It keeps you on your toes. You think about doing stupid things like abandoning the company, and then you come back to your senses.

So, what did we do?

We started looking for a new metal shop, of course. At the same time, we turned on the *Backordered* notice on the site for the first time, and pushed the Valhalla release date out a month. *Little did I know how used to being in backorder we'd get. Nor did I realize how often new product release dates would slip.*

To find a new metal supplier, we used both MFG.com and personal contact with local suppliers. Most could be eliminated from a first round of quotes—four to seven times higher than what we were paying. What this meant was that they were an aerospace supplier, usually. Not a good fit. Nor was it a good fit if they were only making machine tool front panels and industrial controls—they weren't able to show any examples of "consumer finish."

In the end, Mike found the metal guys we use to this day. They were only about twenty minutes away, so Mike took the initiative to meet with them. They'd already made up an unanodized sample from our print…and it was beautiful, with consistent, perfect grain. For the first time, I saw what our stuff could look like—and it was very nice indeed.

The problem, of course, was the wait. No metal vendor is fast, unless you bring wheelbarrows full of cash and park them outside their offices. And even then, maybe not.

What's worse about the wait is the nail-biting part. Wondering, *Will it look like the sample, or will they screw it up too?* Because that could easily happen. They could buy the wrong alloy and temper, they could try to fix it too, they could mess up the anodizing, a hundred things can happen. And you won't know until those boxes show up at your garage (er, I mean, "loading dock.")

Metal and Manufacturing, a Triptych

Comment 1: there are many ways to finish metal. There's no right way or wrong way. Graining, bead-blasting, etching, etc.—as long as it produces a consistent, consumer-level finish, it's fine. But the way we do ours is somewhat unique. We grain the aluminum first as a flat sheet, then bend, anodize, and screen it. This requires unique tools that won't mar the grain, as well as a specific alloy and temper so the aluminum doesn't crack when it's bent. This method is a very inexpensive way to produce good-looking chassis.

Comment 2: the importance of an inexpensive chassis. An inexpensive chassis is key to a high-value product. At the higher-end of high-end, it's not uncommon for the chassis to cost three to ten times more than the parts that go in it. And that's fine, if what you're looking for is audio art. But if you're looking for value, you have to drive the chassis cost down to a level below the rest of the components—you know, the stuff that *actually makes the product work*. This is why our chassis cost a *lot* less than what goes in them, across the board, at all levels.

Comment 3: this is the reality of manufacturing. If you're looking for a get-rich-quick, work-two-hours-a-week-from-home deal, making things ain't for you. Stuff *will* go wrong. You *will* have to deal with it. Oh, you say you're going to make it yourself on your own machines for full control? Yeah, let us know how that goes when the machinist quits / when you get the wrong metal / when the machine breaks. As Mike says, "Bringing a product to market is like screwing a gorilla. You aren't done until the gorilla's done."

The New New Normal

"The new metal's here," I told Mike, about five weeks later.

"And?"

"And I don't want to open it," I admitted.

"Pussy."

I said nothing. We were in deep backorder, and well past the intro date for the Valhalla. People were screaming. If the metal was junk, we might not recover from it.

"Open it," Mike said.

I did…and it was perfect. It looked just like the sample. The anodizing was great, and the screens were even better than the old suppliers. We were back in business!

Rina and I went back to work. Soon, there was another "new normal," with two different amps on the line. We were working late into the night, almost every night. The Valhalla got some very good reviews. And I was finally happy about the quality of the metal we were shipping.

In the midst of that euphoria, I got a second call from Jude at Head-Fi.

"You know, CanJam is coming up," he told me. "It's at RMAF in Colorado."

"I don't know if we're ready for shows," I said.

"But a lot of people are asking about you," Jude told me. "Maybe you could share a space with Sennheiser. They were asking about amps."

Wait. *Did he say what I thought he just said?*

"With Sennheiser?" My voice cracked a bit.

"Yes, Sennheiser."

I was still in shock. "*The* Sennheiser?"

Jude laughed. "There's only one, as far as I know."

For a long time, I couldn't say a thing. Sennheiser…and Schiit amps? Would they laugh us off the table when they first heard the name?

But I couldn't let the opportunity pass by. "Let's do it," I told Jude.

"Cool. I'll have you ship out one of each of your amps to Sennheiser at the hotel, and it'll be great to meet you there."

And that's how we got roped into our first show—where we screwed up Sennheiser's plans, and insulted at least one industry bigwig…

CHAPTER 8

We Screw Up Sennheiser and Insult Some Big Guys

HAVE ANY OF YOU GUYS been to a trade show?

If you have, you're probably groaning and nodding right now. You also may be sheepishly recalling some boozy 4:00 a.m. nights out, when you knew you had to be in the booth the next morning at 9:00 a.m. sharp. If that's the case, skip the next few paragraphs, unless you want a particularly snarky take on what trade shows are actually about.

On Trade Shows

Trade shows are where people come together and meet, face-to-face and in-person, to demonstrate products that are usually targeted at a specific niche. As in the companies actually fly people from all over the world to get together, swap flu strains, go out to expensive and uncomfortable company dinners, embarrass themselves by drinking too much in front of current and prospective customers, chase union labor trying to find their products and their booth, bribe union labor to make sure they get their stuff first, work like dogs to set up and tear down the exhibits, stand on your feet all day and try not to look miserable as people talk crap about your company as they walk by, clean up after the one guy whose hangover got a little out of hand, lose the briefcase of the new CFO in your booth storage, get new pants when you realize your stuff doesn't actually work (or blows up in front of your biggest prospect), and be derided by all your co-workers for being chosen to go on such a wonderful vacation on company expense.

Sounds like paradise, doesn't it? Well, for all the different kinds of shows they have, you wouldn't think it was so bad. In addition to the big shows that everyone knows about, like CES, Comic-Con and the various auto shows, some trade shows include:

- The Natural Food Expo
- The National Work Truck Association
- SEMICON
- Conspiracy Con
- The National Coffin Exhibition
- The World Toilet Summit

Now, you might be thinking in this Internet-driven, mobile-aware, Amazon-grocery-delivery day and age, trade shows seem like, well, a buggy whip shop in the automobile era. But they keep happening.

Why?

Part of this is the "well, we can't not be there" theory. As in, "Well, if we don't show up, people might not think we're doing so well, and all the competition is going to be there, and we might miss out on something important." *Hint: people know exactly how you're doing, whether you're there or not.*

Part of this is the "I get to see all my old friends in the business" theory. Yeah, and if your company just flew them all out once a year, it would probably be cheaper than going through all the logistics of a show. *And they'd have more fun.*

And part of this is the, "Hey, I wanna close some new biz," theory. And this is still a pretty good theory if you're on the distribution side of things. Stores and distributors do come to shows, and you may get a chance to meet with them there. You may even close a deal. *But if you're selling direct, that's not a good bet.*

So, let's get this out of the way: if you're selling direct and you're at a trade show, you'd better (a) have something you want the press to see, or (b) really, really like trade shows.

So Why The Hell Did You Go?

So why did we go to CanJam, if we hate trade shows so much? Because CanJam is a lot less stressful and insane than being on the main floor at CES. And it didn't cost a fortune, when trade shows can eat you alive. Centric has helped tons of companies produce, market, and exhibit at trade shows, from SEMICON to SEMA, with budgets ranging into the $250,000 range.

Yes. Read that again. *A quarter million dollars.* For one show. Audio, we got it easy. Now you see why I say it'd be cheaper to just fly your colleagues out.

There was one little snag. I was still working full-bore at Centric, and there was a client meeting I couldn't get out of on Friday, the first day of CanJam. I could be there for the weekend, but not on the first, opening day.

No problem, I figured. Rina and I would fly in Saturday morning, but before that, I'd send two boxes—an Asgard and a Valhalla—to the show hotel, attention Sennheiser. They could grab them and set them up Friday, and we'd join them on Saturday.

Aside: Looking back on it, I can only shake my head at all the things we missed—like "What sources would Sennheiser be using? Should we bring one?" and "How about signage?" and "What about literature?" If I'd had our trade show specialist at Centric running the show, she would have strung me up.

But hey, it was our first show. Jude was going to be there. The Sennheiser guys had a big outfit behind them. What could possibly go wrong?

Waiting While Rome Burns

As it usually is with such things, our flight was later than expected. Which meant we touched down in Denver International at about 11:00 a.m. Getting a rental car and going to the hotel ate another hour. So, all in all, it was about noon when we arrived. We grabbed our badges and headed for the show floor—but we hadn't even walked into the CanJam ballroom before Jude came shooting out of the room, blinking in recognition.

"Hey, are you Jason?" he asked. "From Schiit?"

I barely had time to nod before Jude added, "Hey, I thought you were bringing some amps for Sennheiser."

My stomach flipped over. *What did he just say?*

"I shipped them," I croaked out.

"Where?"

"To this hotel, to Sennheiser's attention."

"Hmm, they didn't find them." Jude didn't seem really upset, but my mind was still in full panic mode. *The amps weren't there? The Sennheiser amps? The ones they needed for the show? That SENN-HEISER needed? Needed before half the show was over?*

"I'll go check at the desk," Rina offered, and took off looking for the amps.

"Well, let's go to the booth," Jude said. "We got Sennheiser set up with some loaners, so it's not the end of the world. I'm glad you guys could come…"

Maybe this would be all right, I thought, half-listening as I followed him into the room. CanJam was being held in a giant hotel ballroom. That year, it was set up as a series of tables along all the outer walls, with a few outrigger table clusters. There was also what looked like a band setting up in the large open area.

Jude saw my look. "Oh, don't worry about that," he told me. "It's a set of instruments that play through headphones, so you can play live and not disturb anyone."

And he was right. Over the next day and a half, people would beat on the drum pads and produce no noise other than an anemic thwack of a stick on a hunk of plastic. But they looked like they were having fun.

The Sennheiser booth was just another single table that year, as were most of the exhibits. The headphone revolution had only really started, and even Sennheiser seemed a little surprised to be there.

Sidenote: It's really amazing how much the industry has grown up since then. Now, professional banners, back walls, table graphics, custom tablecloths, and a much more carefully or-chestrated presence are the order of the day.

They didn't have anything other than the show-provided, block-printed SENNHEISER sign up on the black drape behind the table. Two guys stood there, hands behind their backs, in the classic I'm-bored-at-a-tradeshow pose. Another guy was hunched over in one of the two chairs that fronted the table, listening intently to the Sennheiser HD800s. On the table were some acrylic headphone stands holding a set of HD600s, the then-new HD598s, and a pair of wireless headphones—maybe the RS180s, I think. They were being driven by a small amp I didn't recognize, connected to a massive CD player.

Jude made the introductions, while my mind raced on, full of doom-laden scenarios where the amps had gotten lost in transit, they wouldn't be at the show, we'd lose even more face in front of Sennheiser, etc. I recall him saying something about how they'd borrowed another amp and the CD player to get them up and running. Disaster, total disaster.

But even then, Jude didn't seem to think so. He took me over to the Head-Fi booth, where an early Schiit fan was demoing an Asgard. That was cool, but all I really wanted was to deliver on what we promised to Sennheiser—a couple of amps.

That's when Rina arrived—thankfully carrying a couple of fa-miliar boxes.

"Got 'em," she said.

"Great! Let's get them to Sennheiser!" I double-timed it back over to the Sennheiser booth, where we started the process of swapping out the amps.

The Sennheiser guys took a listen, nodded and said some nice words, and we were set.

Rina Runs the Company

"So, do you work for Sch...ah...I mean...ah...how do you pronounce it?" the lead Sennheiser guy asked Rina.

"Schiit," she said. "Schiit Audio."

Senn guy grinned, a little unsure of how to take it from there. Rina rescued him. "Yep, I make the products," she told him.

"Make?" he asked, even more off-kilter.

"Yeah, I stuff the boards and solder them," she said.

"Sometimes with some help," I said, not wanting to look too small.

"And I print the orders, and do the shipping," she added.

The other Sennheiser guy laughed. "So you run the company, while he"—pointing at me—"plays with designs?"

"Pretty much," she agreed.

They got a good laugh out of that. From there, we lapsed into comfortable show-small talk: the traffic seemed slow for a Saturday, it was busier yesterday, where was everyone, etc. A show can be jammed like Comic-Con on opening morning, and show staff will still complain it was slow.

I slowly relaxed. *This was more like it. I could do this.*

And, to be honest, we had our share of interesting visitors. One was John Broskie, of tubecad.com fame. I was thrilled to meet him, since I'd used his software for some early Valhalla calculations.

Another aside: want to get into audio? Start hanging out in places like DIYaudio.com and reading sites like tubecad.com and Nelson Pass's DIY site. The leading edge of audio is really at places like these—usually not fully worked out, sometimes completely unrealizable, buried in tons of other cruft and bitching— but it is there. Then, start building stuff. You'll quickly learn what works and what doesn't. Then get yourself a QuantAsylum QA400 or some other inexpensive analyzer and start seeing how your designs actually do on the measurement side. Then try to break them, loan them to friends and see what they say, and start figuring out what separates a "consumer-friendly" product from a hobby product, if you want to produce it.

Broskie seemed astounded by our products—in that they were quite inexpensive, and made in the USA. He wrote about them in his blog, and comes back every year to see what we've come up with.

And, of course, we met the press. Some seemed skeptical, some seemed impressed. By the next day, I had the "inexpensive, made in USA" spiel down pretty good. Back then, we were the vanguard of inexpensive, made-in-USA product, so it was really surprising for a lot of people to hear.

The First Ragnarok...Was Lyr

That CanJam is also where we met Audeze for the first time. It was funny, because they were the first company that wasn't impressed by the staggering 1W power output of the Asgard. "Four watts is more like it," they told me. "And our driver will take 15 watts."

That was the eye-opener that led to Lyr, just a few months later. I'd been playing with higher-power designs, truly insane stuff by headphone standards (you know, like 6-8W), but I hadn't really planned on selling them, except as a stunt. Like "this thing has so much power, you have to take off the protective sticker with the disclaimer that you might blow up your headphones if you use it."

So—there you go—the truth is, Lyr was originally going to be our Ragnarok. An insanely powerful amp that people would buy simply because it was nuts.

And then Audeze happened, and changed our plans. That's why we accelerated the development of Lyr—because of the orthodynamic revolution.

The Anonymous Guy

And then there was the one incident, with the company CEO that shall remain nameless. Like I said, the "inexpensive, made in USA" spiel was going well. Most everyone who heard it seemed thrilled that we were trying to bring back affordable, high-end products. So it kinda threw me for a loop when someone didn't seem so pleased about it.

Late in the day on Sunday, a guy came up to the Sennheiser booth. His name tag was flipped around, so I didn't know who he was (note, this probably wasn't a deliberate thing—name tags have a habit of doing that.) If I was less green, I probably would have recognized him from another show, or from his company's press materials. But that day, he was just another anonymous dude.

Anonymous dude picks up the Asgard roughly and squints into the vent holes in the top, as if trying to read tea leaves. And from his expression, he didn't like the fortune he saw. He turned it over and over, ran his hand along the grain, and twiddled the volume pot, all the while his expression getting more and more grim.

"How can you make this for this price in the USA?" he barked out, finally putting the Asgard down, then moving on to inspect the Valhalla.

And—it's funny—nobody had asked me that yet. So I took this as a chance to show off and be a little snippy.

"I think it's because most manufacturers are lazy," I said. "They don't even try to make things here anymore. It's easier to just throw up your hands and say, 'well, just make it in China, because everyone else is doing it.'"

This didn't improve Anonymous Guy's mood. His brow furrowed even more deeply as he scowled at the Valhalla.

"That's it, huh?" he asked, as if in challenge.

"And," I added, throwing gasoline happily on the bonfire, "a lot of companies are really bad at production engineering—it takes a lot of work to make something simple and inexpensive, but if you go to China, you can simply throw parts at it until it works."

Anonymous guy glared at me. His jaw worked, as if he wanted to say something but couldn't get it out. Finally he just shook his head and walked away.

"Who was that?" Rina asked.

"Hell if I know," I told her. Not really caring. There are always some angry guys around. Who could he possibly be?

It wasn't until a few weeks later that I saw Anonymous Guy's picture and found out what company he worked for. And the light came on. Because not only was that company manufacturing product in China, they *were also selling their own expertise in helping other companies move their own manufacturing to China.* So, it was like I'd peed in his Cheerios and then kicked him in the nuts for good measure.

No wonder he'd looked less than happy.

CHAPTER 9

Powering Up: Lyr

OKAY. SO IT'S TIME FOR A new amp. But before we get into this, let's talk about product roadmaps. Yeah, more boring business stuff. But this kind of stuff is important—that is, if you're interested in building a few amps on a hobby basis.

What's A Product Roadmap?

In brief, it's a plan for what products you'll have, when you'll introduce them, and when you'll obsolete them. Yes. Products have life cycles, and you need to plan for how long you expect them to be in the market. Now, this doesn't have to be some elaborate stack of Gantt charts or backed by tens of thousands of dollars in market research. But the reality is, you need to at least have an idea of:

- **What products you intend to sell.** If you did two headphone amps and then, say, decided to make a deep fryer, this may not be the best strategy. If you did two headphone amps and then decided to extend the line with another amp or a DAC that works with them, this makes sense.

- **Where they fit in the line.** Are the new products upmarket? Downmarket? Why would someone buy the new product? What need does it fill that the others don't? Note: "I wanted to try this crazy new topology" isn't a recipe for a logical product line. Having a 1W Class A amp, and a 1.1W Class AB amp, and a 0.9W Class S amp probably doesn't make a lot of sense.

- **How many years they'll be around before you refresh them.**

Planning on selling something "until it doesn't," isn't a recipe for success. How long do you think your products will be competitive? In mass consumer industries, you see major updates every year. In some cases, this makes sense, since the market is changing so rapidly (smartphones, tablets). In niche audio, every year is too fast. Every eight years is a little too slow.

So, coming back from RMAF, we knew we had to have a new product—one set up from the start for the high power needs of orthodynamics. And we knew where it fit in the line: above Valhalla. We didn't know how long it would be around, because, let's face it, we were only about six months old as a company. Nothing was obsolete yet, nor would be for a long time.

The question was: what the heck should we do?

Lyr Challenges

Deciding to do a new product isn't really worth much. You also need to have a set of target goals for it. For Lyr, our early notes were as follows:

- At least 4W RMS into 32 ohms power output
- Tube hybrid design with rollability—this was in response to early Valhallas being non-rollable, which many customers saw as a negative
- Retain as many of the key features of our other designs as possible: no overall feedback, non-Class AB output stage, etc.
- A more direct signal path than either Valhalla or Asgard, which were capacitor-coupled designs
- Same chassis size as the other products
- Sexier cosmetics, without costing a fortune

The first point (4W into 32 ohms minimum power), coupled with the "same size chassis" spec was the biggest sticking point.

Asgard was about at the limit of heat generation into that size of chassis. And Asgard was only 1W output. Multiplying output by 4X would result in a small hotplate or grill.

Of course, Asgard was Class-A, which means it runs full out all the time.

An aside: "Class A" is easily the most abused term in all of audiodom. "Class A" is used variously to describe:

- Real Class A amps like Asgard and Asgard 2, which run full bias all the time and cannot come out of Class A mode, ever
- High-Bias Class AB amps that run part of the time in Class A, but transition out of Class A for higher output
- Low-Bias Class AB amps that have some kind of "sliding bias" arrangement to try to keep the bias in Class A all the time
- Preamp Class AB stages that never come out of Class A operating ranges, but are technically Class AB
- Op-amps that are internally Class B, but have the output stage biased into Class A
- Op-amps that are internally Class B, but do not have the output stage biased into Class A
- Anything they think they can get away with calling Class A

Here's a hint on how to spot real Class A amps: they are big, hot, and heavy. Period. Anything else, and "Class A" is probably just a slogan.

Now, Where The Hell Was I?

Oh yes. Lyr. Four times the output power and not enough heatsinking for Class A operation. Plus the heat of tubes. The logical answer would be to change over to a Class AB output stage and set the quiescent current at a level where the amp wouldn't become a George Foreman Grill.

Of course, being a little (a) stubborn, (b) slow, (c) petulant, (d) affected by Not Invented Here syndrome—choose one or all of the above—we decided *not* to go with the logical answer.

Instead, I wanted to create something new. Something that kept most of the characteristics of single-ended Class A operation, but seamlessly transitioned to Class-A push-pull, then finally into Class AB, as power needs increased. And I didn't want it just to be a high-bias Class AB output stage.

Why? Several reasons:

- Class AB output stages, by nature, use complementary transistors (BJTs, MOSFETs, or, in some cases, more exotic devices)

- Complementary devices are never truly complementary— or, in other words, the "inverse" equivalent isn't just an inverted version of the other

- Since they are not truly complementary, they introduce nonlinearities as you switch from one to another in a Class AB amp

This is why you'll see us employing noncomplementary output stages where possible. In Asgard 2, we use only N-channel MOSFETs, one as a current source. In Mjolnir, we use Circlotron-style topology to use only N-channels as well. Same with Ragnarok. Of course, this doesn't work all the time, so Magni has a conventional Class AB output stage, with complementary devices.

So, what I wanted with Lyr was an all-N-channel output stage that would be able to "slide" out of Class A when necessary, to deliver additional power.

That's easier said than done. I investigated various sliding-bias systems and dual-mode amplifiers, building and measuring about twenty different breadboard prototypes. Most of them worked to some extent, but all of them had some significant limitation—they couldn't make it out of Class A, or distortion was too high, or they required four different trimpot tweaks per channel to make them work.

The problem was that we were working "off the roadmap."

Class AB amplifiers are well-understood. Class A amplifiers, ditto. Something in-between doesn't have a lot of references in literature. Especially when you're talking about such low power output. And, to make it more complicated, some of the best sliding-bias arrangements are tied up in Nelson Pass's patents, which of course we can't infringe on.

The Lyr project dragged on until late December with no listenable prototype. It was getting to the point where I was considering just throwing in the towel and using a Class AB output stage, because nothing was working well enough.

The Critical Stage

Sometimes the place to look for inspiration is in implementations from earlier eras in audio (sometimes not—there are genuinely better ways to do things now.) Because, in the old days, NPN and PNP components weren't just mismatched—they were sometimes not even in the same zip code. A lot of early work avoided complementary output stages entirely. Some of these found neat ways to improve the power output of a Class A circuit. The problem was that none of them really worked the way we wanted them to.

This is where we went back to the closest match and started tweaking. Part of it was actual analysis, and part of it was building and testing additional prototypes.

(If this was a movie, insert montage of boring engineering work with fancy camera angles, fast cuts, and a driving, heroic soundtrack.)

(Re above: ha. Engineering is a lot of heads-down work. There's not a lot of heroics or drama. You know, like everything in real life.)

And, late one cold night in the garage, I finally had it—a stage that would do 43.2V P-P into a 32 ohm load. Sharp-eyed readers will do the P= V^2/R calcs and say, "Hey, that ain't 4W, that's 7.4W RMS!"

Right. But then when you have two channels driven, the output falls due to power supply sag, so 6W is a nice round number.

And that's how Lyr ended up being 6W and not 4W—it over-performed.

On Power Ratings. Okay, please let me vent about this one thing. **Power. Ratings. Are. Done. In. RMS. Per. Channel.** You do not (a) rate at peak power, (b) add power output together for both channels, (c) use an artificially low load impedance to make the output look higher.

The Path to Production

Back in those early days, the path to production was pretty streamlined. As soon as I had a fully working PC board, we drew up some renderings of what Lyr would look like and announced it.

Yeah. Before the metal was in-house. Before we had boards in-house. Before we actually made a single Lyr.

And yeah, we're idiots.

But, in this case, it actually worked out. We sent out press releases on December 27, and the renderings were sexy enough to get picked up by *Wired, Engadget,* and Gizmodo. We promised delivery by March 1, and actually started shipping in late February. It was the only product we ever preannounced that met its delivery date— and the first product that *sold out the first run before we started shipping.*

And, it was the last product that had a run made by hand. By the time we'd started shipping, it was becoming completely clear that we couldn't do this by ourselves anymore.

CHAPTER 10

Our First Employee, Our First Board House

IN BUSINESS, THERE ARE A lot of invisible lines that, once crossed, it's hard to go back. So let's talk about what's arguably the biggest invisible line: having employees.

A business can be quite successful without employees—there are some single-person consultancies and specialized job shops doing excellent work and making good money while doing it. And there are plenty of advantages to working that way. Not least of which is that you absolutely know who's doing the work (you), what their capabilities are (yours) and who's responsible for delivering on time and on target (again, you.) You don't have the additional burden of a payroll, or the additional administration of managing payroll taxes, withholding, etc., or paying a service to do so. It's simple. It's easy.

But it's also very limiting. *What if you want to go on vacation? What if you are laid up? What if you get a once-in-a-lifetime opportunity that's simply too big for you to take on?* That's when the single-person consultancy or job shop model breaks down.

So, you get employees. Sounds easy, doesn't it?

Nope.

With employees comes a lot of responsibility. The baseline is that you have to meet payroll—and, with a growing business, you're probably running most of your profits back into production to expand. *Can you afford it? Will it affect your ability to keep expanding?* You need to run some numbers before you hire anyone, and plan for putting in money if things get thin.

And with employees, you have more administration.

Sure, payroll taxes, withholding, etc., can be handled by a payroll service at minimal cost. But you'd also better:

- Keep records of who you interviewed and who you ended up hiring.

- Have an offer letter that spells out duties and expectations.

- Make sure the language in that letter doesn't end up binding you in an implied employment contract

- Have a clear probationary period, and make sure the employee knows it

- Provide clear sick leave and vacation policies

- Provide health care

- Plan on keeping a record of any feedback or disciplinary actions you take, in case things go south

- Have an employee manual, so that everyone knows the rules of the game

Sounds terrible, I know. I made the whole thing sound like a war between employer and employee. In reality, it usually isn't. Most of the time, people are fundamentally decent, and you usually don't need to worry about armor-plating your ass in five inches of legal armor.

But if things go bad, you want it there. In the twenty years at Centric, we've been threatened with legal action twice by employees. Nothing ever came of either, but I'm very, very glad we had policies and procedures in place, just in case.

So, did Schiit have all that in place when we brought on our first employee?

No. Of course not.

Beyond the Invisible Line

Before Lyr, Schiit could have existed comfortably as a no-employees "hobby business." In fact, we planned for it. We modified our house and added storage in the attic to house some of our stock. We also seriously looked into building a shop in back of our house in order to be Schiit's permanent home. This 400-square-foot box sounded palatial in comparison to the fifty or so square feet we were eking out between the cars in the garage at the time.

An aside: It's pretty hilarious to look back on it today, as we start reaching the limits of 8300 square feet—even with every-thing racked three levels high and a forklift to manage our space better.

After the Lyr introduction, it quickly became clear that Schiit needed help. Rina and Jean couldn't build boards fast enough. And I was getting tired of coming home every night from Centric and building ten or twenty amps. And I needed to spend more time with Mike, getting our first DAC hammered out. And the next run of Lyr boards had just come in, and we needed to do runs of all three amps. And the order rate continued to accelerate.

Bottom line: we needed help, and we needed it fast.

As luck would have it, a very old friend of mine had been watching our progress (not coolly and dispassionately, like Wells' Martians, but actively helping along the way, making some custom tools that made assembling the early Asgards much easier.) He was a frequent visitor at the house, coming up for barbecue or wine or just to hang out. This old friend was Eddie.

Time Machine: Set Dials for 1989

Okay. Imagine you're just out of college. You've been into audio for a few years. You have big Carver amps and you build speakers. You've even sold a few of them. Some of them actually sound pretty good. You have no money at all, and no experience with running a business.

So what do you do? *You start a company, of course.*

You try to run it while working another engineering job full-time. In the pre-Internet, pre-direct-sale world of 1989. You know, no email, no Internet, cell phones the size of bricks that cost $1200 and $45 per month if you didn't use them at all, and $0.45 per minute when you did, and had like two hours of battery life.

What's more, you decide to build them all yourself. First on the patio of your parents' house. Then in a 300-square-foot unpermitted, unheated, uncooled, unpowered shed you built with $1000 of lumber from Home Depot in the back of a friend's house, and finally in a run-down, 1000-square-foot industrial space in Sylmar, next to a meat packer and a body shop. And by build, I mean build. As in, sheets of MDF and gallons of paint would come in, and speakers would come out. All made with a Frankenstein arrangement of pin router jigs and templates, coupled with the world's most hot-rodded and dangerous table saw (no shields, no guards, five times the power it was designed for, blade usually sticking out at least four inches above the table surface, and an eight-foot extension built for the guide.)

This was Odeon Loudspeakers, my first company.

Eddie worked at Odeon.

Odeon had no money. Almost literally. We were so strapped, we cut our own Styrofoam for packing material using the table saw. Yes, the modded table saw. No, nobody ever lost a hand. We should have. Of course, the place should have blown up any amount of times when the air was full of sawdust (we had no dust collection system) and the kerosene heaters were going full blast.

Odeon is why I always win the "we once did this stupid thing at CES" stories. If you've been to a CES dinner with a bunch of other audio industry guys, you know what I mean. "Well, there was this one time when nothing got delivered for the booth, we had to make do with rental plants and couches," or "Well, there was this one time when the prototype wasn't ready, so we had to assemble it the night before in the hotel room." Things like that.

Our Odeon / CES story goes like this:

In the old days, there were two CESes per year. One in Vegas, one in Chicago. Vegas was pretty easy. Throw stuff in the back of a van and drive there. An easy four-hour trip.

Chicago? Not so much. Odeon couldn't afford airfare, much less freight for over a thousand pounds of speakers (yes, we made some big stuff.) But Odeon couldn't afford *not* to go to CES, either. We lived on orders made by distributors and dealers, and the only place we had contact with them was at shows.

(Pre-Internet, remember? Distribution held all the cards.)

So we *had* to be at Chicago. Which meant, in the infinite wisdom of less than a quarter of a century on this planet, we pack up the van and drive. From California to Chicago.

Or, more precisely, Eddie and Jose drove. (Jose, my other business partner at the time, now runs a very successful specialty costume shop...you've probably seen their work in tiny little movies like *Thor, The Avengers, Tron, Spider-Man*, etc.)

Why didn't I go with them? Because I was able to fly out with Sumo. Sumo had money. Sumo shipped things and flew places. Odeon didn't.

Now, the sheer insanity of driving from L.A. to Chicago in an overloaded 1970 Dodge van that was literally held together with Liquid Nails would be funny enough, but what wins the Stupid CES Stories Folly is what happened once I flew in.

After dropping stuff at the Sumo hotel room, I headed down to the show sub-level, which was where the high-end stuff was being shown that year. I found the Odeon room, and two very tired-looking co-workers.

"Dude, Zagnut bars are real!" Eddie said, proudly whipping up a table skirt to show me what looked like ten gross of Zagnut candy bars, most still bundled into factory display packs.

"What?" I asked, completely confused.

Eddie pulled out one of the candy bars and dangled it in front of my eyes. "Zagnut! Like in *Beetlejuice*! They're real!"

"Uh..."

"So we picked up a bunch of them," Eddie said, gesturing at the boxes and boxes of candy bars.

I didn't know what to say. They'd found a candy bar...that they saw in a movie... It didn't make any sense.

Jose came to the rescue. "So we need some money."

"Money?" I asked.

"Dude, you gotta try one, they're good!" Eddie cut in.

"We ran out of money," Jose said, waving him off. "We're staying at a friend's house, but we really need to get a motel or something, and it would be good to have some real food for a change…"

"You ran out of money?" I echoed.

Jose nodded and pointed at the giant pile of Zagnut bars.

Suddenly it clicked. "Wait. You spent all the trip money on candy bars?"

Jose nodded.

"But it's worth it!" Eddie said. "Everybody's gonna trip when we get home. These are real!"

"And you didn't have money for a motel."

"No."

"And you've been eating nothing but candy bars…" I said, trailing off.

"For a day and a half," Jose said. "Since we got here."

Right. These were my business partners. Now you see why I win the Stupid CES Story Award, every time. And why that business didn't last long.

So Why'd You Hire Eddie?

Because 1989 was a long time ago. People change. And, most importantly, Eddie was:

- There
- Willing to work
- Okay with piecework

"Piecework?" you're probably saying. "What's that?"

Piecework is where you tell someone, "Hey, I'll pay you $X for each product you finish." It works great in cases where you're confident your employee isn't going to sacrifice quality to make numbers. And Eddie was, if anything, an insane stickler for quality. So we didn't have any worries there.

Now, to do piecework legally, you still need to either pay someone at least minimum wage (with piecework on top), or you need to have them not as an employee, but as a contractor. Which is what we did to start: Eddie worked for us as a contractor. Which had a lot of benefits in itself. Since he wasn't an employee, we didn't have to worry about withholding, health insurance, etc.—just pay him and give him a 1099 at the end of the year.

"Well, that's great!" you say. "I can avoid all the headaches with employees by using contractors."

Not so fast. There's a pretty specific legal definition of what a contractor is, and it may vary state to state. If you're trying to skate by and call employees "contractors" to save cash, and the Powers That Be decide they're not contractors, but actually employees, you're in for a world of hurt.

Contractors must typically, among other things:

a. Be able to set their own hours

b. Use their own tools

c. Not have to work in a specific facility

With Eddie, we were pretty much in compliance on all three, though he never really took products home to work on them. He could have, though, and we wouldn't have cared.

But the fact was, we were still a small business. Eddie was working in our garage. It wasn't such a big deal—he was happy for the work, and we were happy for the help. The first few hundred amps he made standing up, between the 1966 Corvette and the garage shelf where we burned-in and shipped the amps. His total work area was probably about ten square feet. I sat at the bench, testing, and Rina took his space during the day to ship orders.

And we slipped into that pattern for a while—Eddie coming in every evening, throwing something on the grill, then going out into the garage to work on Schiit. It wasn't a bad setup. And Eddie was very helpful in pointing out ways to make things easier, stuff we could change to make assembly go more quickly.

So, yeah, Eddie. He's the kind of friend who'll show up at 3:00

a.m. to fix your busted car, or hop out in the middle of an intersection to pick up a pipe wrench someone dropped, or tell you everything the body shop did wrong to your car, or will put together amazing things on a weekend just because he can, or hook you up with machining or bead-blasting, or make Schiit. He's also been the go-to guy for ultimate finish work on specialty costumes, like on *Thor*, and he was the reviewer in Centric's experiment with Internet video back in 2006 or so, called *Wineass*. A quick YouTube search will pull up a few of the 140 episodes we shot. He's a bit of a character—and a great choice for our first, well, contractor.

Completing the Story: The Board House

With Eddie on the team, we were now able to keep up with production, and even get ahead. The bottleneck was now in boards. Rina and Jean were overloaded—in fact, I probably ended up stuffing about twenty Lyrs out of the first run.

So we had the choice of either adding more staff, or going to a PC board assembly house. Mike Moffat was always in favor of the latter, and on the second Lyr run, I finally took his counsel.

"I used to use these guys—Robert, he's still in Simi Valley, I think. We could have them do it," Mike said.

"But how much will it cost?" I asked. "Do they even do through-hole stuff? How fast can we get it done?"

"Dunno, dunno, dunno," Mike said. "But you can pick up that antique communication device that you loathe—the phone—and ask them."

"Why don't you do it? They know you're legit."

"You're just being lazy. You can't email for everything."

"Right. And when was the last time you helped put stuff together? And how about that DAC we have to do?" I shot back.

"I have ideas for the DAC," Mike grumbled. "But I hear you. I'll call them."

"Don't call them. Go ahead and take them the Lyr kit."

"Without a quote?"

"If we want to ship, without a quote."

And here's the funny thing. The next day, Mike went down to the board house and dropped the Lyr kit with them. A week later, we still didn't have a quote, but we had a full run of boards. Beautiful boards. Better than we ever did.

I was sold. We'd never make boards by ourselves again.

(And when the bill came in a few weeks later, it was insanely inexpensive. Lesson learned: there are some things that it's best not to do yourself.)

That's how, in the process of a few weeks, we went from a hobby business to something much more real. We were still a tiny diversion in the board house's big runs, and Eddie was still working primarily with Jose, and Schiit still wasn't producing enough money to pay Mike or me a salary, but it was starting to feel like something that was, well, going to go somewhere.

A final aside: today, we're the board house's #2 customer...a fact I find pretty hilarious—and appropriate.

CHAPTER 11

USB Sucks! Or, Mike Joins the 21st Century

OKAY. TIME FOR ME TO take a step down. Until now, most of the book has been about my designs, but now, it's time to talk about Mike Moffat and DACs.

But first, a scorecard. At this point in time, we're early in 2011. Say, nine months old. We've introduced:

- Asgard
- Valhalla
- Lyr

And I'd talked about upcoming DACs and other fantasy products with 6Moons, further deepening my "don't talk about it" dilemma. Again, if I could go back and punch myself in the face, I would.

Anyway, on to Mike.

If you know a little bit about the history of digital audio, you know that Mike was one of the first guys to take digital seriously, and the first to introduce a standalone DAC. Yes, you can thank Mike for all the separate DAC vs. CD player, DAC vs. sound card, DAC vs. the D/A in your phone / computer / Blu-ray / oven arguments we have today.

This same Mike Moffat also designs all the Schiit DACs. So, it's not like we just decided to get into the DAC market—we have the guy *who started it all.*

It's funny. Shortly after we introduced the Bifrost DAC, I got an email from a prospective customer that went something like this:

"Hey, this looks interesting, but I'm wondering what your credentials are in digital design...let me know, please?"

To which I replied something like this:

"Well, other than having the 'father of the DAC,' Mike Moffat, on our team, we can recount all the stuff he brought to the table in terms of DAC design. This includes:

- Much experimentation with early 2-chassis player / DAC designs with shared clocks before the SPDIF standard was approved
- The first standalone DAC
- The first to use custom digital filters in a DAC
- The first to use DSP to run those digital filters
- First true time domain optimized digital filters, based on math perfected with a U of Iowa Professor Emeritus of Mathematics and a RAND Corp mathematician
- The first to identify jitter as a cause of audio degradation— before Mike, 'bits is bits'—you can thank him for literally every jitter argument we have today
- The first to work to minimize the causes of jitter
- First to use a Stanford interval counter for jitter analysis, before 'convenient' measurement via JTest
- Presented an AES paper on jitter in digital audio
- The first to introduce the AT&T ST-optical interface to address jitter issues
- The first with upgradable DACs at Theta (from the beginning in 1986)
- The first to make an upgradable surround sound processor at Angstrom
- The first DTS-capable surround processor at Angstrom
- Multiple firsts in entertainment digital media distribution engineering at Digi-Flix

But even before Mike was doing digital, he was doing audio, at Theta:

- One of the first in the tube revival in the 1970s
- The first non-12AX7 implementation for audio (revolutionary in its day)
- The first 'no overall feedback' tube stage in the 1970s
- One of the first passive preamps
- Worked in the Chilean jungle looking for oil using the first 8-bit A-D converters prior to Theta
- In 1934, many years before he was born, God appeared to Mike and revealed to him the formula for amazing digital audio, which he has inscribed on twelve lead tablets..."

The prospective customer's response:

"Oh, then you're going to annihilate pretty much everything, then?"

Ha. If it was only so easy.

When Mike Says USB Sucks, You Listen

Okay. Enough of the bragging. The fact is, I'm excited to have Mike Moffat as a partner, and I'm proud of his resume. He's contributed quite a bit to the digital audio realm—just look at Sony's original stance of "perfect sound forever," and their current frank discussion of jitter-reducing measures in their audio products. Quite a turnaround.

But to get back on topic, let's talk about DACs. Not Mike's original idea for a DAC, the one he came up with shortly after we started the company, but Bifrost.

An aside: Mike's original idea for a DAC is what eventually turned into Yggdrasil. Yes, we've been talking about it for that long. Yes, we're really late. But it has grown and morphed over time. And, in the early part of 2011, we weren't ready for a DAC that cost ten times as much as an Asgard.

Once we were focused on the real goal—an inexpensive DAC in the same size chassis as Asgard, Valhalla, and Lyr—that's when the arguments started.

"And it'll have optical, coaxial, and USB inputs," I opined to Mike.

"USB?" Mike gagged, miming sticking a finger down his throat to induce vomiting. "USB is for children and fools. Why would you want to use USB for audio?"

"Because it's really popular," I said. "Everyone has it—"

"If everyone was dressing up in tutus, would you?" Mike shot back.

"No, but…"

"No, but you'd say you did, just to be popular."

"We *have* to have USB," I pressed on. "There are a ton of people who only have laptops for sources, and most of those only have USB."

Mike grumbled something under his breath, then spat out: "But USB sucks. It just sucks. It was never meant for audio. It's an all-purpose, packet-based grab bag that might be fine for printers or hard drives, but it's just crap for streaming. You can recover the clock from the packet clock, barf, or you can have the computer and DAC do some negotiating and guess at the clock, barf, or you can turn the whole car around and drive it from the back seat with the computer providing the clock, barf."

Note: the above, for the more technical, is Mike's take on iso-synchronus, adaptive, and asynchronous USB implementations.

Second note: also, remember, this is early 2011 we're talking about. Adaptive USB 1.1 was kinda the de facto "good solution", with most audio components using the truly terrifying TI USB input receiver / DAC / headphone amplifier / car washer chips that weren't even adaptive. Some guys were fooling around with USB 2.0, but implementations were thin and software was iffy. We know. We tried all of them.

"We *have to have USB*," I told Mike, firmly.

Mike grumbled again.

"Remember Angstrom," I said, bringing out the big guns.

Angstrom was Mike's surround processor company. It would probably still be around today, except for various life issues that aren't mine to talk about. But it's also the company where we discovered that going against the grain might not be the best idea, even if it ends up being the *right* idea.

Angstrom brought out one of the first inexpensive Dolby Digital decoders on the market, the Angstrom 100. It was a great product. But Mike didn't want to do video switching. Video switching, he said, had no place in a no-compromise home theater audio product. What's more, the new HDMI standard was imminent, and that was a whole new ballgame. The whole video-switching deal was going to be changing, and fast. So why put it in a product when it was going to be obsolete in less than a year?

Yes, it made sense. To us. Unfortunately, to customers, it made a lot less sense, especially when Angstrom never brought out the promised separate video switcher.

"But Angstrom *was* right," Mike said. "Look at all the processors today, you throw them away when HDMI changes. Now we have the same thing with USB. You know there's gonna be a better way to do it in a few months."

"I know. But USB is a must-have. We're dead in the water without it."

Mike sat for a long time, saying nothing. Then his eyes lit up. "Make it upgradable," he said.

I shook my head in confusion. "Make what upgradable?"

"The USB input. Put it on a separate card. So you can change it when the technology changes." Now, Mike was excited. He jumped up. "No. Not just USB. Make the whole thing upgradable, so you can swap the DAC as well! That's the way you do it! Not just a throwaway product, something you can keep for as long as you want."

"The whole thing? Upgradable?" I was skeptical. "Mike, you

know we're talking about a product that only costs a few hundred dollars."

"Right. And that's the brilliant part. You can buy a throwaway DAC, or you can buy ours."

"And," Mike continued, pointing a finger in the air, "We'll also make sure it's bit-perfect to the DAC, instead of using an asynchronous sample rate converter."

"Is that good?" I asked. (Remember, I'm the analog guy.)

"Is it good? Is it good, he asks?" Mike said, recoiling from me as if I'd just asked if a Michelin-star restaurant was better than McDonald's. "It's *an absolute necessity* if you don't want to throw away all the original music data, and create some mathematical-abortion mishmash of interpolated crap, especially if you're at a nonbinary multiple of the original sample rate, like going from 16/44.1 to 24/192. No, wait. Let me guess. You're gonna tell me, in your infinite marketing wisdom, we have to crap everything up to 24/192 so we can have a number on a datasheet. Oh, boy."

"No, I'm not gonna tell you that," I said. "But what are we talking about here? How hard is it to keep everything bitperfect?"

"It's a pain in the ass," Mike said. "We'll need a microprocessor to switch the clocks, we have to reset the DAC when sample rates change, we'll need a hard relay mute, stuff like that."

"Expensive?"

"More than just throwing in an ASRC chip and being done with it," Mike said. "And we'll need firmware."

I sat quietly for a bit. Firmware meant Dave, the unsung code / digital hero of Schiit Audio. He's the third guy on the engineering team. But bringing him on meant even more expense, and we were still struggling to simply keep shipping on time.

But if Mike wants something, he gets it.

So we got Dave. And we started working on the first prototype of what would become Bifrost. This was a bigger project than anything we'd taken on before, involving digital design, firmware, system integration, and analog design. I did only one thing on Bifrost—the discrete analog output stage. And that was plenty.

Analog electronics in a digital box, being fed by the relatively noisy output of a D/A chip, is a whole different ballgame than a preamp or power amp. So, many iterations of compensation and filtering were in order.

While I was working on that, Mike and Dave were doing the rest. This included:

- Evaluation of the various USB input solutions
- Integration of the SPDIF inputs
- Microprocessor-based clock management
- DAC evaluation (one of the good things about a modular DAC is that it lets us try all the leading candidates for D/A ICs out there—we settled on AKM because it's what sounded the best, plus it's one of the best-measuring DACs out there)

Fun fact: the first layout of Bifrost had the input selector switch backwards, pointing inside the chassis. I joked with Mike that we could put a cantilever behind the front panel button to activate it, and I think for a few moments, he actually believed me.

Of all "the rest," what took the longest was by far the USB input. Back then, you had the option of licensing code for USB 1.1, using a standard USB 1.1 input chip (the one I mentioned that has all the other stuff tacked on to it), or using one of three different USB 2.0 input solutions. The problem with the USB 2.0 inputs was that they were all kinda beta-ish in one way or another. One needed drivers for Mac and PC, despite Macs supporting the USB Audio Class 2 natively. One was really ambiguous about their drivers and licensing.

And then there was C-Media. C-Media was an obscure Taiwanese company that had just introduced their flagship USB 2.0 input receiver. And by "just introduced," I mean, "the datasheet was labeled Version 0.9, and the USB firmware programmer crashed after successfully programming one device—every time."

"Version 0.9 on a datasheet," Mike said, grimly, when we got the first docs. "It's a beta. Run away. Run far, far away."

But C-Media was helpful, providing the support we needed to get their device up and running. And when it was running, it sounded pretty good. And by "pretty good," I mean "as good or better than anything else we tried."

Mike was less impressed. "It's not complete crap," he grumbled.

Later, we'd make it the USB input better with some tweaks, to the point where we thought we had one of the better-sounding implementations out there. That was where we launched with the original Bifrost—but that happens much later in the story.

A USB Mode/USB Audio Standards Primer

Okay. Let's go to the "useful data" side of things. A lot of people are monumentally confused about USB audio input. So here's a guide to the whys and wherefores—something I should probably put on our site.

USB Mode Versus USB Audio Class. A ton of people are confused when I say things like, "Modi uses USB Audio Class 1 over USB 2.0." They think I mean that it uses USB 1.0 as a transmission protocol. Actually, it doesn't. It runs USB 2.0 at 480MBPS, but transmits audio using the USB Class 1 audio standard.

Still confused? Okay, let's break it down.

USB Modes. This is all about data rate. This has nothing to do with audio.

- **1.0:** The earliest standard. So slow I forgot what it was. Not used for audio.
- **1.1:** Transmits data up to 12Mbps. Can be used to transmit audio up to 24/96.
- **2.0:** Transmits data up to 480Mbps. Can be used to transmit audio up to insane torture-the-cats-and-hard-drives rates like 32/768 and such.

- **3.0:** Transmits data up to 5Gbps (ha.) No USB Class 3 audio standard. No USB Audio 3.0 receivers. However, USB 3.0 ports are backwards-compatible with USB 2.0, so they can be used with anything using USB Audio 2.0 standard.*

- **3.1:** New reversible fantasy USB spec created out of Apple envy and support for people too dumb to insert a cable the right way. No products out yet. Looking forward to all the confusion coming our way because of this.

USB Audio Classes. These are *standards* (hello, Microsoft) created to enable the transfer of audio data over USB. They are not USB modes.

- **USB Audio Class 1.** Supported by everyone. Plug a DAC using USB Audio Class 1, like Modi, into any Mac or PC, many Linux systems, some phones, etc. and it will be recognized and play audio with no drivers required, up to 24/96.*

- **USB Audio Class 2.** Hello, Microsoft. There is this not-so-new-anymore standard called USB Audio Class 2. And you really should support it. Because you look really dumb when anyone can plug in a USB Class 2 DAC to any Mac, many Linux machines, phones, etc. and expect it to work without drivers,* while you still rely on kludgy workarounds that require drivers, ASIO setup or WASAPI setup, etc.

So what is it with all these asterisks? Well, it's because, in Microsoft and Apple's infinite wisdom, they've decided to save us from the threat of extreme power dissipation through USB ports with a new innovation called "port power management." What this means is that the USB port, rather than delivering the full 500mA, or 1A, of power, as required by the USB standard, can be throttled down to use less power. Which plays merry hell with some DACs. Yes, including ours. Which means we get to educate everyone about how to turn off port power management, or, in some cases, ask them to go out and buy an externally powered USB hub to completely mitigate it. Maybe they should label the ports as "really full power / real USB spec," and "battery-lifetime-promoting, save-the-planet USB port that doesn't really provide full power." No, wait, that wouldn't fit. Never mind.

And, you know what? After writing that, I agree with Mike. USB sucks.**

**About 80% of our customer support is helping resolve Windows USB issues, from driver installation to port power management, so I'm biased. But now you know why Fulla is locked down to driverless USB Audio Class 1 operation.

USB 2.0, 24/192, and Beyond (and the Silliness of it All)

For Bifrost, though, locking it down to 24/96 wasn't an option. 24/96 was becoming the de facto entry level for digital audio via USB. I wanted to start with 24/192 capability from Day 1. And I got that.

But USB still had some oddities. The earlier C-Media USB receiver chip didn't work at 24/176.4, even though it did 24/192. Why? No idea. But at the time it wasn't a huge consideration.

Fun fact: the CM6631A can easily do up to 32/384. Why don't we enable it? Two reasons: (a) There is no 32-bit music, and never will be.*** (b) There is no 384k PCM audio for sale that we know of. Sure, there's DSD 2X at 352.8k, but that's a whole 'nother discussion.

***There's a napkin-scribble by a famous analog designer floating around out there on the Internet somewhere, regarding the noise and precision of analog circuitry necessary for different digital resolutions. I can't find it at the moment, but it went something like this:

14-15 bits: standard parts and layout

16-17 bits: attention to power supply noise, premium parts, careful layout

18-19 bits: extreme measures taken with low-noise parts, multi-layer boards, and exceptionally fine layout

20-21 bits: God's domain

Fact is, 24 bits is 144dB dynamic range, which is about the limit of our Stanford analyzers. The best DACs, to date, manage 19.5-20 Equivalent Number of Bits (ENOB), even if they are "24 bit" or "32 bit" spec'd. 32 bits is 192dB dynamic range, which ain't gonna happen, no way, no how, not even in temperature-controlled circuits sitting within two feet of solid lead shielding. Consider that a stun grenade is 170-180dB, and you'll see how crazy this is.

Perhaps it's a matter of capability. With SPDIF, we had some finite, and rather low, limits to amount of data we could transmit reliably in the past, especially if you were talking Toslink optical. That's why Theta went to AT&T glass-fiber optical to get more bandwidth. Now, Toslink is better, but it's a rare Toslink that can do 24/192 reliably.

But with USB 2.0, and even more so, 3.0, we have no such restrictions. How big a data rate do you want? How many bits? No problem. We can make up silly numbers all day. But don't think it'll be meaningful in musical terms, if, say, we can transmit 64/1.544Mbps bit depths and sample rates.

But, you know what? If you have a Bifrost, you don't have to worry. If aliens from the planet Zebtron land on our world tomorrow, bringing physics-defying technology that enables 64/1.544Mbps audio transmission over USB, we'll have a USB Gen X card soon enough to handle it.

But I wouldn't hold my breath.

The Problem with Not Invented Here

Finally, let's talk business. Thanks to Mike's insistence on being different, we ended up with a truly unique DAC. And sometimes it takes that stubborn insistence, that rejection of everything "not invented here," to make something great.

But "not invented here" can bite you in the butt too.

It's something to watch for, if you're going to start your own business. Too much "not invented here" hubris can delay products, reduce efficiency, and interrupt operations. Sometimes the right answer is only an Internet search away. Or a great idea might be just a small tweak to a similar product.

"But wait," you say. "Are you saying…steal from other companies? Plagiarize?"

No. It's a balancing act. You should be aware of what your competition is doing, how other people have solved problems like yours, and what the basic industry benchmarks are. At the same time, you should have your own ideas.

And—here's the hard part—you have to have a feel for whether or not your ideas are better than the prevailing wisdom, and also if your ideas are realistic to implement.

"So how the heck do you do that?" you ask.

Believe me, I wish I had a formula. Some companies will spend tons of time benchmarking against their competitors and running focus groups to try to determine if they're going to be successful, but I believe this is more likely to result in mediocrity rather than brilliance. You can't assume your competition has all the right ideas, and you can't assume a focus group is a microcosm of your entire prospect base. What's more, you can't assume that a truly great idea will make it through a focus group, because they're more likely to be confused about something that's truly unique and has no point of reference.

Case in point: until the original iPhone was announced, everyone was wondering what kind of keypad and stylus it would use. Nobody guessed it would have neither one. It was simply insanity to consider it, at the time. Love or hate Apple, they changed the game.

I think the best way to decide on when to stick to your guns on new ideas—to be stubborn, and pound the table, and insist on "if it's not invented here, it's not for us," comes down to weighing the risks and rewards.

Here's an example, using Bifrost.

Rewards of doing what everyone else was doing:

- **Faster product introduction:** If we'd done what everyone else was doing—using USB 1.1 and upsampling everything with ASRC, in a non-upgradable platform—we would have had a product out much sooner.

- **Easier development:** We wouldn't need code, integration, multiple boards, custom connectors, etc.
- **Easier support:** No explanations about why the DAC has to be reset, resulting in the famous "clicking".

Risks of doing it like everyone else:

- **Prospect disappointment:** People were already expecting great / different / innovative products from us, not a rehash of what everyone else was doing, so Bifrost might have flopped if it had been like a lot of others.
- **Undershooting the bar:** If someone else introduces a game-changer right before your me-too product, you're gonna be in a world of hurt.
- **No story:** Going with the crowd means you have no ideas of your own. No position. If you have no ideas of your own, what is your value? Sometimes you have to stand up and say, "This is what we believe in."

In the end, we decided to stand up and say, "We believe in this, and we'll take the pain to make it right."

Which is good. Because it was a pretty painful path getting to the Bifrost introduction, which was several months late. But the anecdotal results are that we did something right. Have you noticed that most of the better DACs these days are avoiding sample rate conversion, or allowing you to turn it off?

And now, on to the next chapter. Our most humbling experience.

CHAPTER 12

Schiit Goes Evil?

NO STORY ABOUT SCHIIT WOULD be complete without talking about NwAvGuy and the infamous Asgard Incident. Although the latter sounds like a neat title for a modern dark fantasy / conspiracy movie, it wasn't a joking matter at the time.

If you want to look at this from a business perspective, this is about how you handle adversity. I've said it before, but it bears repeating: even if a Bernanke helicopter drops $100 million in your lap with a note saying, "start-up capital for your company," business is a series of challenges. Some of these are gonna be company-changing. This one was.

But first, the scorecard: we're about thirteen months into Schiit at this time. July of 2011. We still have the same three products:

- Asgard
- Valhalla
- Lyr
- And a prototype of the Bifrost (no chassis)

In terms of human years, we're still a baby company. Still working in the garage, still putting everything back in to make more products and develop new ones, still with the 1.2 person crew (if you count 20% of my time, 30% of Eddie's time, and about 70% of Rina's time.)

So, we're cruising along, with Eddie building stuff, me testing, and Rina shipping, and Mike and I working on tweaking Bifrost so we could get it shipping (originally planned for July, but hey, you know, we're late on nearly everything), when we get an email.

This email has a video pasted into it, showing an AKG K701 driver flexing. With the email, there's a short message, asking if this is normal behavior when you turn an Asgard on and off.

Also, although I didn't know it at the time, the emailer also posted the same video on Head-Fi, asking "what causes this?" The whole thread is still available for your browsing: www.head-fi.org/t/562736/what-causes-this-amp-related

It's an insane day, so I send off a quick response: *Yep, it's normal.* Thinking at the time, *Yep, of course it's normal, many amps have transients when you turn them on and off.*

Anyway, back to the email...

The buyer wasn't thrilled by my response, so I offered to let the buyer return the amp for a refund, even though the sale was of a B-stock product, which we don't normally offer a fifteen-day return on.

Eventually, he took me up on the offer—but not before the Schiit hit the fan on Head-Fi.

Enter NwAvGuy

On the weekend after our buyer posted the video on Head-Fi, NwAvGuy appeared, pronouncing Schiit all a bunch of knuckle-dragging morons building dangerous amplifiers. Of course, I'm being a bit hyperbolic, but here's the actual first paragraph:

> *"My professional engineering opinion, having done both amplifier and speaker development, is this is potentially harmful and a serious flaw with the Asgard. The Schiit amps are clearly not designed for good objective performance. And when designers have other goals in mind there are often some serious side effects. NuForce doesn't seem to care the uDac-2 has serious channel balance problems for example. They claim that bad channel balance was necessary for the best sound at the price. The Asgard may have been designed with similarly misguided, or sloppy, priorities."*

Of course, Head-Fi went nuts.

I was lucky enough to see this post shortly after it happened, so I jumped in, citing the turn-on transient as a relatively minor one (which is what I remembered from the engineering notebook—in retrospect, I should have just grabbed an Asgard and tested it—but it was a weekend, I was tired, blah blah), defending our design against his assumptions about us putting all the cost in the chassis, and bringing up some reasons why we didn't want to use relays (most of all, contact degradation from outgassing, which NwAvGuy dismissed out of hand, although it is clearly present on the datasheet.)

The war escalated as a Head-Fi moderator stepped in to defend us (he owned an Asgard), and others weighed in. Mike Moffat even posted (as baldr) an emotional tract, calling out NwAvGuy as a coward and a bully, hiding behind anonymity with unknown agendas. Perhaps a bit over-the-top, but I think it's important to say that engineers are no less passionate about their products than an artist or performer. Attack the product, attack the person.

On Monday, more data came to light. The Head-Fi moderator tested his Asgard and found that the DC offset was more like 1-2 volts, not 150mV.

I confirmed this measurement. *Crap.* What now?

The notes on the prototype didn't jive. So I tested a few more units, then went back and tested the prototype. All the same—an order of magnitude higher than I remembered.

The explanation for the discrepancy between what was in our notebooks? I don't know. Maybe I wrote the numbers down wrong. Maybe I was measuring the wrong thing. The bottom line: never assume the old data is right. I shouldn't have. And I shouldn't have dismissed the question out of hand.

But, then again, I had no reason to suspect we had a problem. We'd tested about 1000 Asgards by this time, all through the full on-off cycle, through a single pair of Sennheiser HD650s. The 650s were fine. No problems. Bottom line on this: don't trust anecdotal results. And don't assume everyone has HD650s.

An aside: to this day, nobody has ever blown up a headphone with Asgard, at least to our knowledge. Lyr, yes—which is why we added the relay mute to it before the whole Asgard Incident.

After this, I went back on Head-Fi, apologized for my misrecollection, and said we'd:

- Warn people about the need to unplug and re-plug headphones in the owner's manual
- Investigate adding a relay mute to Asgard
- Refund anyone who had ever bought an Asgard, from the start, if they were disturbed about its performance

The third item—an unconditional refund on every Asgard— wouldn't have killed the company, but it would have come very close.

So, why did I offer it? Simple. I was done.

I was making no money from Schiit, Centric was going great guns, and along comes an anonymous blogger and calls into question our competence and reason for existing. What other crazies would be coming out of the woodwork, I wondered? When would the next attack come?

Maybe this whole audio thing wasn't such a hot idea, I thought. *Maybe better to pull the plug completely.*

But, I sat down with Mike over dinner at a local Korean BBQ (I still remember going there, but I don't remember the food at all, or even if I ate—I was really, really upset). And Mike talked some sense into me.

"This isn't the end of the world. We have Bifrost coming," he said.

"If we ever finish it," I moaned.

"It'll be done. And when it's done, we'll laugh about ever considering quitting."

I sighed. "That's easy for you to say."

"No. It isn't." Mike sat back. "Theta had its share of attacks over the years. We were reported for FCC noncompliance by a competitor, and the FCC came in and shut us down. Hell, our offices were broken into, and our engineering computers were stolen. Someone was trying to get our digital filter code. The thing is, these days, the hounds are invisible. You can't touch them. They can drop in out of nowhere, say whatever they like, and have no repercussions."

"So what do we do?" I asked.

"We be better than them," Mike said. "Add that relay. Kill the current run. Don't sell another Asgard without it. And offer to update everyone's current Asgard."

"The whole current run?" I asked. That was a pretty big investment.

"Yes. The whole current run of headphone-killing amps."

"But they aren't headphone-killing—" I began.

"It doesn't matter that they are or aren't. What matters is that everyone thinks they are. Or at least enough people to matter. So, we go above and beyond. And make it good."

I nodded. Mike was right.

The next day, I called the board house and had them scrap the current run of Asgards. Then, in a sixteen-hour fit of engineering, prototyped a relay mute, added it on to the Asgard PCB, and ordered new boards, rush, from the board house.

While I did this, the thread on Head-Fi grew and grew. Supporters, detractors, people bringing up other amplifiers that needed headphones unplugged, replugged, etc.

Finally I was done. That was when I posted this to Head-Fi:

"That said, we now understand that the precautions common to ultra-high-end (where it's well-known that turning on your multi-kilobuck amp before you turn on your multi-kilobuck preamp may involve having a very bad day) simply won't fly with inexpensive gear, so we're making the changes necessary to have our stuff be as user-friendly as possible.

Asgards will now ship with the same relay mute as Lyr, when we are back in stock. We will also offer a retrofit relay mute for

Asgard and Lyr, for customers who want the convenience, and install it on any current owner's amp for free."

An aside: This offer continues to be in force for all Asgards and Lyrs. Because, even though we've alerted the owners in our database, there are (a) second- and third-hand products out there with owners we don't know about, (b) many owners who didn't want the relay, and (c) our database is never 100% accurate—people move, etc.

But the biggest thing that happened in this thread was that NwAvGuy got banned.

Now, the reason for his ban wasn't his criticism of our products, but that isn't what mattered. Because the ban happened during the Asgard Incident, and because of what NwAvGuy posted on his blog afterwards, he'll be forever connected to us, rather than the other manufacturers and DIYers whose products he's criticized.

Oh, I don't believe you, you might be thinking. *Head-Fi protects its sponsors, that's why he got banned, end of story.*

Nope. If Head-Fi protected its sponsors, that thread simply wouldn't exist—and it certainly wouldn't exist now, almost three years later. If Head-Fi protected its sponsors, lots of negative stuff wouldn't happen. Are the threads still there? Yes.

And—consider this—Jude contacted me, bought our products, and talked about them before we were ever sponsors. This is something Head-Fi does very well—uncovering new, interesting products and getting them out in the world, even if the companies that make them are not sponsors.

Coda: What We Did Wrong...and Right

What we did wrong:

- Relying on memory of a measurement that was incorrect
- Minimizing a valid question because we're busy / tired / etc.
- Not immediately checking the performance of the amplifier

What we did right:

- Throwing away the current run
- Redesigning and shipping ones with relays
- Recalling and retrofitting Asgards and Lyrs, free

NwAvGuy: The Good and the Bad

"So, you guys really, really hate NwAvGuy," you might be saying.

The reality is more complex. NwAvGuy did a lot of good for the industry, including raising awareness about output impedance matching and the importance of measurements. And, as with the Asgard Incident, he helped make Schiit Audio a stronger company. For those things, I'm thankful. And, if he ever surfaces again, I'd buy him a beer.

But, he also brought a lot of absolutism to the fore, like the oft-stated idea that an amp (or DAC) with good measurements is audibly transparent, and cannot be improved upon. The "us vs. them" mentality of objective and subjective, audiophile and engineer—the objective-subjective divide widened considerably during, and after, NwAvGuy.

He also assumed a lot, without confirmation. Like our "expensive" chassis. Yes, they look expensive, but they are not. Like our "design by ear" philosophy. In actuality, it's more "confirm by ear." The speculation that we don't have, or know how to use, test equipment. The reality is that we have better equipment than the vaunted dScope.

And the bigger reality is: NwAvGuy, by his own admission, never touched a Schiit product.

Also on the good side, he helped kick the inexpensive headphone / DAC world into high gear with the open-source O2 and ODAC. Although neither of these designs is like anything we'd make, they're very popular.

And that's why you made Magni and Modi, you're thinking.

Actually, no. Modi is why we made Magni, and Modi actually appeared before the ODAC, at least in prototype form (see the upcoming chapter, DAC in a Toilet Paper Roll.) I doubt we would have done Magni much differently if the O2 wasn't around (more on that in another future chapter.)

I guess the biggest difference is in one of philosophy. We have a "live and let live" attitude at Schiit. We don't think we know it all, and we don't believe that our answers are always the best ones. We know how much work it takes to bring something to market, and we salute every company out there. It was only after NwAvGuy, though, that we enshrined our basic principles here: schiit.com/about/principles

So, if someone else can come along, kick us in the pants, and help us make things better, let me say in advance: thank you!

Where Did He Go?

Despite the joking about "Schiit had him offed," the reality is we have no idea who he is, or why he disappeared. But let's have a little fun and speculate, because some of these ideas I haven't seen in other places:

1. **Muzzled by a retainer.** As an audio consulting engineer, NwAvGuy's retainers would have heart palpitations if they saw him attacking other companies. If they found out about it, they may have said, "please stop doing that," without the please, and with a threat of contract termination.

2. **Hidden in plain sight.** Maybe he's now working in the industry and knows the ramifications of attacking other companies (in short, lawyers, lawsuits, expenses, bad stuff all around, see Apple and Samsung.)

3. **Gone to the subjective dark side.** Maybe he heard some gear that was incredibly magical, but measured like crap. Maybe that rocked his world enough that he'll next be reviewing at *The Absolute Sound* or 6Moons.

Coda 2: Business Lessons

So, what did we learn from all of this? I can joke and say, "Well, we learned to put relays in everything," but that's not entirely true.

We did learn a lot on the engineering side, and it did push us to put one of the most advanced, analog-computer-style protection system in Mjolnir, and perhaps the most advanced protection system ever in Ragnarok, fully microprocessor-controlled for all operational and fault states, running proprietary algorithms that both manage thermal runaway and conditions that may cause de-biasing of the output stage (such as when playing loud, compressed music.)

But most of what we learned was on the business side. It reminded us that we don't have all the answers, that we can and do make mistakes, and that we have to stand up, admit them, and make it right when we do.

Because no business, no matter how great the engineers, no matter how skilled the production team is, no matter how solid the logistics guys are, no matter how enlightened the management is, is infallible.

You screw up. Bad things happen. And you make them good.

CHAPTER 13

"Isn't the Symbol for USB the Long Flat Rectangle?"

STRANGE TITLE FOR A CHAPTER, right? It'll become much clearer—and funnier—later on.

This chapter is really about three things:

- Transitioning from a "headphone amplifier company" to a "DAC/amp company"

- The difference between a hardware company and a software company, and some of the decisions you have to make if you're going to be both

- Products that really, really, really, really don't want to ship on time—see "development time is proportional to the square of complexity"

I'd announced the Bifrost DAC on June 30, 2011, with a delivery date projected to be in August. Because we'd been running the prototypes for a while, I was really confident we could ship the Bifrost early, and was looking forward to a July launch.

So, starting June 30, 2011, prospective customers were able to preorder a Bifrost. This immediately caused several problems, as exemplified by these questions:

- **Hey, I just bought a Bifrost and an Asgard, do you hold them and ship them together, or can I get the Asgard early?** Problem: this broke our shipping quote system, which was still in the archaic realm of "guess a range, and hope you don't lose too much money on it."

- **Hey, if I get that Asgard earlier than my Bifrost, when does the fifteen-day money-back start?** Problem: Oops. Kinda broke that model, didn't we? We didn't have a great answer for this, and ended up making all sorts of extended deals. Which gets fun if you're trying to refund money, say, after sixty days.

- **Hey, do you have an exact date when you're going to ship, I need to plan…?** Problem: No, of course not. We didn't even have metal. So what did we do? We said we'd probably ship early, in July. Very dumb. *Do not do this.*

- **Hey, do you charge my card before you ship?** No, we never charge before we ship, but the problem is—the authorization on the card expires. Go back and try to capture transactions that were authorized a couple of months ago. Guess what? Sometimes they don't reauthorize. Customers don't like these complexities.

- **Does Bifrost work with the GigaComplex Server X-2000 running a modified Amiga operating system with Rubycon Black Gate capacitors and opto-coupled USB 2.2 outputs?** Problem: Yeah, I'm having a little fun with this, but you get the drift—lots of people asking questions about Linux, phones, etc. We'd only tested on Macs and PCs using the three most popular PC OSes at the time (XP, Vista, 7). And that was a hell of a lot of testing. So we really couldn't say.

Which is a great segue into the difference between hardware companies, software companies, and what happens when you have to do both. So let's talk about that for a bit.

Hardware, Software, and Restaurants

Restaurants? Yes, restaurants. Although I'm a foodie, I have exactly zero desire to ever open a restaurant. Why? Because restaurants combine the problems of manufacturing with the problems of service with an extra problem of *the stock actually goes bad.* No thanks. So, a tip of the hat to anyone who can make it as a restaurateur. That's a helluva business.

What does that have to do with hardware and software?

Well, the problems with hardware are largely a matter of manufacturing (buying / holding stock, assembly, margins), while the problems of software are largely a matter of service (finding and keeping a team happy, support, dealing with a constantly changing OS and software regime.) Of course, I'm oversimplifying, but you get the general picture.

Hardware Business Problems. When you're making hardware, like analog headphone amplifiers, your problem really comes down to this: *can you make enough margin on what you're making to run the company and keep it growing?*

Because, when you're talking hardware, you're talking stock. You have to buy chassis, transformers, boards, transistors, ICs, and a myriad of other parts before you can ship anything. That means there's a lot of money up front in hard bits. Then you have to assemble it, test it, ship it, and support it. If you're doing it right, your support will be minimal—your failure rate should be much less than 1%. And, if the products are simple, your tech support should also be minimal.

But for parts, you could be looking at 33-50% of the cost of your product. So if you're making a run of 100 $1,000 amps, you'll be out $33-50K at the start. Then you have the added costs of personnel, facilities, support, and shipping on top of that.

Note: *never discount the importance of shipping—this is not a trivial task, and it can get very complex. And "free shipping" should be called "cost-inclusive shipping." Offer it at your own risk. Because Hawaii. And Alaska. And Canada. And every other country in the world. And what about returns? And...hell, I'll just say it. Don't offer it. Period.*

In a hardware business, you're out a sizable investment before you've shipped anything. More so when you find out the parts you specified aren't available, or you ordered the wrong parts, or something's wrong with them. But once the product is shipped, you should be able to make money, if you're doing it right. And you can keep doing it, as long as there is market demand.

Software Business Problems. Software's a bit different. Your "hard costs" are actually salaries for the programming staff, your facilities costs, your admin costs, etc. These aren't tied to the amount of software you sell. If you spend $50K developing software, it doesn't matter if you sell 100 copies or 1,000,000 copies at $99 each, because you're going to be distributing it via download or via inexpensive media.

But—and here's the *big* but—you have to support it. Unlike simple hardware, you have to assume that it won't install on some systems, it will conflict with other software, many customers may need hand-holding. And, as an added bonus, the OSes change from year to year. This means that what worked yesterday may not work today, and vice versa.

What this all adds up to is that software is an ongoing business—you need to keep programmers constantly employed and engaged, you need to test your product against changes in OSes, you need to issue updates to deal with incompatibilities, and you need to have a significant service staff to provide technical support. So, with software, even if your costs are not directly related to how much you sell, you have to sell enough to cover your costs and make a profit.

Note: *of course, there are different models (open-source, SaaS, etc.) that I'm not covering here, and admittedly I've never had a software company, but the principles are somewhat similar on the agency side (heavy service, overhead unrelated to amount of revenue.)*

So, back to restaurants. They have hard costs (ingredients), service costs (chefs, servers, etc.)…and as added bonuses, their stock goes bad over time, and they have additional regulation (liquor licenses, inspections) and accidents (sick people) to deal with. So, no restaurants in our future. But I'm certainly hoping others are up to the task.

What the Heck Does This Have to Do With Anything?

Yeah, I figured you'd ask that. What it has to do with Schiit is that, with the launch of Bifrost, *we became a software company by default.* A very, very lightweight software company, yes, but we had new complexities of firmware and drivers to deal with.

"Oh, waah, big deal, you get the Giant Baby of the Year Award," say the real software developers now.

Yeah, that may be true. But by using firmware to run the Bifrost, and planning to release drivers for Windows, we were crossing another invisible line in business: from a pure hardware company, to a hardware / software company.

With this driver came tons more support, all for Windows users. And no less than eight updates to the driver as of this writing. This may not be a big deal in software-land, but it's a big deal for a hardware company.

In fact, Bifrost almost remained capped at 24/96 for this exact reason. The discussions went something like this, usually in a summer-hot garage:

"Mike, we need to offer 24/192 support. There's 24/192 music available on HDtracks," I told him.

"What, seven tracks of it?" Mike sneered.

"It's limited, yes, but people are asking for 24/192 support. And it would be a good differentiator for Bifrost, now that we've nixed the balanced outputs."

"Balanced should only be hardware-balanced," Mike pontificated. "Two DACs. Summed single-ended. That's what we did at Theta."

"I know, but don't change the subject. 24/192."

Mike doesn't change course fast, though. "If we're going to do balanced, we're going to do it right. Hell, I want to do a DAC that has two DACs per channel."

"You can do that one later. For now, Bifrost. 24/192."

"24/192 uses a half-rate master clock to the DAC," Mike said. "24/96 probably sounds better."

"Is this a limitation of the AKM?" I asked.

"No, it's a limitation of most delta-sigma DACs. The master clock can only be so fast."

"I still want 24/192. Period."

Mike sighed. "Who's going to do the tech support for the Windurrs users?"

"Me, for now."

"You're going kill yourself," Mike predicted.

"Maybe. But we need 24/192. It works. Let's support it."

"Ohhh...kay," Mike said, shaking his head.

And that's how Bifrost got 24/192 support. It seems funny today, with 32/384 or even higher sampling rates. Not that there's any PCM music available there, but hey, it's like megapixels. Meaningless numbers to use in marketing. Buzzword compliance.

Hardware, Firmware, Software

With Bifrost, though, we didn't just have software. We had hardware (the DAC—chassis, motherboard, USB daughterboard, DAC / analog daughterboard), firmware (for the motherboard and USB daughterboard), and software (Windows drivers.) This was a level of complexity higher than anything we'd ever done before. Complexity was one of the reasons we were late.

Yes, I'm getting back to the late part.

But first, some of you are probably saying, "Software? Firmware? What the hell is the difference, anyway, and what do they do?"

- **Firmware** is embedded code you don't expect to change very much, if at all. Examples of this include the code that runs the LCD display on your refrigerator, or makes the buttons on your sprinkler controller work. Firmware runs behind the scenes, usually never needing updating.

- **Software** is installed code that can change quite a bit. This is everything from your NVIDIA driver to your copy of Microsoft Office. You update software from time to time, or even switch to different versions.

In the case of Bifrost, we had to develop two different sets of firmware: one to run the motherboard, and one to run the USB input.

The motherboard firmware runs the front panel button, the bitperfect clock management system, and the hard mute protection system. It's programmed via an Ethernet jack inside the Bifrost (intentionally placed, because we don't expect to ever update it.)

The USB firmware runs the USB receiver, generating the specific clocks and formats that we need for our D/A implementation. It's programmed via the USB port.

And firmware is where we get into the genesis of the title of this chapter. But let's talk about problems some more, first...

Products That Don't Want To Ship

Okay, back to Bifrost problems. Announced in June, said to be shipping in August. When did it ship? Late October.

Doesn't sound like much, but when you're already ordered into backorder before shipping and you have hundreds of angry customers yelling at you, it's a very big deal indeed.

Aside: *Haven't I said something before about opening your mouth and preordering? Well, it took us past Mjolnir and Gungnir to finally learn that lesson. Mainly because, "Nothing could be as bad as Bifrost." Yeah, right.*

So, what went wrong?

First, it was the DAC / Analog board. My first attempt at a hardware summer (from the DAC's differential output) was simple, elegant, good-sounding—and completely useless, because it would have fixed Bifrost at 1V out, rather than the industry-standard 2V

RMS. So I had to go back to the drawing board.

Then, the way we were going to attach the daughterboards didn't work out. We'd expected to use press-in connectors, like I did back in the Sumo days. Those didn't work so well, because the Bifrost daughterboards stood a lot taller than the Sumo ones. We played around with various plastic options before saying, "the hell with it," and using metal standoffs and screws instead.

Next, the board interconnections themselves. Now, there are plenty of header options out there, but not at the length we wanted to use. Which meant Bifrost headers were custom. Which meant an eight-week lead time.

Note to other guys who want to start hardware companies: check the lead times. Some parts are fourteen to sixteen weeks. And sometimes they don't come on time.

Then the metal came. Unlike Valhalla, it was beautiful…but it didn't fit. I'd gotten used to getting the metal "done in one," and we hadn't done a first article for fit. So, now we were sitting on hundreds of chassis that didn't fit…and we had boards already out for assembly.

This was by far the biggest problem. Because when you're in a situation like this, you either have to redesign the board (and throw away the assembled ones) or redesign the chassis (and scrap the chassis).

In the end, we did a modification to the inner chassis that allowed it to work, then made a longer-term change—the only running change we've ever done to metal.

Another note to other prospective manufacturers: don't change the metal if you can help it. Having two (or more) versions of the same chassis plays hell with production—as in, "Hey, we found a box of chassis, but the boards don't fit."

And, when the modified metal came, we found that we'd inverted the left and right designators on the output jacks. Argh! Back for rescreening.

In short, Bifrost really didn't want to ship. It was a product from hell.

But, by RMAF 2011, we had a working Bifrost, in a cosmetically perfect chassis. Time to show it off!

This time, we weren't exhibiting with Sennheiser. We'd grown up enough to have our own booth! But we hadn't grown up enough to do anything other than take the products there. We had no signs, no literature, nothing. Rina clipped a couple of 8.5" x 11" printouts of the logo to the curtains behind us, but other than that, there was no indication of who we were. *Great marketing, dood!*

It was also the last show that we took all the products in a single backpack. Literally. Asgard, Valhalla, Lyr, Bifrost, a pair of LCD-2s and a couple other cans—all in Rina's backpack.

That was her idea. "It'll save on shipping, and it won't get lost," she told me.

"So what happens when Homeland Security takes one look at the X-Ray machine and stops you for having forty pounds of electronics in your bag?"

"Then I smile nicely at them and play dumb."

I sighed. "Then I'll tell them I don't know you."

"It'll be fine," she insisted.

And—frighteningly enough—she was right. They didn't even blink at LAX. Didn't stop us. Didn't ask about what all the electronics were. Not a single question. Nor did they stop her, or ask anything, at Denver International, when we were coming back.

Makes you feel really good about flying. *Three-point-five ounces of shampoo? Bad boy, go to the little room. Forty pounds of aluminum, steel, copper, transformers, and wiring? No problem, move along.*

Isn't the Symbol for USB...

The day we put together the first ten Bifrosts, I felt about 1000 lbs lighter—and about ten years younger. We were finally shipping! The nightmare was over!

At least until the next day.

Rina was listening to the Bifrosts, prior to cleaning, bagging, and packing. But instead of looking happy, she looked uncomfortable.

Finally she stopped cleaning and asked, "Isn't the symbol for USB the long flat rectangle?"

"What do you mean?" I asked.

She pointed at the icon on the front of the Bifrost to clarify.

"Of course it is!" I said, thinking, *That's a dumb question.*

"It's not the round circle?"

"No, that's the coaxial input. Why?"

"Because this Bifrost is playing USB when it's on the round circle."

What? I stomped over to take a look. She was right. It was happily playing music from the USB input, with the front panel LED indicating that it was on the coaxial input.

My heart skipped a beat. "Are they all like this?" I asked.

"I think so," she said, and grabbed another.

In a few minutes, we confirmed: yes, they were all like that. Including the show Bifrost. Which we'd never noticed.

Great, just great.

I knew what was happening. The front panel LEDs were controlled by the microprocessor. It was simply lighting up the wrong LED. It could be fixed with a simple firmware change.

But...firmware took Dave. I had to get ahold of him, tell him about the latest fire drill, and get a new copy of the firmware. Which only took hours...but then we had to take apart every Bifrost so we could get to the Ethernet connector and reprogram them.

And...*what about all the other Bifrosts we shipped yesterday?*

Yep. You got it. They all had the wrong firmware.

We offered to replace it, but many customers didn't want it changed...as if it was a Bifrost Special Edition or something. By my estimate, there's six to seven Bifrosts out there still with reversed LEDs. As well as my personal Bifrost, the original show unit. I've simply never bothered to change it.

So, if you buy a used Bifrost and see that the LEDs are wrong, let us know...we'll change it. Or not. You have a piece of history.

CHAPTER 14

Technical Help Via Time Warner, and The World's Most Irritating Failure Mode

THIS IS THE STORY OF Tony, our second employee and first technician. It's also a story of an amazingly hard-to-diagnose production
problem that, to this day, is not fully explained. You'll see why
soon, but first, the wrap-up:

- At this point in time, it's late October 2011
- We have four products: Asgard, Valhalla, Lyr, and Bifrost
- But, we are both thinking about what's next...the bigger,
  badder, as-yet-unnamed balanced amp and DAC
- We're still in the garage, though Eddie has been banned
  from smoking Djarums now
- We've reorganized the garage to give Eddie more space and
  a real table to work on—which meant moving the Corvette
  to Mike's extra garage space for a while

Even before we brought out Bifrost, it was clear I couldn't do all
the testing and repair. At least not do it and remain sane. I was
running the marketing company full-time—and, with it being busy,
sometimes more than full-time.

I was also contracted by Penguin to write a couple of crazy
books about giant robots. Just because.

Yes, I am an idiot. But hey, might be fun, right?

Yoda and Rain Man

In any case, this is how we got Tony: me freaking out from insane time pressure, and Mike stepping in to help. Now, for all of you who think Mike is a Yoda-like sage who comes in with words of wisdom and a perfect plan, consider this conversation…

"Mike, I can't do this all," I told him. "Between Centric, the books, and the orders ramping up, I'm doing sixteen-hour days."

"Well, we should look for a tech," Mike told me.

"To work in a garage?" I said, doubtfully.

"Eddie does," Mike shot back.

"Eddie is special," I said. And he was. Eddie had long worked in the entertainment biz, so he was used to weird hours and spotty schedules. And he liked the free food.

Mike's expression brightened. "I think I know the perfect tech for us."

"Who?"

"Tony," Mike said. "He used to work for Time Warner Cable. He did all the tough installs that nobody else wanted to do."

I shook my head doubtfully. "Mike, a Time Warner tech is a little different—"

"He's a little like Rain Man," Mike said. "But once you show him something, he never forgets it."

Rain Man? I thought. The image of a Time Warner-uniformed, confused Dustin Hoffman flickered through my mind. It wasn't a reassuring thought. "Um, Mike—"

"He's a good guy, I'll call him," Mike said, whipping out his phone.

"But he's still gotta work in a garage," I protested, as Mike put the phone to his ear.

"No problem," Mike said. "He's my stepson."

Oh, great. Better and better. "But Mike, we can't guarantee hours, and we don't have healthcare and stuff—hell, we don't even have real employees—isn't he better at Time Warner?"

"Doesn't matter," Mike said. "He's been laid off." Then, into the phone: "Hey, Tony, want to come down and work on some Schiit?"

"Mike!" I snapped.

Mike held up a hand. "Yeah. Sure. Now is good. I just spent half an hour listening to my girly business partner talk about how he's overworked. Yeah. Here's the address…"

When Mike hung up, I grumbled, "Does he even know how to solder?"

"Probably," Mike said. "And if not, you only have to show him something once."

"What if he doesn't work out?" I asked.

"Then he doesn't work out," Mike said. "Look, I'm not trying to stuff him down your throat. But I figure, Tony's available, let's give him a shot."

I sighed. "Rain Man? Really?"

Mike grinned. "Yep!"

The Tequila Bottle Theory of Hiring

Okay, you don't need to be a brilliant CEO to know that what we just did there isn't how you hire people. Not if you want to be successful. Or at least not by the rules of any manual on *Getting the Best and Brightest,* ghostwritten for a CEO who got the reins of an established $10B company by his friends from Harvard.

Because, of course, you have to have a rock-solid vetting process that includes questions like "How many marbles fit in an average toilet?" and psychological profiling to determine if the candidate is a right fit. You have to set Goals and Responsibilities and identify Key Result Areas. And you must carefully analyze the results in order to determine the best possible candidates, then offer them a can't-refuse package that includes all the latest perks, from a fitness club to a concierge.

(Or you can go play some basketball with the founder and get a job offer, or have gone to school at Stanford with the CIO, or have compromising pictures of the CMO with a chicken. The real world doesn't always work by the numbers.)

In my businesses, I've hired probably a couple hundred people over the last twenty years. In the early days, I went by the formula and the checklist. I agonized over who to hire. And, a lot of the times, the formula won over my gut.

And *every time* the formula won over my gut, I screwed the company.

Because people can't be distilled down to a two-page resume and a one-hour interview. There are a ton of candidates skilled in the art of looking good on paper. There are plenty who can be friendly, intelligent, and make all the right noises in response to the standard interview questions.

And then fall on their face. Because it's easy to recite a formula, but a lot harder to deal with the unpredictable real world. People who interview well usually fall down at one of these things:

- **Only Doing it By the Book,** or "This is how we've always done it in my previous jobs." Yeah, that's fine, but the world is changing. Open your eyes. If you're incapable of adapting, then it's going to be a bad day.

- **Stunning Lack of Initiative,** or "Well, you didn't tell me to do that" syndrome. Look. You're not computer software. You're a person. Small businesses don't have time to program your every move. You know what needs to be done. Take some initiative.

- **Prima Donna-itis,** or "You're so lucky to have me." Hey, I know you're a rock star, but that doesn't mean you need to redecorate your entire division before you do a single ounce of work. And no, we will not sort your M&M's. You're here to work. Get over yourself.

Your standard interview—or even the creative Google-esque interview—isn't going to identify those kinds of people. They're not even particularly good at identifying the go-getters, unless you get off the script and ask them *why* and *how* they did something, rather than just focusing on *what* they did.

For example, let's look at this scenario:

- **Laid off from last job.** Big red flag, in traditional hiring. *Do not interview.*

- **Laid off from last job**—for recognizing the inefficiency in the ordering system and building a custom database to automate it, thereby eliminating their own job. *Hire this person. Immediately.*

Today, when I'm hiring, I don't ask any of the traditional questions, or the stupid you're-stuck-on-the-moon-with-a-banana-and-inner-tube trick questions, or give people tests.

What do I do?

I just sit and talk to them, usually about what they're most interested in—which may or may not be work-related. Because you won't get to really know someone until they're comfortable talking with you.

(I joke that my ideal interview would be sitting down with the interviewee and a bottle of tequila. But of course we can't do that. Regulations. Decorum. Horrors! Ia! Ia! Cthulu fhtagn!)

The result? Today, we have a lot less churn in both businesses, and a lot more long-term employees. Selecting people with potential and ambition beats experience every day.

Tony and the Popping Lyrs

So where does that put us with Tony, you ask?

Well, Mike gave me a hint at his potential with his comment about "he used to do all the difficult installs." That's not the behavior of someone who just wants to collect a paycheck.

And Tony was excited to work with us. He'd been hearing about Schiit from Mike for a while. And even before he was laid off from Time Warner, he was done. He wanted to be part of something where he could make a difference.

And Schiit, yes, he could make a difference. Mike was right. Tony didn't take long to train at all. By putting Tony in the mix, all I had to do was look at a few broken products from time to time. My schedule was back to a manageable level, and everything seemed to be going well.

And, when we introduced the Bifrost, Tony loved it—because it involved programming and computers. Tony is our resident Android / Linux guy, though he also has PCs and Macs as well. He's the guy who qualified our DACs on Linux.

So everything was going great, until we get the next run of Lyrs in from the board house.

Tony came into the house, jiggling a finger in his ear. "The Lyrs are popping," he said.

"A small pop is normal as the relay engages," I told him.

"No," Tony said. "Popping. Blow-out-your-ear popping."

"It's probably a bad servo. I'll look at it later."

"They're *all* doing it," Tony said.

"*All* of them? And they've been through the pretest?"

Tony nodded. "Yep. I pretested them, then Eddie put them in the chassis, and I set the bias again, just like you showed me."

I frowned. If they passed the pretest and biased okay, they pretty much had to work. We hadn't changed anything since the last run of Lyrs, and those had worked flawlessly.

I went out to the garage to have a look. I grabbed a Lyr—one labeled with a Post-it note saying, *"popper,"* and took the back chassis off so I could probe around and see what was happening, and put it on the bench.

It tested perfectly. Right gain, right bias, right voltages, THD looked fine, no DC, no popping, no problems anywhere.

"Are you sure this is a popper?" I asked Tony.

"Yep!"

"Check another one, then give it to me."

Tony ran another Lyr through the sound check. As the relay engaged, a loud POP! came from the open-backed HD650s—loud enough to echo in the garage.

Tony winced, taking the headphones off his head.

"You know you can test it without putting them on," I told him. "Or, better yet, run it on the scope."

"Okay," Tony said, handing me the Lyr.

I took the back off and tested the "confirmed popper."

Like the first one, it measured perfectly.

What the hell? I'd just heard it blast a headphone so loudly it was amazing the thing still worked.

I turned off the Lyr, then put the scope in one-shot mode to see what kind of DC spike was happening when the relay engaged.

A few millivolts. Nothing to worry about.

"What is it?" Tony asked.

"I don't know. It's fine. No problem."

"You just heard what it did," Tony said.

I nodded. *Yep, I'd heard.*

I power cycled it a couple more times, and the Lyr continued to behave. No problems at all.

"I don't know," I told Tony.

"Maybe it fixed itself."

"Maybe," I said. Knowing things never fix themselves. I buttoned the Lyr back up and handed it back to Tony for sound check.

BANG! Another explosive pop reverberated through the garage.

"Is that the same one I just gave you?" I asked Tony.

"Yep!"

"You sure?"

"Yep!"

Great, I thought, *an intermittent problem.* Those were the worst. I took the back off the Lyr and ran it through its paces again.

No problem. No DC spike. Nada.

This made no sense! There wasn't anything different about our test rig and the listening setup.

Except—*I'd taken the back chassis off the Lyr.*

Nah. Impossible. It made no sense.

Shaking my head, I put the back chassis back onto the Lyr, and plugged it back into the test rig. I powered it up and waited for the relay to click on.

BANG! A huge pulse of not-just-DC, but multi-megahertz oscillation hit the scope, the moment the relay closed.

"Oh, you've gotta be kidding me," I groaned.

"What?" Tony asked.

"It only pops when the back chassis is on."

"Huh?"

I nodded. "Exactly."

I went back to the bench and quickly confirmed that three out of three Lyrs all worked fine with the back chassis off, and oscillated when the back chassis were on.

"Why does it do that?" Tony asked.

I shook my head. MOSFETs are weird. Something as simple as the chassis being close to the output devices might cause enough parasitic capacitance or inductance to make the amp unstable. But that was extremely unlikely. None of the rest of the Lyr runs had shown this kind of instability.

And, the biggest problem? When you have an oscillating amp, you can usually poke around with a finger to see where the problem lies, or at least the basic area. But with the Lyr bolted all the way together, there was no doing that.

"How are you going to work on it, if you can't get into it?" Tony asked.

"I don't know," I admitted.

The Brute Force Fix

The "how" of fixing Lyrs that only oscillated in the chassis turned out to be a tedious, trial-and-error process of endless disassembly and reassembly. I did all the normal stuff you do when you have an amp that isn't behaving—additional bypassing, bigger gate stoppers, etc.—and none of it worked.

The only thing that worked was to replace the MOSFETs. And, since many of the "poppers" also took out the servo and part of the Dynamically Adaptive stage through oscillation, we replaced those too.

That finally killed it—the brute-force replacement of about a dozen critical parts.

Why did it fix it? *No idea.*

Yes, that's right. To this day, I have no idea what caused the problem. That single run of Lyrs is the only run that ever popped. Nothing before, nothing since. No parts were changed, the board house was the same—it should be absolutely, totally the same. But it wasn't.

I have some theories, of course, but they're all pretty iffy.

The most plausible idea is that the output MOSFETs were somehow damaged by static. And that's not saying much. Our PCB assembly house is an ISO-certified facility. I doubt if their assemblers suddenly decided to leave off their static straps and wear angora sweaters to work en masse. And we usually don't handle the parts outside of their own protection.

Or, it could have been a bad run of MOSFETs. The ones we replaced them with had a different lot code. Again, not very plausible.

Finally, tolerance stacking—the boards, the solder, the parts, and the assembly were just different enough this one time to make it unstable. Again, not very plausible, probably the most farfetched of all.

I suspect we'll never know what the problem truly was, for the most irritating failure mode in the world.

CHAPTER 15

DAC in a Toilet Paper Roll

SHORTLY AFTER WE STARTED SHIPPING Bifrosts, Mike brought me something that would change the company.

"Take a look at this," Mike said, handing me a Bifrost USB card.

I didn't think anything of it. We were making Bifrosts, we had tons of Bifrost USB cards, they worked, and that was that. And I knew we weren't going to be suddenly introducing a new USB card, only a few weeks after we announced the Bifrost itself.

"It's a USB card. So?" I asked, not taking it.

Mike waggled the card at me. "Just look at it."

I took the card and sighed. And that's when it sank in: *this USB card had RCA jacks on it.*

I looked closer. The USB card also had a few more parts added onto it. I recognized one: an AKM4396 D/A converter.

"Is this a USB DAC?" I asked, incredulous.

Mike nodded his head vigorously and cackled. "Yeah, it is!"

"USB powered?"

"Yep! And it sounds really good!"

"Wait a sec," I said. "I thought you were Mr. Anti-USB?"

"Yeah, but sometimes you just gotta say, 'what the heck!'" (Except without the h and e, replace with f and u.)

An aside: this was really the beginning of Schiit's ongoing "WTF" phase, where we'll try a lot of different things—and, if we like them, make them into products. This is what got us Mjolnir, Vali, Fulla...as well as a shelf full of experiments that may never get turned into products.

Anyway, back to the frankensteined USB card. As I held it, three thoughts immediately came to mind:

- How inexpensive could this be?
- How do we keep the cost of the chassis from dominating the cost of the product?
- This is a whole lot smaller than anything we currently make, what would the chassis look like?

"What's the BOM look like, cost-wise?" I asked Mike, using corp-speak for the Bill of Materials, or, in English, *All that stuffs ya gotta put together to makes it.*

Mike cackled again and told me.

My head exploded. If we could get a chassis cheap—I mean, really cheap—we could sell that little DAC for $99.

Ninety-nine bones. That was a whole different part of the market.

I didn't know how many we could sell, but I knew, even then, it would be a hell of a lot more than Bifrost.

"And we could put it in a toilet paper roll," Mike said.

"What?" I asked, coming back to reality.

"Well, you know, for those guys who want something cheaper than a Bifrost. Here you go. DAC in a toilet paper roll. You don't want to upgrade, you want cheap and disposable, we have cheap and disposable."

I had a brief mental flash of a (thankfully) alternate future in which we'd be selling cardboard tubes with electronics inside of them.

"A toilet paper roll wouldn't pass FCC," I said.

"So wrap it in foil," Mike suggested.

"No."

"Or machine it out of aluminum tube."

"No."

"We can cut the little spiral on the outside so it looks like a toilet paper roll."

"No!"

Mike frowned, looking offended. "You don't like my new DAC," he whined.

"Oh no, I like it just fine," I told him. "Assuming it sounds good."

Mike laughed and grinned. "Just plug it in."

So I did. And it sounded good. Really good. I knew right there that this would be our next product. I knew we had to make it. It wasn't a case of 'why,' it was a case of 'why not?'

But *not* in a toilet paper roll.

The Challenges of a Changed Game

That first modified USB card completely changed Schiit as a company. Arguably, it's the biggest factor in us moving from a "hobby business" to a "real company."

But note when this happened: November 2011. Modi (and Magni) didn't show up on the scene until late in December 2012—over a year later.

Huh? Our simplest products took over a year to develop?

What's up with that, you ask? (And some are snickering in the background about how long it took to get a sellable Ragnarok. Hey, bite me. I almost did an April Fools' announcement that the Ragnarok and Yggdrasil were cancelled.)

Bottom line: developing even simple products can take a good long time—that is, if you want to get them right. Especially if they're clean-sheet designs that move you into entirely new spaces as a company.

Modi itself was a challenge, on several fronts:

- **It required an entirely new, and hella cheap, chassis design.** When we started the development, I didn't know if we could meet the very aggressive price point I set— especially without going to China.

- **It had to be as simple as possible,** which meant surface mount and very easy assembly. We were already doing surface mount with Bifrost, but it was brand new to us at the time. Chassis-wise, even our insanely simple chassis for Bifrost, Asgard, etc. were clunky and slow to put together—we needed something simpler and easier.

- **It required huge production runs**—in the thousands—much more than we'd ever done before. Huge production runs meant (comparatively) large investment—we had to be ready for it.

So what did we do? Well, let's start with the one thing we *didn't* do: we didn't sit back on our asses and say, "You know, we have a pretty good thing going here. Why take chances? Iterate the current products, keep milking the products for all they're worth, and take the money."

Because, like it or not, that's what most companies do.

They're scared. *Risk-averse*, they call it, in typical corporate doublespeak. Hell with that. Call it what it is. *Scared.* You're scared to jeopardize your accomplishments to date. You're scared of burning your profits on something that might not work out. You're scared to step out of the mold you've made.

Hint: the mold you've made is a coffin. Break out, or die.

"Okay, fine, I get it," you tell me. "Go ahead and write what you did, already."

Fine.

Chassis: Set A Target, Stick To It. On the chassis side, the first thing we did was to actually set a price target. If we could bring it in at or under the target, we had a product. If it came in more than the target, we'd have to think again.

This is the first time we'd set a price target on a chassis, instead of just sitting back and saying, "Well, let's see where it lands."

To maximize our chance of hitting the target, we put the chassis design up for bid at MFG.com, as well as with our two local chassis vendors at the time.

It ended up that several vendors undershot our target price, some significantly. One of the local guys was under the target, and one was over. The local guy who was under the target price wasn't the least expensive bid, but I knew already not to gamble with quality. We went with the one local guy, even though the chassis could be cheaper.

Corollary: Don't be frigging cheap. If you set a target price and your most preferred guy comes in under it, don't grind them for the couple of bucks you might save if the long-shot new guy across the country works out. Just place the PO.

Assembly: Simple At All Costs. I'm doing this out of order, because the chassis design comes before the chassis. But you get the picture here. Assembly time is a function of chassis design. The simpler the chassis, the lower the assembly time.

We first experimented with variations on our current chassis—a U-shaped piece of metal wrapped around an inner sleeve. But, in that case, you were still talking sixteen screws or so, between the ones that connected the chassis, the ones that connected the boards, and the ones that, well, connected the connectors. That's a lot of screws.

That's why we decided to have a "sled" design quoted—a new concept that used only a front "L" shape, rather than a U-shape. The main advantage of this is that it eliminated the bottom screws. The end result? Seven screws, not sixteen. I know, it doesn't sound like much, but it makes a huge difference in production.

At the same time, we decided to go to an all-steel chassis. Why? Lower cost...and it can be repainted if it's damaged.

And that's how Modi ended up in a steel box, rather than in aluminum and steel: simple economy.

Production: Bite the Bullet. Yep, big runs are pricey. There's no way around that. And that took us to another point that could change the company.

When you're talking big production runs, you really have two choices:

- **Save your own money.** Funny, this is the way that businesses used to do it all the time. Seems it's gone out of fashion today.

- **Borrow the money.** Go to the bank, get a line of credit, or get a loan against your inventory or receivables. This is what our accountant advised, citing all the normal reasons for getting in bed with a bank:

  1. You're growing fast, this allows you to grow faster

  2. Keep your own money for other stuff, like building spaceship-styled campuses, Porsche GT3s, and vacation homes

  3. At current interest rates, it doesn't cost that much

Guess what we chose?

Yep, right in one. As in, #1.

We chose to save our own money for this, because either (a) we're a little stupid / touched in the head / out of touch with thems modern ways of doin' things, or (b) we don't think a bank should pay for our own dice rolls.

Okay, I'm being flippant. But I have seen what happens when a company gets addicted to bank financing. Once you're on the take, you don't get off. And then the bank comes in and starts dictating what you should sell, and when.

No, thanks.

So, that's my long-winded way of saying that there's no easy way around the capital outlay necessary for large production runs. We bit the bullet and made the investment—an investment much larger than we ever could have made when the company started.

We were growing up.

Ego Talking

But, in my mind, there was something even bigger: Modi needed to make sense…as part of a whole line. Mike's original idea was a tiny chassis (much smaller than today's Modi) that could be used with any of our larger amps. But I had noticed—already—that people were stacking Asgard, Valhalla, and Lyr atop Bifrost...and they looked very good together. Which meant only one thing:

"We need a matching amp," I told Mike.

"A matching amp for what?"

"The little DAC. We need a small, cheap amp to match it. Ninety-nine bucks as well. A sub-$200 stack of an amp and DAC."

Mike looked thoughtful. "How are you going to do any good headphone amp that cheap?"

I waved a hand. "I have a bunch of ideas."

It turns out I shouldn't have dismissed the "amp problem," because that was arguably what set the Modi back a good four to six months. It took a long, long time, down many dead-end paths, before we had an amp we could pair with the Modi.

But that's a story for another chapter.

CHAPTER 16

Growth, Garage Style

YOU MAY HAVE SEEN THE video I posted of the early Bifrost era / Lyr-debacle era in the garage, and thought, "Holy moly, these guys are really cramped in there."

In reality, it wasn't so bad. Most nights, there were just two or three of us—me, Eddie, Tony. Rina shipped during the day, so she usually wasn't in the garage with us in the evenings. And we'd gotten our space efficiency down pretty good, storing some chassis at the Centric office, some in the built-out attic, and some outside on the patio (yes, it doesn't rain much here…)

So we didn't really feel the pinch that much. At the time (late 2011), it seemed like a sustainable business for the midterm, without taking on separate production space. Still, a little voice in the back of my mind kept whispering, "You'd better start looking."

What did I do? I ignored it.

If I have a failing in business, it's in being too conservative. I'll wait until we're completely overloaded until hiring, until we're so cramped we can't move until expanding, and so on. Part of this is simply being raised by parents who were, well, tightwads / intelligently thrifty / not using the house as an ATM. Part of it is seeing the consequences, firsthand, of what happens when you "hire forward" or "expand forward."

The Penalties of Optimism

In 1999 and 2000, Centric was in the middle of the biggest boom we'd ever seen—the first Internet wave. Companies were panicking, declaring, "We gotta get on the web, damn the budgets!" and spending money like, well, like someone had turned on a money shower. We got a ton of work, and expanded like crazy, going from 2800 square feet to 7100, and prepping to hire a lot more people if the boom continued.

Even then, though, I was conservative. We took no business from Internet start-up companies that weren't funded (or, in other words, we weren't suckers taking stock options as payment—stock options that soon would be worth less than toilet paper.) Because I know what a bubble looks like, and we were most definitely in a bubble. And I wanted to avoid the inevitable bursting of the bubble, when everyone had their website, looked at the cost, passed out, and said, "Never again!"

Hint: in marketing, if corporate says, "We don't care what it costs," there's something very, very wrong—as in, you're panicking for no reason (like the first Internet boom, or the social boom, or the mobile app boom, etc.) or your CMO is soon going to be shown the door.

Instead, we were doing business mainly with companies that worked on the hardware side of things—from the people who built the process equipment and metrology products to make and measure hard drives, semiconductors, and optical fiber, to companies doing optical networking chips and new processes for connecting the "last mile" at high speeds.

(Remember, this is fundamentally the beginning of the DSL and cable era—we were still running a T1 line at the office for Internet.)

Because we were conservative, and because we didn't take a lot of Internet business, and didn't get big bank loans to expand like crazy, people thought we were, well, kinda stupid. I got comments like this a lot of the time:

"Wait a minute, you're doing web development, and you're only twenty-two people? What's wrong with you? Why aren't you hiring forward like those guys with 300 or 600 or a thousand people?"

I just nodded and explained we were an integrated marketing company that did web development, so we were selective and didn't take all comers, we wanted to grow organically, and we saw the web boom busting soon.

Their response (in 2000):

"What? Are you kidding? Everyone has to get online, I just read a *Fast Company* article about billion-percent growth rates and so-and-so being bought for a trillion dollars or something like that!"

Yeah. When you're in a bubble, most people don't see it. Rah rah, buy everything in sight, leverage all, and grow! Because it will never stop. *Uh-huh.*

Fun fact: the "you're a web development company, and you're only twenty-two people, you must be doing something wrong?" comment changed in 2001 to "you're a web development company and you still have twenty-two people, wow, you're doing well!"

By being picky and conservative, we managed to avoid the web bust almost entirely. We lost only a single client in that morass.

But...we should have been even more conservative. The reprieve was short-lived. Remember I said we were working with a bunch of optical networking and tech players? Well, 2001 wasn't so bad for them, but come 2002, very bad schiit went down. We lost seven clients in one year, either because marketing budgets were slashed, or they went bankrupt, or simply dissolved. One company had taken $200 million in venture capital and never produced a product.

And—these are the "hire forward" companies. These are the guys who had the executive chefs come in and cook for everyone, every day. Who had the fully stocked juice bars and all-you-can-drink beverages. Who had masseuses. Who had foosball and arcade games and lounges full of multicolored couches and beanbag chairs. Who had ultramodern polished-concrete-and-glowing-translucent-walls-of-glass offices. Who had Porsches as the "car allowance" car.

Yeah. Because it will never end. *Uh-huh.*

Back to 2011...

Okay, fine. Enough reminiscing. But you start to see why I didn't want to go out there and sign a lease for office space. Because it *could* end. Booms die. Competitors come out of nowhere. We could screw up again. It could all just be a fad. And so on.

"What's the big deal?" you ask. "It's just industrial space, it can't cost that much per month."

And no, it doesn't. Not per month. So, it sounds like it's time for a quick primer on leasing space for your business.

Point One: Know what a lease is. Distilling down the seventy pages of legalese, here it is in simplest form: *You will pay us $XXXX per month for XX months on or before this day of the month.*

Point 2: Note the lack of any outs. The lease doesn't give two craps if your business is in the toilet, if your cash flow sucks, if your sales forecast was wrong, or if you're late on your mortgage as well. *Pay us. Every month. Until the end.*

Point 3: Subleasing sucks. Someone who's never had a lease before sez, "Well, you can always sublease the space." Yep. Have you ever tried? By the way, you're on the hook until it subleases—and even after. They crap up the place? *Your problem, not theirs.*

Point 4: You'll have surprises, and they won't be good. Instead of hearing "hey, you get a free month of rent this month," from your landlord, be prepared to hear, "Hey, well, I don't care if the plumbing isn't working, that's inside the building, so that's your problem," or, "We had to refurb all the air-conditioning units, here's your prorated part of the bill.

Point 5: There's less space than you think. Even before you sign a lease, you'll quickly find that many spaces won't fit your needs. They'll be too big, too small, not air conditioned, in a bad neighborhood, etc. That big long list gets very small, very fast.

And—an unwritten fact of life—*you'll* probably be on the hook for the lease, especially if it's your first business lease. They'll want you to sign what's called a "personal guarantee." That means that even if the lease is in Arglebargle Inc's company name, you have no corporate shield. Fold up? They come after you. Can't pay? They come after everything you've got.

Leasing a space is very much one of those invisible lines in business. Once you do it, you won't go back. Nor will you back out. So you'd better be damn ready to do it.

So why would you ever lease anything? Because you need the space.

We were just on the edge of needing the space, but we were doing well enough. We could squeak by. And we could rationalize a lot of stuff for the future, like:

- We could move more cars out of the garage
- We could have the PCB assembly house do even more—to the point of completed products

And we had one huge advantage, late in 2011: we ran out of stock all the time. Since we ran out of stock all the time, we didn't have to keep stock. That saved a ton of space.

Fun fact: running out of stock and going into backorder became so bad that we actually were out of stock on every single product at the end of 2011. That's right. No Asgards, no Valhallas, no Lyrs, no Bifrosts. The holiday rush crushed us.

Still, I knew the end was coming. Mike and I were talking about the next step-up products, the as-yet-unnamed Mjolnir and

Gungnir. I wanted to do a balanced amp, and he wanted to do a balanced DAC. We knew they would be bigger than our current products. Bigger products meant more space.

And—there was Modi, the DAC in the toilet paper roll. And an amp. If I could get one to work, that is. Bigger runs meant more space.

But for the moment, we stayed put, as 2011 ended, and 2012 began.

CHAPTER 17

Resurrecting the Circlotron and Other Mid-Centuryisms

OKAY, LET'S START WITH A disclaimer: this chapter's gonna be highly technical. The engineers and technology-minded in the audience are gonna love it. For everyone else, it may be a little hard going. However, there's a lot of useful information here that might make some of this "Class A, JFET, circlotron, etc." stuff more understandable, so you may want to have a look.

Let's set the stage first. This is the beginning of 2012. We're still in the garage, we're still selling the same four basic products: Asgard, Valhalla, Lyr, and Bifrost. Mike has a mini-DAC prototype that I know I need to design a little amp for. But before that amp, I wanted to do a be-all, end-all balanced amp design that was substantially more ambitious than what we'd done before.

"Balanced." "Substantially more ambitious." Yep, that's about as much of a design brief as I had, when I started designing Mjolnir.

In the real world, a design brief can be tens to hundreds of pages, spelling out everything from measurement and power output goals to detailed feature sets, form factor, cosmetics, producibility requirements, and company best practices. But that's a lot like telling an artist, "Sure, do anything you want. However, it has to be done in soapstone in a Bauhaus style, not more than 360 total square inches, with symmetry appropriate to production using not more than a two-piece silicone mold. And it has to be orange."

And, in our opinion, it's why you get a lot of stuff that looks a lot like the last product the company made, with nice fit and finish, but no real surprises. No stunning advancements.

And so, in the spirit of exploration that Mike started with the Modi, we set out to design an endgame-worthy balanced amp with really only five words in mind.

Whys, Wherefores, and Design Goals

"Balanced," someone is probably saying. "Why did Mjolnir have to be balanced? I've heard that single-ended amps can be better than balanced, most headphones aren't balanced, etc."

Okay. Here's the deal. Everything has advantages and disadvantages. Period.

Everything. The Ferrari you paid $400K for is going to be hard to get into and out of. The clutch packs on the robotic manual transmission will need adjusted every 8,000 miles. The brakes will cost $20,000. The parking lot attendants will hoon it around. People will make jokes about compensating. Blah blah, woof woof. Guess what? If it's right for you, it's right for you.

(And, you know what, same goes for Lexus, Tesla, Mercedes, or any other car. All have their advantages and disadvantages. There is no perfect solution.)

So what does this have to do with balanced versus single-ended? It gets down to tradeoffs. Single-ended has advantages, and balanced has advantages too.

Single-ended advantages:

- Can have lower noise (only one active stage and ground)
- Simpler to design and implement (usually)
- Easier to connect (most headphones are single-ended)

Single-ended disadvantages:

- Ground path management can make or break the design (ground is not perfect 0V—where do the currents run?)

- High rail voltages required for high power (runs into device limitations)
- Balanced input is problematic (feedback connects to one side)

Balanced advantages:

- Four times the power for the same rail voltages
- Rejection of common-mode noise on the input (if differential)
- Elimination of most ground path problems

Balanced disadvantages:

- More parts, more complexity (except for maybe circlotrons)
- Gain difference between phases if two-stage amp is fed balanced or SE input
- Most headphones ain't balanced, duh

But, you know what? The main reason we went with a balanced design is that, in our experience, balanced designs offer better sonic performance than single-ended designs…as long as it is a purely balanced design.

Yes. A subjective reason.

Aside: Note the *"a purely balanced design."* "Balanced" is probably the most abused term in audio, other than "Class A." There are tons of amps out there with balanced input and output connectors that aren't really balanced. They take a balanced input signal and sum it back to single-ended. Or they just hang single-ended outputs on a Neutrik 4-pin connector. These aren't really balanced amplifiers, and performance of a truly balanced system shouldn't be judged by their capabilities.

Escalating the Headphone Power Wars?

Some have accused us of firing the first affordable shot in the headphone power wars (Lyr) and escalating it with Mjolnir and Ragnarok. But there never really was a headphone power war at all, at least in our minds. I never had a power output goal for Mjolnir, other than, "About as much as the Lyr would be fine."

"Well, the fact is, you do a bunch of high-powered amps, and most headphones don't really need it," someone says.

Yes. True. And that comes down to the First and Second Laws of Audio, as espoused by John Chen at Grado:

- First law: you can never have too much power
- Second law: see the first law

Now, I'm being flippant here, because the law should read something more like, "More power is always a good thing, as long as there aren't any tradeoffs to get that power."

Yeah. More tradeoffs.

The tradeoffs for more power are usually:

1. **Higher noise** (higher power = higher gain to reach that power output, so higher noise.)

2. **Greater need for protection** (muting, DC detect, automatic shutdown, etc.—although a 100mW op-amp headphone amp can destroy a headphone if it lets go, something with 100,000uF of filter capacitance and 50V rails is gonna be very, very bad news)

3. **Paralleled output devices** (really only in the speaker amp realm here—bottom line, paralleled devices, even matched ones, are never quite the same)

From the start, Mjolnir was going to be a high-power amp, so we were aware of the tradeoffs. #3 didn't apply, but we paid a lot of attention to #1 and #2. Because, after all, we were in the middle of the Orthodynamic Revolution, and many of those orthos weren't that efficient. Also, many great headphones were still 300 and 600 ohm models, which need plenty of voltage to run them. Both mean big rails, and a big amp.

Today, orthodynamics are actually becoming more efficient, so the need for extreme power is abating. The headphone amp power war, which never really existed, will probably seem pretty silly in a few years time.

And yet still…I'll take the high-powered amp.

Onto the Circlotron

So why was Mjolnir a circlotron from the start? After all, there are plenty of other ways to do a balanced amp.

Well, a big part of it is simply that I have a soft spot for circlotron, or "cross shunt push-pull" amplifier designs. They're simple, high-performance, and neatly sidestep some of the problems inherent in other amplifier topologies (more on this later.)

Back at Sumo, we made circlotron-style amplifiers, but they were Jim Bongiorno's designs. I'd never designed a circlotron amp. And yet they kept drawing me back in. First, because the topology is so different than anything else out there. When you first look at it, your natural reaction is "How the hell could that ever work?" Then, when you understand the principle behind it, you think, "Wow, that's really elegant. Why aren't there more of these?"

And, another big part of the decision was based on the fact that there were no circlotron-style headphone amps on the market. None. Zero. Nada.

"Well, that's being contrarian," someone says.

Yes it is. But I'm a bit contrarian. I mean, hey, look at the name of the company.

But maybe I should explain a bit more about amplifier topologies, so you can better understand why Mjolnir was always a circlotron.

Some Solid-State Amplifier Topologies. Disclaimer: this is not intended to be an exhaustive summary, so yep, if I missed your favorite topology, sorry.

- **JLH.** A great example of an early transistor design by John Lindsay Hood. Underscores two facts about early transistors: (1) They were pricey, so it uses only four transistors, (2) The PNP versions sucked, so it used only NPN output in a quasi-complementary arrangement. This topology is much more like a tube amplifier than a modern solid-state amplifier—capacitor-coupled at the input and output, using a single voltage rail.

- **Lin / Blameless.** About 99% of all audio amplifiers today are Lin amps. A Lin topology uses a differential amplifier at the input, a second voltage gain stage, and an output stage that is usually complementary and biased with a Vbe multiplier. This describes virtually every speaker amp on the market. Of course, there are endless variations: complementary, quasi-complementary, symmetrical, buffered, linearized, output-inclusive-compensated, etc....but at the heart it's a Lin. This topology offers a lot to like, including easy DC-coupling at the input and output, and a convenient terminal to run the negative feedback to.

- **CFA / Current Feedback.** This relatively new topology dispenses with the Lin's differential amplifier, which is usually the limitation on a Lin design's slew rate, and replaces it with a diamond buffer and current-feedback architecture. This topology can provide excellent performance at low parts count, but its advantages and disadvantages are hotly debated on, say, DIYAudio. Typically has better bandwidth and slew rate, and worse distortion than a Lin design.

- **Supersymmetry.** This is a patented Nelson Pass topology that is inherently balanced, and has a fundamental simplicity that is very appealing.

- **CSPP / Circlotron.** Note that none of the topologies discussed above, except supersymmetry, is inherently balanced. Now we get to the cross shunt push-pull amp, which is a very old topology (from the 1950s, Google "Circlotron patent" for more info.) First applied in tube amplifiers and named

"Circlotron" by Electro-Voice, the CSPP topology at first looks like a mistake. Oversimplifying, all of the topologies measured above use the output devices as, well, "valves" that control the flow of current from one or two voltage rails to a single output node. The CSPP uses these devices to "unbalance" the flow of current from two cross-coupled power supplies to two output nodes, one positive and one negative. Thus, it's an inherently balanced design.

- **Chip / Integrated, or Chip and Buffer.** Today, it's easy to get a headphone amplifier output chip that pretty much does it all. That's fine, but then you're beholden to what's on the chip—it becomes a "black box" topology, which can only be tweaked via power supply and ancillary components. Boring.

So, we went with a circlotron because it was inherently balanced—and also very simple. It uses only N-channel devices, so there's no worry about the N-channel and P-channel devices being mismatched. It does, however, require a complex power supply—two separate non-ground-referenced power supply rails for each channel.

And why did we call our version of the circlotron "Crossfet?" Because it's not really a circlotron if it's not tubes. We wanted something that expressed "cross-shunt" and "MOSFET" in a short phrase. It wasn't because the MOSFETs were mad.

Amplification Devices Disambiguated. And, with that, why don't we talk about amplifying devices for a bit, because I'm sure that you guys wonder if we engineers just make up silly acronyms like JFET or MOSFET for fun:

- **Triode.** This is a tube with three elements (hence the "tri"): anode, grid, and cathode. A heater heats the cathode so that it emits electrons, which flow across naturally to the anode due to the overall circuit potential (voltage.) You can control the electron flow by applying a voltage to the grid. Triodes are very, very old (nineteen-teens), and, in some forms (such as the 6SN7, 6DJ8, 417, etc.) are the most linear amplifying devices out there. Some tubes can do 0.005% distortion open-loop. So, while many tube amps have higher overall distortion than solid-state, it's not due to the tubes' inherent linearity—it has more to do with their current output capability (low) and the use of output transformers (necessitated by their low output current.) Tubes are also interesting in that there is no physical connection between the elements—the grid, anode, and cathode are all in a hard vacuum, so a tube can be considered almost a perfect voltage-controlled device.

- **Pentode.** This is a tube with five elements: anode, control grid, screen grid, suppressor grid, and cathode. These types of tubes have much higher gain than triodes, but are inherently less linear. These were more commonly used as output tubes (driving a transformer) in audio power amps. Some can be run in triode mode with good results.

- **Bipolar, or BJT, or just "transistor."** The Bipolar Junction Transistor was the earliest successful solid-state amplification device. Formed of three doped regions of silicon (negative-positive-negative, or positive-negative-positive, or NPN and PNP, respectively), it uses current input (not voltage) to control an output current. The gain of a BJT is expressed in current gain, or beta. Betas of 20-500 are common. BJTs are used almost everywhere in discrete amplifier design, and if you avoid common problems (beta droop, nonlinearity, etc.), they make great components.

- **JFET.** Junction Field Effect Transistor. This takes a hunk of n-doped silicon and uses it to control the current flow through a channel of p-doped silicon. The input terminal is essentially a reverse-biased diode, through which virtually no current flows. And JFETs act a lot like a tube—but, to be precise, it acts more like a pentode than a triode. These can

145

be made very low-noise, and are frequently used as inputs on an amp's differential stage.

- **MOSFET.** Metal Oxide Semiconductor Field Effect Transistor. In this case, the control terminal—the gate—is insulated from the drain and source, so it can also be treated as essentially a voltage-input device. With a catch: most MOSFETs have significant input capacitance, and care must be taken that you have enough current capability to drive them at high frequencies. Like a JFET, these devices operate kinda-sorta like a tube, with curves that look like pentodes. Commonly used as output devices in audio power amps, MOSFETs come in two basic flavors: enhancement-mode (meaning they do jack squat if they don't have a pretty big bias voltage on them) and depletion mode (which will run current even at no bias, like a JFET or a tube.) MOSFETS can be made very robust and very fast, making them a good choice for output stages (as long as you watch for parasitic oscillation—did I say "fast?")

- **SIT.** Static Induction Transistor. A relatively new device that has some characteristics of both JFETs and MOSFETs—with an interesting twist: the curves these devices produce look a lot like triode curves! Unfortunately, when available, SITs are eye-wateringly expensive, leading to limited use in commercial applications.

- **Op-amp.** The Operational Amplifier is an amalgamation of hundreds or thousands of BJTs, JFETs, MOSFETs, capacitors, resistors, and other devices on a single chip. Available with gains in the tens of millions, these are complete amplifiers on a chip that offer very good performance in terms of traditional measurements. However, if you want to tailor a topology to your own application, or reduce loop gain to ensure constant feedback across the audio band, you're out of luck.

Okay, so what does this mean for Mjolnir? What we ended up

doing in the early Mjolnir design (and we're talking breadboards here, not PC boards) was trying two different topologies:

1. High-voltage JFET front end and MOSFET output with no overall feedback.
2. JFET front end, BJT VAS stage, and MOSFET output, with local feedback around the VAS and output stage only.

We focused on these two topologies because both were simple, and both sidestepped the "different gain per phase" problem inherent in balanced amps that are driven single-ended.

What do I mean by this? I mean, if you drive a differential amp with overall feedback with a balanced signal, it produces a balanced output. 1V in, gain of 10 = 10V on either side.

But, if you drive a differential amp with overall feedback with a single-ended signal, it produces an unbalanced output: 1V in, gain of 10 = 10V on one phase, 11V on the other.

Huh?

Yep. Look it up in an op-amp cookbook. You'll see the different gains per phase and ways to compensate for them.

However, since we wanted to have an amp with both balanced and single-ended input, we wanted to avoid having different gains per phase. That would mean we'd have to switch the feedback resistors (say, with relays) to compensate if a single-ended input was used. No, thanks. I didn't want to have ten relays inside a Mjolnir. This was supposed to be a simple, no-frills, performance-is-everything kinda amp.

What was interesting about those two topologies was how closely they measured. We found that by using 95V rails and a special high-voltage JFET (which I think we own the world stock of), we could get very, very close to the measured performance of the amp with the VAS stage—without any feedback.

This made for a very simple amplifier. The path was set. Mjolnir would be a no-overall-feedback, single-stage amp design.

So Is It Class A?

One of the things we get asked about all the time is "What class amp is it?" It's a terrible question—not because we hate to answer it, but because manufacturers have misapplied amplifier classes, especially Class A, to the point where there's a ton of confusion out there. I won't repeat my screed about Class A amps from a few chapters back, but I think it'll be useful to go through some common amplifier classes.

Amplifier Classes Explained. While class is in session, why don't we talk about amplifier classes a bit? This will be fun. Like everything else, this isn't exhaustive—I won't be talking Class C or S or T— look 'em up!

- **Class A.** Class A amps run full-out all the time. They never turn off. They're hot. They're big. They're heavy. And they are, by definition, no more than 25% efficient. So if you have a 125W per channel Class A amplifier, it's going to be sitting there dissipating 1000+ watts at idle. It will get cooler the harder you run it. There are no shortcuts, no excuses, no easy outs.

- **Class B.** This type of amp really isn't used for audio. This is where the output transistors turn off as soon as they cross zero, because they are completely unbiased. The problem with this: huge crossover distortion, as the transistors turn on and off.

- **Class AB.** This is Class B, with bias on the output transistors so they run Class A some of the time. Fun fact: BJTs have an optimal bias for linearity, so "cranking up the bias" doesn't necessarily translate into better sound. MOSFETs don't. Crank them! When a Class AB's outputs eventually shut off, the transition is managed much better than in a Class B amp. This is the most popular audio output stage, because it combines high efficiency (up to 75% theoretically) with good performance. Mjolnir is technically a Class AB amp. It runs in Class A up to about 1W, then in Class AB thereafter.

- **Class D.** Switching or PWM amps. These "digital" amps have gone past the "exploding parakeet" stage (based on a comment from Mike Moffat about seeing one of the first commercial Class D amps, which output so much RF noise that it would probably cause a parakeet to catch on fire), and can provide good measured performance. They can also offer 90-95% efficiency, so your thousand-watt amp can fit in something the size of a cigarette pack. Still, barf.

- **Class H.** This is Class AB with voltage rail switching. These amps run at lower rail voltages to increase efficiency and reduce heat, then switch to higher rails when output demands. A neat way to get high efficiency without the drawbacks of Class D, but necessarily more complex.

So what does all this pedantic BS have to do with Mjolnir? Think of it as some of the stuff an audio engineer has to hold in his (or her*) head as they work on a new design. How crazy you wanna get? How many chances you want to take? Should it be an all-BJT, Lin topology, Class AB amp, because that's the best-known and most-documented design option out there, or a whackazoid tube-input, level-shifted, DC-coupled hybrid supersymmetry circlotron with a Class H output stage?

Yeah. You get the picture.

*Too bad there aren't more female engineers. When I was in school, one of my classmates snarked, "You've dated all the girls in engineering." To which I replied, "Yeah. Both of them." Which wasn't far off the mark. Come on, guys can do this. It can't be that hard. And they teach you wayyyyy more math than you need. Don't be scared by nonlinear differential equations. You'll never use them…well, unless you plan on being the Ph.D in residence and presenting papers before the AES. Which is fine. Me, I'd rather blow up…er, I mean build stuff.

Early Adventures with Mjolnir

"Circlotron?" Mike asked doubtfully. "Isn't that something that only six people in the world know how to do, and even then they have to chant incantations and swing dead chickens over their heads to make them work?"

"No, they really aren't that bad—" I began.

"Famous last words," Mike cut me off.

"They're actually really simple—"

"Except for the keeping it balanced problem, the voodoo transformer, the eight thousand voltage rails, the weird in-the-air outputs, and making sure some idiot doesn't ground the negative output and blow it up problem, you mean."

"Well, yeah, but—"

"But you're gonna do it anyway."

"I already prototyped it. It works fine." Which was true. Circlotrons are really dead-simple. They just scare people, because at first glance they look like a very, very bad mistake that will catch on fire and burn your bench to the ground. In reality, a circlotron using enhancement-mode MOSFETs with no bias and no input will just sit there happily and do absolutely nothing. With a decent function generator, you can program in an offset voltage and two out-of-phase sine waves and run it easily. Really not a big deal. But Mike's scared of weird analog things, and I'm scared of complicated digital stuff. So there you go.

"Really?" Mike said, doubtfully.

"Really. It took like an hour to build it up."

Mike sighed. "Ohh-kayy. How are you keeping it balanced?"

"A differential servo."

Mike's eyebrows shot up. "A differential servo?"

I nodded and explained. I'd found a cool way to use a servo to compare the difference between the two outputs, and set the bias on one of the paired MOSFETs to match the other. That way, you just had to adjust bias on one side, and the other would follow.

Aside: "Servo" is short-speak for "DC servo." This is commonly used in amplifier designs to ensure that the DC offset at the output is very low, without having to use coupling capacitors to block DC, or twiddling pots to null DC (and hope it doesn't drift over time.) DC servos are relatively simple and very powerful, but like most things that are simple and powerful, they demand respect. DC servos are not perfect. They inject some audio back into the servo summing junction, so they'd better be high-quality and well-filtered for best performance (or used at a point that's not an input, like I was doing in Mjolnir.)

"And the voodoo transformer and eight thousand voltage rails?" Mike asked.

"Already have one. Got prototypes from the transformer guys. And yeah, it'll have a lot of capacitors in it, so what?"

Mike nodded. "Is this one of those things where the outputs are 40V in the air?"

"Nope, they're close to 0V."

"How about the shorting problem?"

I frowned. Because Mike had a point. Both of Mjolnir's output phases were active. If someone connected them together (say, by using a balanced to single-ended adapter), it would be a very bad day. And I knew that no matter what warnings we put in the owner's manual, someone would do just that. Even if we put an electronic flashing sign on the top of the amp saying "NEVER USE ADAPTERS THAT SHORT THE OUTPUTS!" it would still happen.

"I'll figure that out," I told Mike.

"And how about single-ended output?" Mike asked.

"This is an endgame amp. I figured it would just be balanced."

"And what if these endgame guys have single-ended head-phones?"

"Then they'll have to get balanced cables, or re-terminate them for balanced," I said. In retrospect, I should have paid more attention to this. Although we tried to work up a single-ended summer for Mjolnir, we were never happy with the performance of the design we had. So it never got single-ended output.

And, you know what? Mjolnir really was a fairly simple amp to get working.** Except the protection. Mike called that one right on. A simple output delay wouldn't protect Mjolnir from shorting adapters. A DC detect circuit wouldn't do it, either.

In the end, I came up with a complex analog-computer-style circuit that continuously monitors output current and DC offset, and lifts the output if the current goes over a preset point, or if DC offset goes higher than a predetermined limit. I think it uses more parts than the original Asgard gain stage.

But it has saved our butts many a time. When we get an email that goes like, "Hey, I plugged in the Mjolnir and it sounded a bit funny, then it went 'click,' in the middle of a song," we immediately ask, "Are you using an adapter to plug your headphones into the jack?" The answer, unsurprisingly, is "Yes."

**Working, yes. Right, not so much. Mjolnir's first appearance was at the Audeze-sponsored meet in Los Angeles. It was running far too high bias, its protection was only kinda-sorta working, it wasn't thermally stable, and the servo was being, well, very un-servo-like (we found out later that it was oscillating.) But it ran through the show and didn't blow anyone's headphones up. Unfortunately, it sounded very strange. It wasn't until May that we had a real, production-intent prototype that made us happy to listen to it.*

Whew. Big chapter. Lotsa tech talk. But hopefully illuminating.

CHAPTER 18

The Pinch-Off Problem

LATE IN THE DEVELOPMENT OF the Gungnir analog stage, I was sitting in the living room, talking to Mike on the phone about a problem we'd been having on the prototype boards.

To me, this was just another day in engineering. Weird schiit happens. You gotta figure it out. So I didn't think anything about our conversation…until Rina walked into the room, laughing so hard she could barely stand.

"What?" I asked her.

She just laughed harder, holding on to the kitchen counter to keep from falling over. Literally.

"What's wrong with you?" I continued.

"You—" she said, gasping and pointing. "You—you—"

"Me me what?"

"You have a company—called 'Schiit'—and you're talking about your—pinch-off problem!" Rina said, through gales of laughter.

I stopped dead. Then I started laughing too. *Schiit had a pinch-off problem.*

Pinch-Off is an Engineering Term. Really.

Well, more accurately, it's an old-guy engineering term, like "plate" instead of "anode" for tubes. What it describes is the voltage it takes to turn off a JFET (or other depletion-mode device.) As described in the previous chapter, a JFET runs current through it from drain to source as soon as it's connected to a voltage. But, if you lower the voltage at the gate of the JFET, eventually it won't conduct at all. That's known as Vgs(off), or, in old-dude speak, the pinch-off voltage.

So Mike and I had been sitting there, talking about our pinch-off problem, and that's what Rina had walked in on.

Yeah, I know, stuff like this surely doesn't happen at Sony…

Now, as far as why we were discussing our Vgs(off) problem, it was simple. I'd built some perfboard versions of the Gungnir analog stage, measured them, and been very happy with the result.

Then we got the PC boards, put the parts on them, and suddenly they were running fifty times the distortion of the perfboard versions.

Stuff like this happens all the time in engineering.

The real world isn't the same as simulations. PC board protos are different than built-in-the-air protos. Manufacturers change processes, and parts don't work the way they used to. If you want a simple life, consider a career as a fisherman in Costa Rica or something. Maybe. Who knows. I've never actually done that, so it might be as bad as engineering.

So, after spending a night with Mike and Dave trying to chase down the distortion (looking at compensation, oscillation, badly routed PCB traces, bad solder, wrong parts, bad parts, etc.—all the obvious stuff that shows up on prototypes), we were all baffled. The circuit worked, but it didn't work well.

So I went home and slept on it. Problems that seem huge at night sometimes become really obvious the next day.

But this one wasn't.

I went back to it that evening, swapping parts and measuring. And a parts swap did make things better. Just not enough better. So I swapped parts again, just for the heck of it. And it got worse.

That was when the light bulb went off. The in-the-air prototypes weren't built with surface mount parts. They were built with through-hole parts. The JFETs we were using on the PC boards were supposed to be a near-equivalent to the through-hole parts…*but maybe they weren't.*

The datasheets told the story: the through-hole parts we'd been using on the perfboards had a pinch-off voltage range that was very small, and spec'd pretty tightly—about 0.2-0.5V. The ones we were using on the surface-mount PCB? 0.5V to 6V.

Yeah. Twelve times different. Like, duh.

And, considering where they were used in the circuit (as followers), that big pinch-off could cause all sorts of problems. I tacked some through-hole parts in their place, and suddenly the boards were acting (and measuring) just like the early prototypes.

From there, it was only a matter of finding a surface-mount JFET with similar specs, which only took a quick web search. A few days later, when the parts came in, Gungnir's analog stage was working as it should.

But only after a painfully hilarious conversation…

Analog Isn't The Real Story

Okay. I front-loaded this chapter with a funny story about Gungnir's analog stage, but that was probably the least interesting part of the DAC's design.

With Gungnir, the real story was on the digital side. Like Bifrost, we started with not much in the way of a product brief, except for Mike Moffat stating that he wanted to "do a proper hardware-balanced DAC." Beyond that, nothing. No sizes. No feature sets. No colors. No 500-page list of specs.

But Mike is very, very specific when it comes to digital. "It needs to be big enough to keep the Hatfields and McCoys out of each other's corrals," he declared. "That means two transformers, one for digital and one for analog. And clock regeneration, we need to look at that a lot harder. And absolutely, positively hardware balanced, none of this single-DAC-per-channel stuff."

Let's translate:

- **Big enough to keep the Hatfields and McCoys away from each other.** In Mike-speak, this means careful segregation of the analog and digital sections. Grounds. Power supplies. Clock routing. Physical space. Mike looks askance at tiny products that mix analog and digital. So, Gungnir was gonna be big.

- **Clock regeneration, we need to look at that.** Bifrost uses a lot of the tricks Mike learned to get SPDIF jitter to acceptable levels, but Mike's work at Theta always featured VCO clock regeneration, and he hated to give that up. Eventually, that grew into Gungnir's unique Adapticlock system, which actually assesses the quality of the input signal (in terms of center frequency and jitter) and routes it to either a VCO or VCXO oscillator. It also meant that Gungnir needed a much bigger and more powerful microprocessor to do this analysis and routing, for all supported input resolutions and sample rates.*

Actually, let's talk about that a bit. In the old days, you only had to worry about 16/44.1 and 16/48. Now there's a LOT more variations. And if you're interested in keeping everything bitperfect, that's a hell of a lot of management. Why do Gungnir and Bifrost click when you change sample rates? Because you have to reset the whole system to run at the new clock multiple.

- **Absolutely, positively hardware balanced.** Hardware balancing, or using one stereo DAC per channel, pays off huge dividends. Lower distortion, lower noise floor, elimination of more of the high-frequency noise that comes out of a modern sigma-delta DAC—these are all wonderful things. It also comes at a cost of using two DACs and twice the analog components, plus discrete summers for single-ended output.

So yeah, digital is the real story. And the real story of Gungnir is probably Adapticlock, its unique feature. That's a Mike Moffat original that he's justifiably proud of. As far as we know, no other DAC tells you if your source is good or bad, and, even if bad, still provides clock regeneration. It took a ton of code to make that one work—and some very expensive VCXOs.

"If it's bad, we'll light up a front panel light," Mike said. "We could call it the 'buy better gear' light."

And "Buy Better Gear" is what stuck. It's technically the "VCO Mode" light, but that's a whole lot less interesting, right?**

**There's not a lot of really bad gear out there, to be honest. Pretty much any computer won't light it. It really only comes on with really, really awful stuff, like satellite receivers and Apple Airport Express sources. And some old CD players that have gone off-frequency. That's about it.*

In the spirit of the last chapter, let's talk about the parts of a digital audio system, so hopefully all of this stuff makes a little more sense:

Storage. Digital music has to be stored, whether it's on a plastic disk, magnetic disc, or in the cloud. At this point, it is no different than any other data you have. And, like other data, it can be lost if your hard drive is made by Western Digital (er, I mean, when it breaks.) Sorry, WD has had the majority of breakage in my personal experience—this is not a statistically significant result, just a personal opinion. The important thing is to make sure it's backed up. Or, if you're still a dinosaur (er, I mean, using plastic disks), don't treat them so poorly as to destroy them.

Formats. Most of you guys already know this, but let's go ahead and be inclusive. Digital music comes in tons of different formats. Let's cover three broad swathes:

- **Lossy (MP3, AAC, etc.)** These formats have had a whole lot of bits thrown away. Lossy formats contain only 10-20% of the data of the original digital file. This means they have to be reconstructed into a semblance of the original signal by an algorithm running on a computer or player, with the losses masked by perceptual encoding. This is in no way, shape, or form a "bitperfect" solution.

- **Lossless (FLAC, ALAC, AIFF, WAV, etc.)** These formats preserve all the original bits, even though some use lossless compression to pack them more efficiently. All of these are Pulse Code Modulation, or PCM, formats. These formats are bitperfect—they preserve the original music samples.

- **DSD.** Instead of using multiple levels to represent the music, DSD encodes it as a high-speed, pulse width modulated (PWM) datastream. Theoretically, a DSD recording made on a pure DSD analog to digital converter and never converted or processed could be reproduced on a pure DSD DAC (or simply via a very good switch and low-pass filter) and retain all of the original DSD "samples"—or, more precisely, information.

Transmission. From the stored digital file, you need to get it to where it's going. This should be relatively simple, but sometimes it isn't.

- **Ideally.** In an ideal (PCM) world, the DAC wants to see three things: bit clock, word clock, and data. In a delta-sigma DAC, you can add a master clock to the list. Which means you'd ideally have three to four BNC cables connecting a digital source and a DAC. However, in the dim dark days of early digital, this was Kevorked for a single-cable solution— simpler, easier, but far more problematic in terms of jitter, since the clocks were buried in with data. Welcome to SPDIF.

- **Internal.** Let's say you want to move data from a CD drive to a DAC internal in the CD player. After recovery of the data from the disk, it's usually moved around via I2S, which is, hey, bit, word, data. Ideal? Sure. Why don't they use this outside of the box? There's no single accepted standard for it.

- **Optical.** One of the flavors of SPDIF. This was chosen in the early digital days because it glowed, looked cool, and in general seemed like a nifty futuristic idea in an era when people also thought the 1980s Corvette digital dashboard was the height of fashion. It's bandwidth-challenged, though, and can only sometimes stretch to accommodate

24/192.

- **Coaxial.** Another flavor of SPDIF. Looks boring, but generally performs better than optical. BNC connections make it seriously good for high-frequency use. Unless there's a ground issue, of course.

- **USB.** And now a left turn into computerland. I've gone on and on about how much of a pain USB is, but it's here to stay. Comes in many, many flavors and implementations. Different than SPDIF in that it is a packet-based system. Bandwidth isn't a problem with USB 2.0 and above.

Reception. Beyond the digital connection, there's a receiver to process the incoming SPDIF or USB signal. In the case of SPDIF, it recovers the clocks that are embedded in the data. In the case of USB, asynchronous transfer controls the clocks locally.

Clock Management. Okay, so you have digital data. Now what? Some manufacturers choose to upsample everything to a specific data rate, no matter what's coming into the box. This eliminates the need for clock management, but...you guessed it...asynchronous sample rate conversion, or ASRC, is not bitperfect—it replaces the original samples. So, for a bitperfect DAC, this means clock management is necessary. In short, this is the process of telling the digital filter and the DAC, "Hey, I'm sending you 16/44.1, get ready, 'kay?" Or 16/48 or 24/96 or 32/192 or whatever. Run through the different bit depths and sample rates, and you'll quickly see that there are many different combinations. Clock management isn't trivial.

Digital Filter. Digital filters are where bit-perfect transfer usually dies. Digital filters upsample the incoming data to higher data rates (typically eight times) to reduce the need for analog brick-wall filtering. This is handy, but again—what it outputs is a mathematical approximation. That is, unless it is a closed-form digital filter that retains the original samples. And we know of only one of those—which is what's in Yggdrasil.

D/A Converter. From the digital filter (which may be inside the DAC chip itself), the data gets passed off to the actual D/A converter. These typically come in two varieties:

- **R2R.** This is nearly dead as a technology today, because it's a pain in the butt to implement, especially with resolution that exceeds 20 bits. But it's the only D/A technology that can be bitperfect.

- **Delta-Sigma.** About 99.9% of DACs (or more) today use delta-sigma conversion. The reason? Because they allow marketers to use big numbers, like 24 bits (or even 32). And because they are inexpensive. However, like ASRC and digital filters, they only output an approximation of the actual data.

Analog. And you thought we were done? No. Some DACs output current, which requires an I/V converter. This is a place where discrete designs, with proper low-impedance inputs, can offer huge advantages over ICs. Some DACs output voltage, but it still needs filtered, and, in some cases, summed. So there is an analog component at the very end—and it is definitely critical to the performance of the entire system.

Although I can go on and on about the engineering side, I'll spare you the huge dissertation, as in the last chapter. Because, the more I think about it, I believe the central thing comes down to philosophy.

"Philosophy? What the heck does that have to do with DACs?" you might ask.

I'll respond: It has everything to do with DACs. And amps. And business in general. So let's move on to that.

Philosophy: Or, Why You Do Something

Okay. Let's say you start a company. *Why did you do it?*

Let's say that company makes products. *Why did you do one, and not another?*

Let's say your products are made a certain way. *Why did you choose that method?*

Let's say your products have certain features, or you choose to leave them out. *Why?*

If you keep asking, "Why?" you might find that there is a good reason behind all of the answers. Or you may find none at all. And, even if you find there is a good reason, you may not agree with the "why." This is why companies have to have a philosophy—and stick to it. Because otherwise, they're rudderless. Aimlessly wandering. Waiting for a magical hit product to pull them out of the morass. You see this in a lot of big companies—ones where products are created and approved by giant committees, endless meetings, thousands of hours of "gaining consensus."

Car companies are a great example. How many midrange cars can you simply swap the badges on, and not even know it's made by a different manufacturer? How many are so completely forgettable? How many seem to lose their way every decade or so—and then suddenly release a flood of models that simply copy the one hit they recently had?

There's no philosophy. Just the endless chase of benchmarking and specs-list-stuffing and crossing your fingers and hoping that somehow, something with enough personality makes it through the bean-counters and second-guessers to make a difference for the line.

If you start a company, make a product, decide on features and specs, ask yourself, "Why?" And be specific with your answer. You'll do a lot better for it.

So what do we mean by this? Fine. Let's use Schiit as an example.

Our philosophy is that *we want to make fun, affordable products that are as true to the musical source as possible.*

Note what comes first, second, and third.

- **First, fun.** Come on, guys, this business is far too serious at times. Let's have some fun with this.

- **Second, affordable.** The elephant in the room in high-end audio. On a recent panel, some guys tried to make the point that "personal audio" wasn't really any younger than high-end audio, citing examples from companies making $1000-5000 products. Like, duh. I reminded them that our audience was much younger than the norm, statistically, because of one simple thing—they're affordable.

- **Finally, true to the source.** In the digital realm, to us, this means retaining the original sampled data as much as possible. In the lower-priced realm, this also means forsaking the totality of this goal, because modern delta-sigma DACs sacrifice the original samples for a mathematical approximation.

Now, this isn't to say these DACs can't sound good. And, congruent with the third part of our philosophy, we choose to preserve the original bit depth and sample rate as far as possible down the chain, and to minimize errors caused by jitter. That's the best we can do with delta-sigma.

"But I don't agree," someone out there is saying. "You might have a philosophy, but I don't agree with it."

Yep. And that's the thing. You'll never have 100% consensus. If you don't agree, simply move on, and find a company that meets your own goals. That's why there isn't one *The Amp Company* out there to rule them all. It's a wonderfully wide, varied world—and that's a very good thing.

What we can say is that we do actively ask ourselves why, and bump up the answers against our philosophy, as we develop products. Let's see how that works:

Hey, a D/A converter manufacturer brought out a new delta-sigma device. Let's build a new product! No, sorry. Just because it's new doesn't mean it's better. Is it a meaningful upgrade? Inexpensive? Then maybe.

Hey, a D/A converter manufacturer brought out a new R2R

device. Let's build a new product! Hell, yes! R2R DACs are bitperfect. So let's go for it—well, unless it's crap or a billion dollars.

You know, some people really like the old, lush euphonic tube sound, let's throw a really nonlinear tube in our DAC! Nope. Although it can be pleasant, and although some prefer it, it's not staying true to the original, is it?

You know, we can make something even better and more fun, but it's even better and less expensive than our top-of-the-line products. You bet, let's do it! Everyone benefits!

Did you see that there's a new Class D module that puts out 300WPC from something smaller than a cigarette pack? Let's throw it in a DAC and make a power DAC. Not gonna happen— throwing away the signal for a nonlinear-control-system approximation of it? Not our bag.

Anyway, perhaps you see where I'm going here. Philosophy is key. Whys are important. But by sticking to them, you won't please everyone all the time.

But then again, trying to please everyone all the time *won't do that, either.*

CHAPTER 19

Every Road is a Dead End:
Early Adventures with Magni

THIS CHAPTER IS A LESSON in hubris—and in the value of chucking it all and starting over.

It happens to every company, I'm sure. There will always be a time when things are going well, reviews are great, and new products are flying off the shelves. We literally couldn't keep Bifrost in stock. Asgard, Valhalla, and Lyr were all doing well. I'd just been contacted by the Arizona Audiophile Society, where the Bifrost had beaten all the other DACs in their blind listening test, with retail prices up to $7,500. We had working prototypes of Mjolnir and Gungnir, and were looking forward to their launch. And we'd just started looking at space so we could move out of the garage (more on that later.)

This is the time when you start thinking, "Hey, this is going pretty well. Man, we're really tearing it up. Wow, maybe we actually are pretty good at this!"

This isn't good.

In fact, this is the time you should be the most terrified.

Now, to be clear, we didn't go completely over the top on the narcissism. We didn't do anything truly stupid. Nobody bought a Ferrari. None of us went out and bought $1,000 bottles of Scotch. None of us created audio product derivatives to sell to Wall Street. And none of us rode to work in a sedan car borne by a dozen acolytes.

But, this run of good luck was enough to have me thinking,

"Heh, a little amp? How hard can that be?"

As it turned out, it was damn difficult. Remember, thirteen months from Modi proto to launch? At least six or seven of those months were spent running down the wrong paths on Magni.

Philosophy Can Also Be A Prison

I spent the last part of the previous chapter nattering on about philosophy. And I truly think that every successful company should have a well-thought-through, concise philosophy that informs everything they do.

But a philosophy can also be a prison. If it's too specific or too inflexible, you won't be able to change when you need to. You won't be able to adapt to new needs, new markets, new competitors. That's also necessary.

It's also why our philosophy is pretty broad. And if I'd done nothing more than apply that philosophy to Magni, I probably would have been fine. Instead, I larded on a bunch of additional "wants" to Magni's initial design brief. Some of these were based on market reality. Some of them were sheer fantasy.

Let's start with the ones based in reality:

- **This amp should be versatile enough for most any headphone.** We already had some very specific amps, like Valhalla for high-impedance headphones and Lyr for power-hungry orthos, but this should really be a do-all amp, since it would likely be a starter amp for many audiophiles.

- **If we couldn't do better than the inexpensive amps already out there, why bother?** To me, "doing better" was a mix of more power and sonics, in a simple, attractive package.

- **This amp needed to hit a very aggressive price point**—a price point unimaginable when we started the company. We had to be careful about design, construction, features, reliability, etc. I had $99 as a target, to match the Modi.

And now, the fantasy:

- **The topology should be as simple as possible**—insanely simple, just a few transistors and a very simple power supply, almost like a solid-state version of a tube amp. That's probably what would sound best, I thought.

- **To keep costs down, we'd use a switching wall wart** to generate a single DC rail. Switching wall warts are so cheap they show up in Cracker Jack boxes these days. I mean, unimaginably cheap. We'd have to use a switcher to keep cost down.

- **It should be a neat, unique topology.** I'd messed around with two-transistor gain cells. Maybe that would be cool. I'd also played around with the old JLH topology, which I remembered sounded good.

Looking back, all those extra fantasy items are really funny.

Simple amps usually have to resort to Class-A output to get them linear enough to work well—and Class A was absolutely out. Magni's tiny chassis wouldn't be able to dissipate the heat.

Switching power supplies are cheap, but absolutely scary in terms of power supply noise—not to mention the fact that a single rail would mean we'd have to use coupling capacitors at the input and output of the amp.

And a neat, unique topology? Yeah, there's a reason those are scarce. The "cool" stuff I'd played with in the past simply had too many limitations—not enough voltage swing, not linear enough, not stable into a wide range of headphone loads, etc.

But I'm An Idiot

So, of course, the first thing I had to do was to try a JLH-style amp with a switching wall wart that I bought off of eBay. I think it was $3. Which meant, in production quantities, it could easily be a fifty cent part. Think of that—a cord, plastic chassis, PC board, switching supply doing 24V at 0.5A for half a buck.

And yeah, it was about as good as you'd expect for that price. It was so noisy that it made the JLH amp oscillate constantly at full voltage, without any input. I'm talking full-scale noise at a couple of megahertz.

To translate: instant headphone fry. Assuming the output stage lasted that long.

I tried a couple of other switching wall warts, but they really weren't much better. So I tried filtering them. Which doesn't work so well when you have half a volt of noise on the ground (the engineers here are cringing).

Finally, I gave up and simply hooked the JLH topology up to our lab power supply. Now it ran fine. No oscillation. Which is what you'd expect from a clean supply.

There were only two problems:

- The JLH topology really, really doesn't like to be transformed to a Class-AB design. It's very nonlinear, with high distortion.
- It sounded like ass.

I mean, it sounded awful. As in, 1960s solid-state awful. I'd forgotten how bad solid state could be. Bright, nasty, confused, muddled…it simply didn't stand up to modern designs.

Yeah. Hubris.

After that failure, I tweaked around with the circuit for a while, and ended up with something that sounded kinda decent. But by this time, the original sixteen-component-per-channel design had ballooned to over twice that. It was more complicated than some of the 60- and 100-watt speaker amps I'd designed. And that was really stupid.

So what did I do? For a while I just gave up. I had a non-optimal topology and an unworkable power supply. I'd wasted a couple of months getting exactly nowhere.

The Non-Lighting Light Bulb

Sometimes when you walk away from a project, the insight will come when you least expect it. You'll wake up one morning and have the answer. Or you'll be driving into the office and it'll hit you so hard you'll say, "Hell, why didn't I think of that before?"

In the case of Magni, walking away didn't work. As Mjolnir and Gungnir moved towards production, and as we started our first move out of the garage, I had plenty to occupy me. I could forget about it.

But the answer didn't come.

Not that I didn't try. Sure, I put together a half a dozen neat circuits. JFET-MOSFET gain cell. Simple current-feedback amp. Etc.

But all of them had at least one fatal flaw. And all of them still wouldn't work with a noisy power supply. Even if one had worked, the supply still killed it.

So I wasted more time—drawing up chassis for the Modi and the nonexistent amplifier, trying still more wall warts, tweaking circuits and hoping that something would work out. Nothing did. And I was starting to sweat. Any day now, Mike would ask me how the Magni was going, and I'd have to tell him. And he'd say, sarcastically, "I thought you said it would be easy, Sparky!"

I didn't want to have that conversation. I didn't want to say, "You know, an op-amp and a buffer wouldn't be so bad."

In the end, I was sitting in the garage one weekend, staring at the perfboard mess that should be a Magni. And I suddenly remembered that one thought I had: *Hell, this thing has more parts than some of the speaker amps I designed.*

So what if I made it just like a speaker amp? I wondered. That would eliminate the topology problem. Lin topologies could be very low-distortion—and Class AB—and direct coupled—and very, very robust.

But that was crazy! A full Lin topology for our least-expensive amp?

What the hell. I opened the schematic capture program and drew up a simple Lin amp.

It was simpler than the mess I'd designed.

But...a Lin amp really needed a bipolar power supply—that is, both positive and negative rail voltages. They didn't like to hang halfway between a single supply and ground. That meant caps in the feedback loop, input biasing, and other ugly stuff like that.

So what if I just said, "The hell with it," and did an AC wall wart (basically a transformer in a box) and a half-wave bridge to create both positive and negative voltages?

Half-wave bridge, barf, I heard Mike's voice in the back of my mind.

But I didn't care. Maybe this was the way to go. Maybe a full Lin amp with a bipolar supply—and, what the hell, a DC servo too, might as well go crazy—maybe this would work. Maybe modern surface-mount manufacturing would make this feasible.

Aside: *I really had no idea. I'd never done a surface-mount board before the Magni.*

I built the Lin circuit that night and ran it on the lab supply. The damn thing worked first shot, as if to say, *Why didn't you just do this from the start?*

And it measured well. Not just well, but spectacularly.

Now, I was excited. This was getting somewhere. If we could get a power supply put together to run it, we might have a product! Except I had no idea what a linear wall wart would cost. They're pretty scarce. Most people have gone over to switchers these days.

But again, like I said in the beginning, most answers are not much more than an inquiry or two away. Since I knew we were shooting for minimum cost, I wasn't going to be able to get it from a US manufacturer. So I turned to a new source—one I'd never used before—Alibaba.com.

Yes, that Alibaba. Chinese manufacturing. Now, there's nothing wrong with that. But it was different than anything we'd done before. Luckily, Alibaba has a pretty good feedback system, so you have at least an idea of the companies you're working with. We quickly had quotes from a half-dozen manufacturers, all at amazingly inexpensive rates. Not as inexpensive as a switcher, but still well within the envelope of a $99 product.

But what would they look like? Would they be any good? Even if they were, how well would Magni perform on a smaller power supply (smaller than the lab supply). I ordered some samples and sat back to wait.

In a week, I had my answer. They looked like standard cheap wall warts, the kind you see on dozens of different products. But these had one big difference: they were AC wall warts.

I did a version on perfboard and verified the performance—and sat back in shock. The Magni prototype delivered nearly 2W into 32 ohms at clipping, and distortion was less than 0.004% at 1V RMS. And this was from the wall wart. 60Hz hum from the half-wave supply was over 100dB down from 1V RMS.

It measured better than anything we made.

Still, what did it sound like?

Into Surface Mount

Before I did Magni, I'd never laid out a surface-mount board. It was a profoundly alien experience. I wasn't used to the parts. I wasn't familiar with the best way to route them. And, most of all, I still wasn't confident it would work. The lesson from Gungnir's pinch-off problem was too fresh in my mind. What gotchas would we find when we went to surface-mount? Would the equivalent parts even be available?

Parts turned out not to be a problem. In fact, they were a real eye-opener. When you hear someone wax poetic about the glory days of Japanese transistors, they don't work with surface-mount parts. They don't know all the cool new stuff that's available right now.

I learned a lot throwing that first board together. But, because I wasn't confident it would work, it wasn't a full design. No muting relay. No servo. Hell, it didn't have a power switch. But I wanted something we could listen to, and decide if it was good or bad.

In a few days, I had PC boards to play with. I threw one together and measured it. It ran pretty much the same as the prototype.

After that, it was the moment of truth. I grabbed a set of Grados and took them out to the test bench. The little Magni prototype drove them shockingly well.

But it should also be able to do better than Grados. It had tons of power. I decided I'd bring it to its knees with the Audeze LCD-2s.

Magni laughed at the LCD-2s.

No problem. No big deal at all. It would easily go to ear-bleeding levels.

I sat there, laughing at the spectacle of this tiny little amp driving the LCD-2s. It looked absolutely ridiculous.

Rina came out to see if I'd lost my mind. "What are you laughing about?" she asked.

"Magni. The little amp."

She saw that I was holding the LCD-2s. "On those?"

I laughed again. "No problem."

"Really?" She took the headphones out of my hand and put them on. "Play my song."

Aside: *Rina has a specific song she uses to evaluate new headphones and amps. It's not what I'd call hi-fi, but she's heard it so many times that it's a perfectly good reference for her. It's Enigma's "Seven Lives (Radio Edit)". Yeah. I know. Talk to her. Hey, those of you with the earliest Asgards had them listen-tested to New Kids on the Block, thanks to her. Think about that the next time you listen.*

I played her song. She listened for about a minute, poker-faced.

I frowned. What did that mean? Did she like it? Did she hate it? Was it really crap? Was I hearing things?

Eventually, she took the headphones off. She shook her head sadly and looked at me.

"So what are we going to do about Asgard?" she asked.

CHAPTER 20

The HOA Problem

WHILE WE WERE WORKING ON Magni and Modi and Gungnir and Mjolnir—through all the troubles and triumphs and setbacks and workarounds—I couldn't fight a growing unease.

Unease about how big we were getting.

Yeah, I know, it's laughable now. But in early 2012, I had very good reasons to be worried. You see, Rina and I live in a neighborhood with a homeowners association, or HOA.

For those of you outside the USA, that's where a bunch of insanely picky buttheads get together so they can determine the acceptable colors of each other's homes, send nastygrams about cracked concrete or broken bricks, and generally act like a bunch of old-timers with bad "get off my lawn" syndrome.

(Of course, I'm being flippant here. My business partner at Centric specifically avoided buying a house with an HOA neighborhood, and later had a neighbor paint their house in Day-Glo sky blue. Yeah. And, in our case, the HOA does serve a useful purpose, since it maintains the greenbelt that separates us from the hillside brush. Which I was very thankful for in 2003, when brushfires literally came within fifty feet of our house—and were stopped by the greenbelt.)

Protip: *If you're having trouble with your HOA, the easiest way to get them off your back is to learn Morse code and get your ham radio operator's license. Hams are protected by the FCC as part of the critical communications infrastructure of the USA, so if you wanted to, say, put a ninety-foot-tall radio antenna in your front* *yard, the HOA can do absolutely nothing about it. Threatening to do that will shut them up good and fast.*

Anyway, what does an HOA have to do with getting too big?

Plenty. Most HOAs prohibit operating a business out of your home. Now, this isn't usually strictly enforced. They don't care if you have a home office or a studio, or if you're shipping some eBay or Etsy stuff out of your house, or selling a few hobby things you make in the garage.

But when you have two employees coming and going every evening, seven days a week, with garage lights blazing and music blaring...well, that's a different story.

It was only a matter of time before the HOA would start complaining. And since the city doesn't really like businesses being operated out of homes, they could absolutely enforce it.

So we had to look at moving...and soon.

Seven Figures in a Garage, and the Reality of Having Your Own Business

What's the limit of a garage business? A lot higher than you might think. When I finally started looking for space, we were still only using one-third of a three-car garage for "production and shipping floor." In that space, we'd just cracked seven figures in sales.

A note on numbers: Schiit is a private business, and I usually don't discuss revenues, because (a) it's gauche, (b) we are not required to, and (c) it's really not that important.

However, in this case, I'm using a specific number to illustrate what you can do with a self-funded, home-based manufacturing business. Remember, we started this with $10K. Eighteen months later, we're into seven figures annually. In a garage.

This isn't intended to be bragging. This is intended to be inspiration for you. Starting your own business is absolutely doable—without taking loans, leasing tons of space, hanging your ass out for bankers, gambling on delivering a crowdfunded product on time, or otherwise betting big on getting big.

But that brings us to what I call *The Reality of Having Your Own Business.*

In my opinion, the difference between working for someone and having your own business comes down to a single phrase: *When you have your own business, you can't say, 'That's not my problem.'*

Sounds too simple? No. Sit back and let it sink in.

When you're working for someone, you'll usually have a fairly well-defined role. No matter if you're a clerk or an engineer or a COO, in all cases, you'll know what's expected of you. A clerk isn't expected to design a new product—that's not his problem. An engineer isn't expected to write the ad copy for the new line launch—that's not his problem. A COO isn't expected to stand up in front of the press when the firm does a billion-dollar acquisition. It's not her problem.

With your own company—especially a small company— *everything* is your problem.

"Well, I'll hire people to take care of marketing, production, operations, etc.," you say.

Yes, and hiring them is your problem. As is budgeting for their salaries. And keeping them motivated.

And who do they report to? You.

Everything is your problem.

And I mean, everything. In this book, I've covered only the top-level stuff—engineering, putting things together, dealing with production problems, space. But let's look at a bigger list of things that will be your problem, if you start your own manufacturing biz:

- Engineering Documentation
    - Prototyping
    - Schematics
    - PC board layout
    - Testing
    - Compliance (FCC and the like)

Production procedures

Testing procedures

Documentation and archiving

Managing changes

Pricing

- Functional Items

    Product manuals

    Product description

    Product setup guides

    Driver installation guides

    Packaging

    Packaging testing

- Design

    Industrial design

    Packaging design

    Collateral design

- Marketing

    Website structure, functionality, copy, design

    Product "sell" copy

    Press releases

    Photography

    Informal communications (blogs, forums, etc.)

    Advertising

    Review samples

- Sales

    E-commerce capability, functionality, testing

    Sales through other sites

    Sales through dealers and distributors (ack)

       Accounts receivable (if you are dumb enough to give terms)

- Purchasing
  - Vendor interface
  - Purchase orders
  - Accounts payable
  - Account setup
  - Wire transfers

- Customers
  - Incorrect orders
  - Technical questions
  - General questions
  - Customer service

- HR
  - Hiring
  - Firing
  - Vacations
  - Benefits

- Shipping
  - Choosing shipping providers
  - Negotiating rates
  - Setup for e-commerce
  - Mis-shipments
  - Lost shipments

- Accounting and Taxes
  - Bookkeeping
  - Forecasting
  - Federal taxes

State taxes

Sales taxes

Yep, it's a long list. And it's not complete. Not by a long shot.

Now, it may seem I'm relatively cool on the prospect of starting your own business. No. Just realistic. It's a ton of work—but I'll reiterate. It's the biggest, most satisfying thing you'll ever do. At least for me. But I'm weird.

Again: *it's always your problem. No hiding. No passing the buck.*

If you're cool with that, go for it. Create your own business. Own it. Grow it. Enjoy the great times—and there will be plenty. And work through the tough times—those will happen too. Hire and build and make it easier on yourself.

But don't do it because you think it's going to be easy. Or because you think you'll have more freedom.

Because, if it's your business, it'll always be your problem. Until you decide to sell it and get out. And when you're small, everything is your problem.

Including looking for space.

Which is another of those invisible lines that, once you cross it, you won't go back. It's a big step that takes you from "This may be a hobby," to "Okay, we're committed, this is a real business."

Our Advanced Search Technique

When I started looking for space to lease in early 2012, I employed a proprietary algorithm using non-Fourier wavelet mathematics, known as DBLFSN, as well as a well-known methodology called BSLA. DBLFSN and BSLA rapidly narrow the lease candidates to a handful of locations best suited for a business's use.

Yeah, I'm having fun with you:

DBLFSN: Driving By Looking For Space Nearby

BSLA: Borrowing Someone's LoopNet Account

Here's the deal. I was still working daily at Centric, which is located in downtown Newhall. Being lazy, I wondered if there was anywhere nearby that we could use to house Schiit. So that's where I started. And, being observant, I noticed a building only a block away that might be a good candidate. Looking it up on LoopNet confirmed that it was about 1800 square feet, but didn't give a lease rate.

Now, 1800 square feet is kinda big for getting started with a small company. But it's not really that pricey. At a standard industrial lease rate of, say, $0.60, plus $0.10 CAM, you're looking at under $1300 a month. Plus electricity, water, gas, etc.

And this space had one thing going for it: the building was a Schiithole. It was a mixed siding-and-stucco one-story building with holes kicked in its sides, dry-rotted eaves, peeling tan paint that revealed five decades' worth of colors underneath, a nasty potholed blacktop parking space or two…

In other words, it would probably be almost free.

I was thrilled. It seemed like the perfect place. I called the realtor listed on the sign. "Hey, that building on the corner of Railroad and 6ᵗʰ, is it available?"

"Yep," said the realtor. "What are you planning to use it for?"

"Um…I have an audio company, we'd be doing some light manufacturing—"

"Manufacturing, nope," he cut me off. "It's not zoned for that."

My heart sank. "We're not talking machine tools and stuff. Just assembly."

"No can do," the realtor told me. "You start doing manufacturing in there, the city's going to come in and shut you down. The whole thing is a mess. We're now technically a flood plain, and the whole Enterprise Zone thing is screwing everything up. We don't know exactly what we can do with that building, period."

"There's no way we can make it work?"

"Nope," he said. "Sorry."

Stupid Rules, and Types of Business Space

Okay, if you've never leased business space before, you're probably shaking your head, wondering what the hell is going on here. Let me 'splain.

What's going on here is zoning. As in, a city divides its space, and decides what you can do in each place. Some common zones will include:

- **Residential:** You can only build houses here. This is where you live.

- **Commercial:** Only shops, thank you. Get your $10 fancy ice cream here.

- **Industrial:** That's where them crazy people build things. Like Schiit amps.

Now, some cities are crazier than others about zoning. Where Mike Moffat lives in Agua Dulce, you could probably build an eighty-foot-tall purple freeform house with a 10,000 square foot manufacturing facility and a Mexican restaurant, and bring in fifteen employees to run it, and the city wouldn't blink. (I'm exaggerating, of course.)

Santa Clarita, which encompasses Valencia, Newhall, Canyon Country, Saugus, etc., is about a million times opposite. In fact, Valencia is entirely master-planned. Which means it has big business areas full of offices and warehouses and manufacturing firms—and not a single restaurant. Everything must be in its place. And they are famous for sending their snoops around to make sure you're abiding by the rules. Yeah, we live in a wonderful place.

And the problem was, that beautiful Schiithole was zoned for commercial use, not industrial. Commercial meant that we could have an ice cream parlor or an office there, but not a manufacturing floor, nor a warehouse.

So did we look for other space? Yeah, sure. We looked in the Valencia Industrial Center, which is where we are now. But I really, really didn't like the idea of driving from Centric to Schiit to get things done. Remember, we had no operations people at that time, so it would be me overseeing things, Rina shipping and doing listening tests, and Eddie and Tony putting things together.

Which brought us back to that crappy little building in Newhall. The question was, how the heck could we get our hands on it?

It took two more conversations with the realtor to get him to agree to let us take a look inside the place. He still didn't think he would lease it to us, but I guess he was either (a) too bored, or (b) pissed that the space still wasn't moving. I still don't know why he did it, but it was that meeting that turned the tide.

And, man oh man, it was at least as bad inside. The tile floor had been cut open to do plumbing work, then roughly cemented over. Everything was covered in dust. A contractor was using it to store parts and equipment, and it was packed floor to ceiling with all kinds of stuff. The heating and air conditioning were nonfunctional. The layout was a weird L shape around a dirt-and-concrete yard. It was next to a barber shop and a thrift store. And the hammering of passing trains across the street made bits of the acoustical ceiling fall like snow.

"I guess this wouldn't be all that great for an office, even," said the realtor, looking at it with new eyes.

"It's perfect," I told him. "If we could just screw a few things together here."

He shook his head. "This is commercial. For shops and such. Places that sell things."

A sudden idea hit me. "But we do sell things," I told him.

"Yeah, but you're a manufacturer," he said. "I'm talking about shops that sell to the public."

"But that's what we do," I told him. "We sell direct to the public."

"Hmm," he said, rubbing his temples. He clearly wanted someone in the space that would pay more than the guy who was using it for storage, but he was still scared of the city. "So people could come in here and buy one of your products?"

"Theoretically, yes."

"Theoretically?" he looked doubtful. "How do you sell your stuff now?"

"Online, mainly."

"Hmm. But you could sell something to someone who came in?"

"Yes."

The realtor nodded. "Huh. Well. Let me see what I can do."

"Great!" I said.

He frowned. "No promises."

But somehow I knew: *this would be Schiit.*

CHAPTER 21

You Catch a Cold, We Die:
Bigger Products, Bigger Problems

THE FIRST AND SECOND QUARTER of 2012 weren't just the beginning of our look into really, truly moving out of the garage—they were also the ramp up to Mjolnir and Gungnir, our two most ambitious products to date. I've already covered some of the engineering challenges presented by these products, but that wasn't where the pain ended—not by a long shot.

First, Gungnir and Mjolnir broke our chassis design. Somewhere in January 2012, I submitted drawings to our chassis provider. Like all of our products, they were simple two-piece designs—an outer "U" and an inner sled. No problem, right?

Wrong. A couple of days after I submitted them for quote, I got a phone call from Russell, the guy we work with at our sheet metal fab shop.

"We can't make these parts," he said.

"Which parts?"

"The 01-25 and 01-30," Russell said, which was code-speak for the Gungnir and Mjolnir outer aluminum chassis, respectively.

Aside: Parts numbers, internal and otherwise. Okay, it's time for a lapse into engineeringland here. If you're going to start a company that makes any kind of custom parts—chassis, transformers, knobs, bolts, whatever—you're going to have to get used to part numbers. Suppliers don't take you seriously without them. They are simply not comfortable with saying, "Hey, the Gungnir outer chassis has a problem." They'd much rather

> say, "Hey, the 01-30 isn't producible, can you make these chang-
> es and send us a Rev B drawing?"

Ah hell, let's talk about parts numbers *and* revisions for a bit. Both are important. Because if you order an 01-18 Rev C when you intended to order an 01-18 Rev F, you're probably going to be boned.

"So what's this weird crap you're talking about?" you ask.

Let's break it down:

Parts numbers. When you create a custom part, you should assign a unique part number to this. Now, this doesn't have to have a bazillion-digit code like a UPC, or be done in hexadecimal or Klingon. But it should have a part number. Some companies break down their internal numbers with a prefix and suffix, like this:

- 01-XXXX: Wire
- 02-XXXX: Screws
- 03-XXXX: Sheet Metal Parts
- 04-XXXX: Milled Parts
- 05-XXXX: Cast Parts
- 06-XXXX: Transformers
- 07-XXXX: Capacitors
- Etc.

Now, that's pretty helpful to you, if you're looking for a part and you forgot what it was. But of course Schiit wasn't so orga-nized. All of our custom parts are simply 01-XXXX. Knobs, chassis, transformers, whatever. It's relatively simple, and we don't have that many parts (though, to be fair, we just did drawings for the 01-132, so maybe we should think about segmenting it.)

But we probably won't change.

Why?

Because that's a whole new bunch of pain, because we'd have to reeducate our suppliers on the new part numbers, which would probably result in some mis-orders. And mis-orders mean backorders for you. No, thanks.

Revisions. These are what happens when parts change. If you're betting you'll get the drawings right the first time, you're probably wrong. (Though, admittedly, the first articles of Ragnarok—yes, Ragnarok, with about ten billion holes and super-complex PC board layouts—fit the first time. This is not called "mad skillz," this is called "damn f'n lucky." Of course, the finish work was so terrifying it was unsellable, but that's another matter.) If you think you won't have to make changes over time, you're wrong.

This means your drawings should have a revision level, usually specified as a letter, like "Rev A" or something like that. So when you change the location of the indicator dot on the knob, it's now "Rev B." And when you find that it doesn't fit the shaft of the pot, and you have to change the drill size, it's now "Rev C." And so on.

Revisions should be specified:

- **On the drawing.** So you know what it is, durr. Protip: add a "Revision Notes" panel to remind yourself what you changed with each revision. Trust me, the vendors will thank you.

- **On the file name.** Seems basic, but you'd be amazed how long it took us to figure it out.

- **On the purchase order.** This may be less obvious. But if you end up with a whole boatload of parts that don't fit because you specified the wrong rev, you're going to eat them—and customers are gonna be howling about the backorder.

Why It's Not Always Bright to Think Everyone's Like You

When I was at Sumo, I thought all this part numbering business was a gigantic pain in the ass that made it impossible for people to know what the hell they were doing. I mean, why call a 121 ohm, 1/4W resistor an 05-1262? Why not call it what it was? Wouldn't that be a lot easier?

Turns out not so much. By thinking "this is a pain, people won't know what part it is," I was actually thinking, "I, as an engineer, think this is a pain, because of course I know it's a 121 ohm, 1/4W resistor, like duh, hell, you can see the stripes on it."

In reality, the people putting the products together (or, today, the robots) don't care what it's called. An 05-1262 has no more or less meaning than a 121 ohm, 1/4W resistor. And when you get into chassis or custom parts, something like "the new, non-screwed-up Gungnir tops" is a whole lot less descriptive than an "01-31, Rev F."

So, if you're going to be starting a business with custom parts, I'd recommend the following:

- **Set up a parts numbering system** that covers, at least, every custom part. It doesn't have to be complicated, but it should probably be segmented. Especially if you plan to produce more than a couple of products. This will get you taken more seriously by your vendors, and (believe it or not) will save you pain in the long run.

- **Document all of your revisions,** and do everything you can to label revisions correctly. There *will* be changes. Yes, even on 3D CAD pre-fitted, pre-qualified-with-the-sheet-metal-module files. Your vendor will need to know what changed between revisions. And you won't want to be ordering 1000 pieces of a wrong rev that doesn't fit anymore. Because those go straight in the trash can. And your vendor will be more than happy to point at the revision level on the purchase order, and say, "We're very sorry, but it's your own stupid fault. Want to place an order for the right part?"

I guess what I'm saying is that working with external suppliers, and working with external assembly, is kinda like writing code. You want to be very explicit, and make sure your syntax is right.

Now, some vendors are gonna be really good, smart, and on the ball. But I still wouldn't want to tell them, "Hey, make this part this new way," and expect that a verbal change will filter through to the final delivery.

Use part numbers. Document changes. Pay attention to rev levels. You'll thank me for it.

Fun fact: *Schiit is up to Rev J on some parts. Yes, even our simple stuff. Revs happen. Keep them straight, and your life will be a lot easier.*

Back to Russell...

Wow, that was a hell of a diversion. Let's get back to Russell and the non-producible chassis.

"Why can't you make them?" I asked. "They're just like our other parts."

"They're too deep," Russell said. "We can't bend something that's eight inches deep on both sides."

Crap, I thought. How the hell were we going to do Mjolnir and Gungnir, then? A boring conventional chassis with a front panel? A front U and extensions? My mind quickly started running through the variations. (No kidding, I frequently think about how to put chassis together in interesting ways. Yeah, not exactly Running with the Bulls, but I think it's fun.)

"Can you get a bigger brake? A different tool?" I asked Russell.

"No can do. The problem isn't the depth so much, it's actually getting the tool in there once it's that deep. If it was a J-bend, sure. But a U-bend won't work."

Note: By J-bend, he meant a piece of metal where one side is much shorter than the other. So, when seen on-end, it looks like a J.

But a J-bend wouldn't work for us. We had to transfer heat from the bottom to the top of the chassis. That was the beauty of the Asgard-style chassis design. It was a heatsink as well. But to work as a heatsink, it had to transfer heat.

A J-bend, with a break in it, wouldn't transfer heat. The Mjolnir would cook.

"Let me see what I can come up with," I told Russell. "I'll see if I can get you a new revision tomorrow."

Then I got to sketching. As in, with a Rotring pencil and big eraser. You kiddies can laugh at the dinosaur now. But I don't think you can iterate ideas any faster in 3D CAD than you can with a sketch.

I took Russell's idea—the J-bend—and sketched up ideas that would allow us to transfer heat between the bottom and top chassis. The first sucked—a 1/8" thick bracket to attach the two pieces. But that was a whole nother piece. And it would have to be tapped, or have PEM nuts inserted into it. Which would drive up cost.

I could do a joggle bend, of course, but that would look terrible. The inner chassis wouldn't be able to hide the joggle...

...unless I did only a partial joggle, and left the outside flush.

There we go.

And that's how Mjolnir and Gungnir got a three-piece chassis with a joggle bend hidden on the bottom. Because it couldn't be done in a single piece.

"Well, I'm sure you could have found someone out there who could do it in one piece," someone is saying.

Yeah. Maybe. And maybe they would have cost five times as much. Or delivered crap. Or a thousand other things. Believe me, in sheet metal, the devil you know is usually much, much, much better than the one you don't. If you're contemplating a vendor change, do it when:

- You don't need them.
- You're very happy with your current supplier.
- You have a ton of extra time.

(Or, in other words, it'll probably never happen. But that's another story.)

To make a long story short, I got new drawings out to our metal guys, they nodded approvingly, and they got started on building the first article metal.

On First Articles and Cheapness

First articles are the first "proof of concept" metal from your chassis supplier. This is what they make so you can:

- Check fit
- See what the finish is like
- Make crappy-looking prototypes and show them to people who won't understand they're prototypes, no matter how big the signs are

First articles you pay for. No metal supplier is going to do them for free. At least not for a small company.

Because we were cheap, we got first articles that were unfinished. As in, no paint on the steel, no screens, no anodize on the aluminum. This saves quite a bit of money.

But, unless you're using the first articles ONLY for fit, it's best to get them done all the way. That way, you can see what the finish is really like, if the screen lines up with the holes, and you can take it to shows and tease people with it, if that's what you're into. This is what we do today. In the past, we were cheap—which resulted in overheating Mjolnir prototypes (unanodized aluminum is a really crappy heat radiator) and a crap-looking Ragnarok that wasn't ready for prime time.

On Metal, Transformers, and Announcing Early

By the time we were ready to think about announcing Mjolnir and Gungnir, we were smart enough to know that preorders weren't a good idea.

"We'll do an interest list instead," I told Mike.

"An interest list?" he said.

"Yeah. We'll put complete product info up, but instead of taking orders, customers can leave us their email and check which products they're interested in."

"Oh, like a preorder, but with no credit card," Mike said doubtfully. "So you'll still have to answer all the questions about 'hey, when's this gonna be out?'"

"No. It's just a list. And we'll set availability at, say, sixty days out. That'll give us plenty of time to deal with any glitches."

"Hmm," Mike said.

"What hmm?"

"Glitches always take twice as long as you expect. That's the Second Law Of Vendors."

"There might not be any glitches."

"Right, and the Pope might convert to Judaism," Mike retorted.

"Look, I think we've got this figured. Lyr was out ahead of time...."

"And Bifrost wasn't. And I know how crazy you get when everyone's hounding you."

I sighed. "I like to think positive."

Mike shrugged. "I prefer to be realistic. But if you say we're doing an interest list, that's what we're doing."

"It'll be fine, you'll see."

"Uh-huh," Mike grumbled.

Of course, you know how this goes. Mike was absolutely right. In fact, he was actually thinking positively when it came to glitches.

Because, a week after the interest list went up, we got the transformers in (01-21 and 01-22, for the parts-number-centric out there.)

And the 01-21s hummed like refrigerators. I mean, if we'd used those transformers in Mjolnir, it could have been a headphone amp / massager product.

Now, of course, the prototypes didn't hum. But production did. And this time, it wasn't our fault. The rev was correct. But the vendor had built an earlier rev. And they were junk.

Okay, not the end of the world. We still had fifty days or so left. Transformers made in the USA can be had in three to four weeks, no problem.

But when you factor in another round of prototypes, and a short run to make sure they were really, really quiet, well…the time stretches out. We ended up getting the replacement transformers only about a week before the initial release date.

Which still would have been fine, except for one small thing.

About thirty days after the interest list went up, we got the metal. And it was crap. The graining was completely random, with skips and hops and slips like tire tread. Completely unacceptable for a relatively expensive product.

I got on the phone again. "Russell, what the hell happened?"

"Ah. Yeah. Our timesaver bearings are maybe a little woppity. We need to replace them. But it's a custom part. It'll take a while."

My stomach sank. "And you thought these were good enough to send to us?"

"We knew you needed them fast."

I groaned. Of course. We'd been pressing them to deliver on time. It didn't excuse the quality, but I could understand why they did what they did. They didn't really know what kind of finish we needed.

After I explained this to Russell, he said, "We'll get new ones to you as fast as possible, but it may take a while for the bearings."

Luckily, they got the bearings in within a week and promised new metal in three more weeks. Which meant we could still make it.

But I could see Mike smirking in the background. And when the metal came in—on time—I had no reason to gloat. Because the bottom chassis were still crap. All of them had a big gouge on the back of the chassis.

It was only days until the release. I called Russell. "What the heck happened? They're all messed up the same. There's this big mark on the back!"

"Oh, yeah, that's where they have to clip them for anodizing."

"Then clip them somewhere else! We're a week away from launch, and on the second set of metal. We can't ship these! Pick 'em up and fix them."

"Will do," Russell said.

"How long until we get them back? Like I said, these are promised in a week. Boards are at the board house. This is the only holdup."

"I'll see."

"Make it fast. Please."

"We'll do it as fast as we can," Russell promised.

Well, 'as fast as we can,' ended up being about five weeks. Those of you who remember the Mjolnir launch remember the delay.

And so, even with the best planning, even with a nice big buffer between announcement and scheduled ship date, even without taking preorders, the launch was still a bust. Mike had been absolutely right. We should have just kept our mouths shut.

That one glitch pretty much wrecked the early summer. If we didn't run with substantial cash reserves (we are *extremely* conservative), very, very bad things could have happened.

Which is maybe the most important lesson. When your vendors catch a cold, you get sick. When they have a problem, it's your problem. Your customers don't care about excuses or The Reality of Making Things Today. They want their stuff. When it was promised. Period.

After Mjolnir and Gungnir, it was clear what we had to do: *never preannounce a new product, ever again.*

CHAPTER 22

Introducing the Schiithole

OKAY, THE LAST TIME I talked about moving out of the garage, I left you hanging—with the realtor saying, "Well, maybe we can find a way for you to do your light manufacturing in a zoned-for-commercial space, but no promises."

To cut to the chase, we got it. What finally sold it was probably three things:

- Persistence
- Not appearing too flaky or insane
- Willingness to take the property as-is

Believe it or not, number two matters quite a bit. There are plenty of flaky, insane people in commercial real estate. Landlords want nothing to do with them. And number three is also a big deal. Landlords don't want to do a bunch of custom buildout—even if you're signing a long-term lease.

And—one other thing: the willingness to take a little bit of risk. Because we were in a commercial space, after all. Not industrial. The city inspector could conceivably come by, decide we weren't conforming, and shut us down.

But it was a risk worth taking, because it got us an inexpensive space near our other office. And the risk, we told ourselves, wasn't high. After all, we were retailers. We sold direct to customers. And if 99.99% of it was shipped via FedEx and USPS, did it really matter, as long as we had a place that someone could theoretically walk in and purchase something?

Perhaps. But that would be up to the inspector. If they ever came by. I crossed my fingers, hoped they wouldn't, picked up our first liability insurance*, and signed the lease.

And that's how, around February 2012, we got the worn and pitted keys to our first Schiit building.

*Hidden Expenses and DIY Dreams

I precede this aside with a * to connect it to the liability insurance mention above. I do this because this is a great corollary to the "everything is your problem" reality of having your own business. Well, here's the second harsh reality of your own business: *there are a hell of a lot of hidden expenses ready to jump up and bite you in the ass.*

I sometimes get taken to task by DIYers who say, "I can build something like that for a lot less than you're charging."

Sure. Well, maybe. No. Wait.

Actually, they can't, because the price on single pieces of stuff like transformers and chassis will make any one-off a budget-busting exercise. Even if you're talking off-the-shelf transformers and project boxes, it really isn't going to be that much cheaper. And that's not factoring in the time the DIYer spent building it, nor the time it took to learn their construction skills, nor the cost of their tools, nor the cost of the new tools they had to get while making it. You get the picture.

(And, just to be clear, I love and support DIY. As far as I'm concerned, we should all be juggling soldering irons and dropping them in our laps, grabbing on to 120V (or 230V) once in a while, putting transistors in backwards, watching capacitors explode, spending endless hours wondering why the new prototype doesn't work quite right, getting excited when the new PC boards come in...)

But DIY isn't production. It's not production in a garage, and it's not a business with all sorts of crazy expenses. Expenses like:

- Liability insurance

- Product liability insurance
- Workman's comp insurance
- Facilities lease
- Facilities upkeep
- Facilities changes / expansion
- Equipment cost
- Equipment upkeep and calibration
- Bookkeeping
- Local gross receipts tax
- Sales or VAT
- Business licensing / registration (if applicable)

And this is on top of the normal, fun stuff like local, state, and federal taxes, payroll, parts cost, shipping, assembly cost, etc.

Yep. Tons of fun.

Mike's Perspective

Mike, of course, saw right through me, as soon as he drove by the place. He took one look at Rina running a Shop-Vac over the cracked and dusty floor (and vacuuming up big pieces of ancient tile in the process), and crowed:

"You got it because it was cheap."

"Right," I told him, not even hesitating.

Rina and Eddie were also arguing over space for shipping versus space for production. Eddie was arguing that we should take all the used, battered Ikea office desks (that I got from Centric's storage unit) back outside and blow the dust out of the space with a compressor.

"There's about a hundred pounds of dirt per square foot up there," Eddie said, pointing up at the sprayed acoustic ceiling. "That crap's gonna fall down if we don't blow it out."

"It may fall down if we blow it out anyway," I told him. The ceiling didn't look too robust. We could be looking at sheets of acoustic cottage cheese if we started blowing on it.

"But it was cheap!" Mike said.

"Yes," I snapped. "And convenient. And it keeps the HOA from shutting us down."

"Until the city inspector comes."

"*If* he comes."

"I'm going to need more space for shipping," Rina interrupted, indicating where she wanted her finished-goods racks placed.

"That's two-thirds of the building," I told her. "Eddie and Tony need more space."

"We need more space for shipping!" she insisted.

Eddie shook his head. "And we should stop this crazy vacuuming and blow this place out. This dust is gonna get *everywhere!*"

"But it was cheap!" Mike added.

I groaned. Thankfully, Tony wasn't there, or would have probably had a comment or three as well. Suffice to say, it wasn't our finest day moving in. The place was really a mess.

Maybe I should step back and describe the Schiithole (the name Rina dubbed it with on that first contentious day—and it stuck.)

The Schiithole was an old, L-shaped stucco-and-siding building on the corner of 6th and Railroad in Newhall. Railroad is named because of, well, the railroad that parallels it. This railroad was instrumental in making Newhall one of the first boom towns of the late 1800s (together with the discovery of oil.) It now carries mainly Metrolink traffic. Many times a day, trains rattle by, shaking the old building. Cars rush by on the five-lane street outside at all hours. With no insulation, it was a hollow, loud, booming space.

Outside, the stucco was fading to an off-white from what had once been a taupe color. Several large holes had been punched in it, whether from frustrated passerby, or by some other mechanism, I don't know. The siding was peeling paint, and much of the external wood was collapsing into dry rot.

Inside, the floor was uneven and patched crudely with concrete. And by uneven, I mean "like, one side was a good foot lower than the other." Some traces of fiberglass tiles remained, but they were rapidly flaking off as we cleaned. The Sheetrock walls were relatively unmarked, but the bathrooms were only partially functional, after the building had been stripped of plumbing and wiring by thieves and only makeshift restored. There was no hot water. No heating. No AC.

Out back, it had a dirt-and-concrete yard full of knee-high weeds and assorted detritus. Of the four doors, one looked out on the back area, two were on the Railroad side, plus a roll-up door the realtor warned us "never to leave open, because that's a sure sign you're making things here," and a door on Market Street. None of the doors matched. None of them were handicap accessible.

I didn't know it at the time, but it had once been the home of the *Daily Signal*, Santa Clarita's newspaper that still survives (barely) to this day. We were later shown the room where they used to melt down the lead plates every night, to recast them for the next day's paper. We were using it as a storeroom.

But, as Mike said, *It was cheap.*

So, yeah, a fun move. But by the end of that first day, we had test equipment plugged in and running, Eddie had his assembly bench set up, and we were moving things in from the garage and the rest of the house.

We had a home away from home. The Schiithole.

Interlude: Business Space Philosophy

Okay, so why did we take such a crappy place (because it was cheap) and tolerate the noise (because it was cheap) and the dust (because it was cheap) and the lack of any typical niceties, like heat and AC (because it was cheap!)

Well, yes. But also because of an observation I've had about business space:

The moment you build a palace is the moment you die.

Now, it may take many years for that palace to kill you. You may end up with some very good years there. It may serve as a very useful way to awe and astound customers or clients that are easily impressed by such things.

But the moment you start focusing on business *wants*, rather than *needs*, you're dead.

It happened to Sherwood. It happened to Marantz. It happened to dozens of ad agencies I've seen come and go. It's happened to scores of clients who spent their start-up money on nice offices and celeb chefs and foosball tables and lounges. We'll see how Apple's "spaceship" campus does for them, but I'm betting right now I know how it ends.

Here's the deal. In business, there are certain things you need. These are things like:

- **A functional space.** That is, one large enough to contain what you want to do. Trying to put a full wood shop in a 20' x 20' space isn't gonna work out very well. Depending on what you're doing, you may need no more than a single office— or a home office—or a whole lot more space for stock, finished goods, production area, machinery, etc. But first and foremost, you need a functional space.

- **Effective places to work.** This may mean an Ikea desk and a Wacom Cintiq and a WiFi router and nothing more. Or it might mean heavy-duty workbenches with static mitigation and ten outlets for work on sensitive electronics. It may mean self-built 2x4-and-fiberboard tables with static mats for accomplishing the same thing. Plus chairs and such.**

- **The equipment you need to do your work.** This may be nothing more than a laptop, or it could be an entire suite of test equipment. Or CNC routers and laser engraving machines. Bottom line, stuff like this is critical, if it is critical for doing your work. Don't skimp.

- **The right connectivity for your business.** This may mean nothing more than a simple DSL line for basic spreadsheets, web surfing, and ordering, or super-high-speed optical cable with dedicated symmetric lines for a phone bank to serve a creative shop with outbound calling.

**I have never seen such a rip-off as high-end office chairs. Please don't get me started on this. Might as well buy audio jewelry lovingly carved from hunks of solid titanium by master craftspeople living in Monterey. Just go to Office Depot, plop your butt in a bunch of chairs that are $150 or less, and pick the ones that are most tolerable and cheapest. Our creative director once tried to talk me into getting Aerons for the whole office. I swapped his chair for a steel folding chair the next day. We bought sensible chairs.

Please notice that none of the above includes things like:

- **A cool-looking building.** Please. Who cares? Save money for your house.

- **A cool-looking office space with polished concrete floors, $16,000 European couches, and iDevice-controlled programmable LED lighting.** See above. If stuff like that impresses your customers or clients, they're not analytical enough to understand:

  a. Every cent of that came from their pocket.

  b. You're making far too much money.

  c. You're not good with impulse control and probably won't be around long.

- **Corner offices for everyone.** Geometrically impossible, anyway. Plus, let the infighting begin.***

- **Nice private offices for everyone.** Yep. Let's give them reasons to close the door and hide from problems. Not a great idea, especially in a start-up.

- **Lounge / recliner / videogame / relaxation / informal meeting areas.** Yeah, you love your employees. But it's more important they love you and believe in what you're doing, without having to be tempted by silly perks. The best person for the job is one who wants to work for you above all others—because of what you're doing, not because of the icing on the cake. If nobody wants to work for you, start looking in the mirror—and hard.

- **A big sign in front of the building.** Might as well advertise "there's expensive electronics in here," in our case. In most cases, this is nothing more than ego.

***Let's talk about this a little bit more. The biggest fights I've ever witnessed amongst employees was regarding "who gets what office," or "who gets which desk." Honestly, this is completely useless and divisive stuff that you really don't need to deal with. Start-ups probably shouldn't have private offices, period.

And that's why we ended up with a space that was really nothing more than a large production floor, with no offices, in an ugly, run-down building. Because it had what we needed. And nothing we didn't.

And it was cheap.

The Earliest Days of the Schiithole

Going to the Schiithole in the early mornings, shortly after we moved in, are some of my most vivid memories of Schiit, beyond the early start-up phase. Why? Because we were finally in our own space—and that opened up so many new possibilities.

And because I was crapping-my-pants busy.

The move, as simple as it was, put us back a few days in production. And in those times of "build tonight, ship the next day," that means that we were very behind. Tony and Eddie would come in during the evening and build the boards that Jaxx delivered, but I was doing all the sound-checking.

So, I'd come in before going into Centric (5-6 a.m.), take the plastic sheet off the pile of finished units on the burn rack, and run them through sound check. If any failed, I'd note it and put it on my desk for later that evening, when I'd come back in from Centric at 6-7 p.m., and fix whatever didn't make it through burn.

Rina would come in during the afternoon and ship, but her time was starting to come at a premium—her own business, Twilight's Fancy, was taking off. She had to spend more time there and less at Centric.

And I was quickly burning out from the long days. You can do fourteen-hour days for a while, but they'll eventually kill you (if your significant other doesn't do so first.)

Tony wasn't going to be able to take over shipping—he had his hands full, especially with Mjolnir and Gungnir imminent, and Bifrost flying off the shelves. Eddie couldn't do shipping, either— he liked to work at night, when it was cooler and quieter in the shop.

Yep, you know where this is going. It was time to grow again.

And this time, we needed to look at it more strategically. Sure, we needed someone who could ship. But what we really needed was someone who could do a lot more than that—someone who could grow to be in charge of operations.

Luckily, Rina had the "perfect" candidate...

CHAPTER 23

"I Didn't Know People In the Private Sector Were As Lazy and Incompetent As the People In Schools"

I'VE ALREADY MENTIONED SOME "invisible lines" in business—hiring your first employee, getting your own production space, etc. Well, here's another: hiring your first employee who won't directly be producing products.

Yes, your first manager.

I can hear the groans now. Well, I hate to break it to the fans of completely flat organizations, but yes, some management is necessary. That is, if you ever want a snowball's chance in a blast furnace of ever having a life. If you ever want to take some time off, have a vacation, or do any of those things that non-workaholic people do, you'll need management that ain't you.

Why? Because, believe it or not, you can't do everything.

Repeat that again: *you can't do everything.*

No, let's turn that up: *you **shouldn't** do everything.*

Now, before you all think I've become some tool relaxing on a beach, espousing the benefits of outsourcing every part of your business and life so you can sit on your ass some more, building your empire on a cloud of a temporary situation in which some places in the world offer very low-cost labor, relax.

Similarly, if you're thinking I'm going to be retiring to the CEO's giant office, reclining in a $6000 Italian-leather office chair, foregoing the day-to-day work, and focusing on creating dream-team org charts while the company is mismanaged into nonexistence by the direct reports under the dream team, oh *hell no* to that as well.

No. Let's be clear. We're not talking about a billion-dollar "hey, I won the VC / start-up / etc. lottery" mass-market business here. We're talking niche. We're talking niches where people get up in arms about the tiniest decisions you make. We're talking an environment where microsocial will dissect everything we do.

Get out of your business and you kill it.

Hire a "dream" CEO to run your brilliant idea, and it's dead meat.

Ignore the nuts and bolts and focus only on a "vision," and you might as well throw in the towel.

But, at the same time, this doesn't mean you have to do *every-thing*. Which means hiring people with responsibility, intelligence, and the ability to make a decision. Call them "managers," "smart dudes," "team leaders," or what-have-you, but you will need them to do things you can't do, don't have the time to do, or don't want to do.

But this is a massive change. Once you've hired someone in management, you've now put on direct overhead. You have a salary that isn't totally dedicated to pushing products out the door.

It's a gigantic change. To put it simply: *once you've hired a man-ager, it's a real business, not a hobby.*

Jason's Thoughts on Business Management, or, Saving Face Before I Get My Ass Kicked By Flat Organization Fans

Now, before we get any further let me be perfectly clear about how I feel about management layers in a business: they're a necessary evil. Extra layers should be avoided at all cost. Like nuclear waste, you don't want to get too much management on you.

The problem is, the vast, vast majority of businesses in the USA have far too much management. Instead of treating it like nuclear waste, they treat it like an all-you-can-eat free buffet...the more, the merrier.

How much management is too much?

- How about a 150-person company with seventeen vice-presidents?

- What about an eighty-person company with sixty-five in management and fifteen in production and shipping?

- How about a 200-person company with six layers of management: C-Level, EVP, VP, Director, Senior Manager, Manager—with anyone below the EVP level unable to make decisions on expenditures that cost more than $1000?

Yep, been there, seen all that. And lots more.

Why do companies have too much management? Three reasons:

- **The 20/80 rule, or hiding in a crowd.** When a company reaches a certain size, and the founding management checks out of the day-to-day reality, it's very easy for groups to form where eight out of ten people are simply hiding in the crowd, and only two people are actually doing the work. Solution: add a manager. All too often from the 80%, though.

- **The "ain't my job" CYA factor.** When something new and scary is thrown at a company running the 20/80 game, the natural reaction of most 80%ers is to run away. It might fail. They don't want to get that on them. (Seriously, at my first corporate job at Magnavox, I was pulled aside by the Senior Team Leader and told very simply, "Never volunteer. It makes us look bad. And you're working too fast.") Good thing there was a manager and senior manager above him, before the department head and then the "real" engineering management.

- **Title inflation.** How do you make someone feel good if you don't want to give them a raise? How about a fancy title? Yeah. It really is that simple.

Mike and I took the titles of "Co-Founder" when we started Schiit, rather than "CEO / President" for the simple reasons of:

- They describe accurately what we are
- They set no limits on what we can or should do
- They are about as anti-inflationary as they can get

So, to this day, and into the foreseeable future, Mike and I are as hands-on as we want to be, or need to be. Mike directly designs pretty much all of the digital products. I do pretty much all of the analog products. When digital problems come up, Mike solves them. When analog problems come up, I solve them.

Will we someday have engineers working with us doing some of that? Maybe. But I don't see us getting out of those arenas entirely, or anytime soon.

Similarly, I do the marketing and the product cosmetic design. Will I get out of that? Probably not completely. But will I hire a marketing person to deal with the mechanics of ads, shows, etc., and to beat off the ad salespeople with a stick? You bet. But not now. Not yet.

So what don't we do?

Well, Mike and I are both what you'd call "administratively challenged." We're not good at detail. Rely on us to make sure the parts show up on time, that we build the right mix of 115V and 230V units, or even that we get to the right show on the right date...hmm. Maybe. Maybe not.

Or to put it in more typical business language: we clearly need help in operations. And that brings us to our first management hire...

Let's Meet Another "Ideal" Candidate

Okay, let's first set the scene. About the time I start thinking, "Hey, I need someone who can do more than test and assemble," we're not even yet in the Schiithole. It's very close, though. Imminent. And I'd really like to have someone in there, ASAP, someone who isn't Rina, Mike, or me.

At the same time, we're starting to think really hard about the Mjolnir and Gungnir launch. Which means the workload was going to get even bigger. The days, longer. Compounding this, Rina's own business was taking off, so she had less time to devote to Schiit.

We needed to hire someone. At least to help with shipping. But I really wanted more—someone who could grow into our lead operations guy. Call him the Proto-COO, or Future Director of Operations, or whatever title sounds appropriate. But I knew we needed someone who was much more than a clerk.

That's when Rina had a brilliant idea.

"Hire Alex," she said. "He could run this whole business."

"Alex?" I asked.

"Jen's husband." Jen was Rina's friend from way back. They've written books together. Currently, they're producing a web series (necrolectric.com). I knew Jen. I'd met Alex before, but I wasn't intimately familiar with his background. I remembered something about computers, but that's about it.

"What does he do?" I asked.

"He'd be perfect! And it would be great. And they've always wanted to move out here."

"Wait." I remembered that Jen and Alex lived in Hesperia. To those not familiar with California, that's a hell of a commute to Newhall—about ninety minutes one way…with no traffic.

"But he could start part-time," Rina pressed. "He wouldn't have to come out here every day…"

I shook my head. "Part-time," and "operations," don't really go together. And anyone who was willing to do part-time…

"What's he doing now?"

Rina frowned. "I told you. He was an assistant principal at—"

Rina kept talking, but I didn't hear her. Every negative stereotype of someone who'd worked in the school system came clamoring to the fore, shouting for attention. *They were overpaid. Lazy. They could never make it in private industry. They'd fold in a second and run back to the land of fat, tax-funded pensions.*

But at the same time, I remembered talking with Alex—and he was sharp.

"Um," I stalled.

"He really would be perfect!" Rina said. "I know it!"

"But…"

"And when they're living here, it'll be even better."

"I really don't know about this," I told her.

"You should give him a chance…"

I knew where this was going. I didn't want to argue, so I pretended that I had something to do (or maybe I really did have something to do) and begged off of making a decision.

Out of the Frying Pan…

But Rina kept hounding me. And that's how, shortly after we took possession of the Schiithole, I found myself talking to Alex over breakfast with Rina and Jen.

And…you know what? Alex was sharp.

What's more, he didn't flinch when I spelled out exactly how it had to be, to start: he'd be a contractor, not an employee. The hours might be a little sketchy, depending on demand. The place he'd be working in was not a palace. He was going to die in the summer heat. And he'd be having to learn the ropes of audio—an insanely picky, somewhat neurotic, completely unique market that he had no deep experience in.

No. Instead, Alex asked reasonable questions, like when we'd end up switching to salary (soon, I was already getting nervous about the "contractor" definition, and I knew it had to go), opportunity to move up (there is no ceiling, I told him the story of Mike and Centric and creating our first interactive department from nothing). And the story of Theta and its bonuses.

And, during that breakfast, I began to get the feeling: Alex may just be one of those diamonds in the rough, like Eddie and Tony…but on a much more functional frequency. He was clearly smart enough to get in and understand our operations.

But was he? Those old prejudices about people who worked for schools kept nagging.

It didn't matter. It wasn't like Mike and I were going to be organized enough to put together a help-wanted ad and screen the applicants. It would be easier to do the "sink or swim" thing again, just like we'd done with Tony and Eddie.

So what did we do? I said something like, "You want to get started now?"

That afternoon, Alex was helping pack and ship Valhallas at the garage. From there, he helped us move all the crap out of the garage into the Hole, then trained with Rina on Mondays, Wednesdays, and Fridays for the next couple of weeks.

After that, it was pretty much the Alex Show.

Alex determined that we needed more racks for better segregation of finished goods—so he went out and bought them. He decided to reorganize the packing and loose parts. He cleaned up the Schiithole to the point where it was much more livable. He oversaw the installation of a security system, told us when we were running out of space, found a place with mobile storage units, and added one in the back. He let Eddie know what to build and Tony what to test. After some short training with me, he took over a lot of the part ordering. He didn't complain, even as the days got hotter and his hours got shorter because things were slow.

And he did this all while he and Jen were looking for a house out here, closing the deal, and he was spending his evenings renovating the house, as well.

And that, my friends, is what initiative looks like.

Alex was the perfect candidate. Rina was entirely right.

Now, Alex got to interact with a lot of our vendors—the metal house, the PCB house, the electronic parts suppliers, the packaging guys...and I think this was a revelation to him in more ways than one:

- **Revelation One:** he didn't have to fill out fifty pages of paper to buy $500 worth of stuff. I'd just say, "If you want it, get it."

- **Revelation Two:** his own assumptions about private business were about as lacking as my own about people who work in schools.

One day, as we were finally shipping Mjolnir and Gungnir (after we'd gone through a couple of rounds of metal incompetence, and Alex had helped us work through them), Alex said something that still stands to this day as The Greatest Schiit Quote of All Time.

He said:

"You know, before I started this job, I had no idea people who work in private industry were as lazy and incompetent as the people who work in the school system."

I busted up.

But I couldn't help thinking: *wow, that's a turnaround from my own prejudices.*

"When I was working at the school," Alex continued, "that's all they ever told us: that we'd never make it in the private sector. That we were so lucky to have these jobs. If we ever lost them, our lives were over."

"They actually told you that?" I asked.

Alex nodded.

"Wow." I shook my head.

"But I get out here, and what do I find? The same bozos."

I laughed. "Yeah, being part of a private company doesn't mean anything. Especially in marketing. You know what we used to say about marketing?"

"No," Alex said.

"You go into marketing because you're not smart enough for science, and not ruthless enough for sales."

"Ouch."

"Yeah. And probably about as true as everyone in the school system being lazy and incompetent. The thing is, everything's a continuum. There are sharp people and not-so-sharp people everywhere."

"I'm still looking for the sharp ones," Alex told me.

"Good. We'll need them."

And that really is *the* challenge, more and more: not letting your company fall to the 20/80 rule, where a handful of good people do most of the work. Not letting the bozos on the bus.

And, to this day, Alex has helped us do that. He oversaw the move into, and buildout of the space we're in today. He spec'd the racking and forklift we needed. He set up the shop layout so it would be more efficient. He's helped us work through half a dozen new product start-ups, and made decisions to hold back on shipping until he was happy with what we are making. He brought on the extra people we need for customer service and for shipping. And he's overseeing the buildout of extra space right now, as I write this. All transparently, without hours of micromanagement from me and Mike, and without us second-guessing everything he's doing.

In short, without Alex (or someone very much like him) we would not have been able to grow as effectively. Schiit would have been much more of a burden on the day-to-day side. We probably wouldn't have been able to launch as many new products as we have, nor the flood of new stuff that's coming.

That's why you hire (good) management. Because it makes things better all around.

Note the (good). Because accepting mediocrity isn't acceptable. Nor is sitting back, crossing your arms, and saying, "You know, we're doing pretty well."

Bottom line: you can't tread water. You can't stand still. You have to sacrifice your babies. You need to look straight-on at cannibalizing your own products. You always have to be asking, "What can we do better, less expensively?" Even if it lays waste to your entire lineup.

Because, you know what? *If you don't do it, someone else will.*

CHAPTER 24

Getting Our Schiit Together

THE SUMMER OF 2012 WAS one of the most transformative times at Schiit, and it was largely due to Alex helping us pull our heads out of our rear ends.

It was the first time we started actually trying to predict demand and buy ahead to meet it, rather than simply looking at the shelves and saying, "Hmm, looks like we're out of Asgards, we'd better order some more."

It also meant major changes on the employee side, the shipping side, the operations side, and on the facilities side. In many ways, it was when we moved from being a "hobby business" to a real company.

In the Beginning (of Summer, That Is)

At the start of summer 2012, we were still operating pretty much as we always had, except for the fact that we were operating out of the Schiithole.

Now, we only had part of the Schiithole (about 1000 square feet) at the time, not the entire building. It was just as crappy, dusty, and miserable as I've described. And, as an added bonus, the Santa Clarita summer was on us, bringing 100-110 degree temperatures during the day to a building with no air conditioning and no insulation.

Yeah, Alex pretty much cooked. Eddie, Tony, and I only came in during the evening when we could prop the doors open and run some big industrial fans to circulate the cooler air outside. Alex stayed there pretty much all day, to keep the shipping going.

Alex tried to combat the heat with a portable air-conditioning unit, but it really struggled in the uninsulated space. We mostly used it to keep the products on the burn-in racks from going full Chernobyl. Indoor temperatures of ninety plus were common.

It was bad enough that we ordered a larger wall air conditioner, but it was delayed, then cancelled for some unknown reason. The delay was good, though, since that was when the landlord came by.

"I'm thinking of sprucing this building up a little," he said. "Putting in heat and AC, painting, doing the floors, stuff like that."

"Great," I said, a little suspiciously.

Because landlords don't do things like that just for the fun of it. Usually such pronouncements are followed by, "And we'll bill you $X thousand dollars for it."

"It'll make the building more attractive to tenants," he continued.

I sighed. *Here it comes,* I thought.

"And I was wondering if you wanted to take the rest of the space," he said, looking at me expectantly.

"At the same rate?" I asked.

He laughed. You know, that landlord laugh. The one that says. *Oh, you silly boy, do you think anything in this world is free? Why don't you just buy a bunch of buildings and sit back and collect money like I do?*

Aside: I have nothing against landlords in general. I'm just not cut out to be one. I've got enough on my plate without having to deal with crazy people on a day-to-day basis. No. Wait. Never mind.

"So what are you looking to get for the whole thing?"

He named a price. A surprisingly reasonable price. A silly cheap price, in fact.

Now, I know that in Biz 101, they tell you to never look impressed, to press any advantage you have and try to grind people down to the lowest possible price, but, you know what? That's also called "being an asshole."

Actually, let's expand on that a bit. Haggling to get a lower price is one of those things that I've done in the past—and I was pretty good at it. But I never liked doing it. It felt bad. Wrong. Slimy.

Because when you haggle, you're saying, "I think what you're doing isn't worth what you're asking."

It also says:

- I don't trust you
- You don't know how to price things
- You're incompetent in general
- I think you're trying to screw me

And it says:

- I'm a cheap-ass
- I don't have a lot of money
- I'm going to be a difficult customer
- I might not pay you

When a customer starts haggling, a truly good and competent supplier does one of two things:

- They reiterate the value of what they're offering, and stand firm
- They walk away

Yes. That's right. I'm actually advocating for *non-negotiation*.

Well, that's nuts, some of you are saying. *There's a ton of companies out there who are set on screwing you, and will quote silly prices. How the hell do you know if you got a good deal?*

First, by knowing the general price of the product you're looking for. If you're looking for a knob you've bought in the past for $2.25, and you're quoted $1.80 by someone who's genuinely eager to make it, guess what? That's a fine price. If you're looking for an industrial space and LoopNet says the average rate in your location is $0.65

per square foot, and you're quoted $1.10, you're probably getting screwed.

Second, by doing your research if you don't know the general price. This could involve putting parts up on MFG.com to see what kind of range you get, or getting multiple quotes from different distributors.

Third, by knowing if something is either "too good to be true" or "worth paying a little more for." If those same $2.25 knobs were quoted by a brand-new business for $0.35, guess what? It may be too good to be true. But, at the same time, if your reject rate on the $2.25 knobs was 35%, it may be well worth your time to take a $3.10 quote.

Fourth, by knowing when to say when. If the quote you get meets what you expect to see on your bill of materials, and it's from a trusted vendor, stop. Don't grind. Just take it. You've accomplished your goal.

Fifth, by being upfront. Okay, so let's say you have a new product that's very cost-constrained, and you've been working with a vendor you're very happy with, but you're unsure if they can meet the cost constraints. Tell them what you're looking for. Don't make it a sixteen-quote guessing game. Their time is valuable too. Also, give them a chance to comment on the part design—they may have a much better idea for meeting your price.

So what did I say to the landlord when he quoted a very reasonable price for more space that was literally next door—space that was going to be all shiny, polished, and air-conditioned?

I said, "Yes."

Like, duh.

Enter Ten Thumbs

Unfortunately, our landlord was probably one of the biz school 101 guys who never grew out of the "grind until you're sure you screwed the bejeezus out of your vendor."

Why? Because he hired a guy for the renovation work who soon came to be known as "Ten Thumbs."

I bet he got a great deal.

Ten Thumbs didn't look much different than your usual itinerant handyman, but he was put in charge of the renovation of the entire building—interior and exterior, structural, AC, and electrical. This is something like giving a kid who's just built his first CMoy set the task of designing the next Audio Research tube preamplifier. Not just scary, but possibly dangerous.

We should have known what was coming when Ten Thumbs started on the outside of the building.

The old structure featured quite a bit of dry rot on the wood beams—something you'd normally remove and replace. Ten Thumbs? Nope. Bondo would be fine. He bought it by the five-gallon bucketload. Similarly, you'd normally re-lay the scaffolding under the holes in the stucco. Ten Thumbs? Fill it with newspaper and wall putty, then stucco over it. Windows? Don't bother masking them, scrape them off later. Roof? Well, you can't see it, so why bother? Paint? Hey, it looks like Home Depot has a remnant sale. Let's mix them all together to get something approximately the color of sick-baby poop. Spray that stuff everywhere. Only add a little lighter green and white accents when the landlord comes by and complains it's ugly. Street numbers? Don't need those. The few decorative trees outside? Cut them down. Trash? It can pile up in the back. If nobody can see it from the street, who cares?

You get the picture.

That's when Ten Thumbs moved inside. Luckily, he started with the area that we weren't using. In came spackling paste in five-gallon drums. In came cheap white primer paint. Use a keyhole saw to cut spaces for the AC vents? That's crazy talk. Just use a hammer. There's plenty of spackle. And nobody will notice they're about five degrees off true. Doors into our current space? Well, we had some leftovers that don't really fit the hole that was cut, but if you sand about an inch off of them, they kinda fit. Of course, they aren't hung on any beams—they're just bolted to sheetrock. Floors? Well, the white paint can go all over it, because it's going to get epoxy-coated. What, you say epoxy doesn't stick to painted floors? Ah well, not Ten Thumbs's problem.

I shook my head. It was crap work, but the space was still cheap.

That's when we had to move into the finished space, so Ten Thumbs could work on the space we were already in. They told us it'd be done in a couple of weeks, so we went ahead and executed the lease and moved into the finished space, in expectation that we'd have the full run of the place on October 1.

Except for Ten Thumbs's little mistake: when he did the epoxy floor in the other half of the building, he didn't mix the hardener in with the epoxy. For those of you who've never used epoxy, *it doesn't harden without the hardener.*

So yeah, we had a big, sticky mess of a floor. Just walking over it caused the unhardened epoxy to lift off and reveal nasty, untreated floor.

After a humorous episode where the landlord tried to blame Alex for the floor not hardening (saying that he washed it down, as if water would change anything), he learned that "no negotiation" doesn't mean "pushover." Because if there's one thing I will absolutely stand my ground on, it's defending our employees.

The landlord caught me on the phone and tried not only to place the blame on Alex, but implied that Alex was sabotaging the job on purpose.

"I don't believe that," I told him.

"And you're just going to take his word for it?" the landlord asked.

"Yes."

"Are you calling me a liar?"

"No."

"Then what are you trying to say?"

"I'm saying that you don't know any more about this than I do. Neither of us was there. Alex was there. He saw what was done.

Plus, the way the floor is behaving is what you'd expect if there was no hardener in the epoxy."

"How do you know Alex isn't deliberately trying to mess up the job?" he shot back, getting frustrated.

"Well, besides the fact that he's packed in there like a sardine, and he needs the space, and we're already a week late on completion, I also trust him implicitly."

"So you're not going to investigate this?"

"No."

"I don't believe this!" he thundered. "I demand you look into this for yourself."

Aside: several clients have tried to pit me against my own employees during my time at Centric. They got the same response. Usually shortly before we fired them. Newsflash: in real, productive companies, you hire competent people, support them, and let them shine. If you have trust issues, you have the wrong person.

"Okay. I'm going to say this just once more. No. I will not spend a minute more on this. I hired Alex to run the show, and I trust him. What did or didn't happen isn't the issue. The issue is that you're two weeks late on a lease that we're already paying."

After some more bluster and spluttering, we agreed that Ten Thumbs would finish at all speed, and we'd stay out of his space. Two weeks later—exactly one month late—we had the full space, complete with a handmade soffit for a new air conditioning duct with runout that could be measured in inches, if not feet.

But the air conditioning worked…

…and it only took two more weeks to fix all the screw-ups in the electrical system

…and since it doesn't rain much in SoCal in summer, it was a couple of months before the roof started leaking.

Ah, bargains.

The Real Work

Okay, so Ten Thumbs makes for some humorous anecdotes, but let's talk about what we really accomplished that summer—taking the first steps towards acting like a real company.

And, for all the hellish renovation work, we ended up in a space that (except for the remaining sticky places on the floor) looked reasonably like a real company for the first time. People could come by and see us, and we wouldn't be entirely embarrassed. It was still far from a palace, but hey, at least we weren't cooking anymore.

But what changed most was on the process side. Now, process is another scary word that conjures up images of big corporate flowcharts, meetings, and managers pounding tables while yelling, "We've always done it this way!" But, in reality, every business needs processes. They just have to be flexible enough to change as the business grows.

In Schiit's case, Alex shored up five major things:

- **Planning and scheduling.** Like I said, the old method was "wait until we're out of something, then start ordering again." This really isn't all that bad of a method when you're very small. It conserves cash flow, and helps generate a perception that things are special, and in demand. That's why we used to go into backorder so often. But as we grew, we realized we had to place larger, timed orders to help ensure better availability. The only problem with that was rising demand. It's hard to project forward when demand keeps growing. And that's why the endemic out-of-stock problem lasted long past summer 2012.

- **Facilities layout and production flow.** It's one thing to have a small truck delivering a few boxes to your garage for one guy to test and another to work on. It's a whole different thing to have multiple vendors delivering many different products at the same time, and having to move them through the shop. Alex set things up so we had a logical flow through the shop, including all the hardware needed to make it happen (you know, "dumb" things like carts, which aren't so dumb when you're handling pricey products, like the then-new Mjolnir and Gungnir.) He also got us set up to handle the anticipated flood of high-volume stuff, like Magni and Modi, and made sure everyone knew what they needed to do.

- **Shipping logistics and relationships.** If you are starting a business that will do volume shipping, you owe it to yourself to be very close with your shippers. Every shipper (besides USPS) offers significant discounts for their volume shippers, and they can tailor your discounts to what you're actually shipping. Alex got us in contact with FedEx, our shipper of choice, and began the process of negotiating better rates…rates that we then could pass along to our customers.

- **General operations and vendor communication.** Before Alex, vendor communication was pretty ad hoc (meaning, I'd talk to them in the spare moments I had between running Centric and writing books.) This isn't great. Especially when you consider the relative laggardness of many metal, transformer, and board vendors. An astounding amount of them still really only respond to phone conversations or in-person meetings. Alex provided a focal point for the vendors to talk to, and he knew much more about our day-to-day needs than I did in short order.

- **Employee management, specifically hiring and training.** Finally, Alex started laying the groundwork for both me stepping back from hiring, and for the coming Salary Apocalypse. Yeah, that's right. As of summer 2012, everyone was still a contractor. Since nobody had set hours (and everyone came in at fairly bizarre times…hell, Eddie frequently worked from 1:00 a.m. to dawn), we could kinda squint and get away with it. But stepping into full-boat employee status, tax reporting, and benefits is a very big step. We didn't make it until January 1, 2013.

The sum total of this was a company much more ready to take on the coming Magni and Modi avalanche. How ready? Well, we've only had one or two short backorders on Magni and Modi since their introduction in December 2012. Which is pretty good when you consider that Magni / Modi volume was about five to ten times what we'd ever planned for in the past.

But all was not well on the planning side. Because sometimes you undershoot the needs…and sometimes you get a big surprise.

Like the one that came next.

CHAPTER 25

Dead Media Ain't Dead: NYT Strikes

LOOK. NOBODY IS PERFECT. NO matter how many degrees they have, no matter how high they scored on their IQ tests, no matter how many years of experience, no matter how many companies they've launched. Period. Puffery and pontification about the One True Way and instant dismissal of any alternative viewpoints may be the sign of great learning—but it's also the sign of a deeply insecure, lazy person.

But, at the same time, a learned caution and reliance on "what you know" can sneak up and bite you in the ass. It's not a light-switch change from being young, enthusiastic, and open to new ideas, to a grumpy, set-in-your-ways know-it-all. It's a continuum.

And I was at least thirty percent down that road to the grumpy know-it-all when we had our butts handed to us on a platter late in 2013.

The further irony? I got bit not because I was old-school conservative, but because I drank the new media Kool-Aid for a bit too long.

What am I talking about, you ask?

Hold a sec, and let's talk a bit about pushing the limits, common wisdom, experience, and the fiction of modern marketing.

Lessons from the Leading Edge of Marketing

I founded Centric, my marketing agency, in 1994, the same year that Netscape Navigator was released. Now, these two occurrences were not coincident; Netscape came on the world about ten months after I started Centric.

This is important because, over the next few years, the world of communications saw the growth of its most important medium, ever.

Yes, *ever*.

If you want to argue with me, name one other medium that disintermediated the distribution of content in the way the Internet did, and one medium that resulted in the significant shrinkage of other media.

The common wisdom of my college years was that all new media was additive—that is, radio didn't replace newspapers, as TV didn't replace radio, etc. I argued vehemently that this wouldn't always be the case, even way back in 1988…but my professor was less impressed about my gut feeling than his statistics. Hey, bite me, Prof. Who's right today?

But it wasn't just the appearance of the Internet that drove Centric to always be on the leading edge. I'd been doing marketing for some time before Centric, and had always relied on "desktop publishing" programs, as the entrenched typesetters and color separators of the time diminutively referred to them as.

"We do *real* typesetting," I was told, with a sneer, more than once, when I asked about camera-ready or film output from my files.

Yeah, and you'll be out of business in a few years, I thought. The economic benefit of computer typesetting, and, later, computer-based full layout and color separations was too compelling to ignore. And those early desktop-publishing programs opened up the field to a lot more people—it democratized design, in a way never seen before.

Aside: If you're too young for this dinosauric crap, just consider that the way you used to lay out brochures included sending your copy out to have typeset and output on an optical typesetter, then actually pasted to an art-board, which you sent to the printer along with any color separations you had done—from film—to make your brochure. The first brochure I did for Sumo had a hand-painted gradient that was sent out for photography

and color separation. Think about that next time you use Illustrator and create one in two seconds.)

In any case, by the time the Internet came around, I was absolutely ready to jump on its leading edge. When I first saw it in early
1995, I literally got chills. *This will change everything,* I thought.

Which is why Centric had one of the first ad agency websites
online (27th listed on Yahoo at that time.) It's why we did some of
the first e-commerce work, including the first online leasing system
for Compaq. It's why we built some of the first customized product
configurators. It's why we built our own content management
systems. It's why we embraced search engine optimization and
online marketing back when you could only buy keywords from
GoTo.com (which Google later copied and turned into AdWords,
the powerhouse that drives most of its revenue today.) We did
some of the first database-connected personalized banner ads. We
did some of the earliest Flash sites, games, and COPPA-compliant
virtual worlds. And we did some of the first social marketing stuff
out there for Warner Brothers, Cotton Incorporated, and other big
names. Hell, we built HP's outpost in Second Life, and created a
virtual environment for David Rumsey Maps that was profiled in
MIT Technology Review.

What I'm trying to say here is that, in terms of marketing, our
leading-edge cred is way, way up there.

Which is perhaps one reason I dismissed the power of the conventional press when I started Schiit. We were *so* past that. It
belonged to the era of paste-up and color separations.

And, to be fair, it was starting to look pretty unhealthy, on lots
of fronts (hell, we had one industry—data storage—in which the
industry print publications all folded up before the turn of the
century, so we knew where things were going.)

So, when Schiit got rolling, we pretty much just ignored the
conventional press, except for sending them press releases when we
launched new products. Yeah, we were happy for the coverage in
Wired and such, but I was far more jazzed about Gizmodo, *Engadg-*

et, and TechCrunch. Those were publications of the present day, reinventing press as we knew it on a real-time basis. They were what mattered. We'd eventually get money to do some AdWords, and roll it into more online, measurable ads as time went by. And that's how you did things in the Shiny New World of the 21st Century.

Or so I thought.

But Social, Oh, Social, and the Fiction of Online Marketing

You may have noticed that I haven't mentioned one of what's considered the most "leading edge" marketing vehicle out there, though: social media.

That's for very good reason. Even as early as 2010, we were pretty much done with social. After four years of pimping MySpace, Facebook, Twitter, etc., we'd learned some hard truths. Namely:

- If you're an entertainment company, social marketing is the greatest thing since sliced cheese. It should absolutely be front and center in your plans. Every entertainment social media program we did produced ten to one hundred times the results of an equivalent investment in conventional media.

- If you're not an entertainment company, social marketing is really, really dumb—easily the biggest time-sink and resource-eater out there, with returns 1/10 to 1/100 of an equivalent investment in conventional media.*

I can't tell you how much hate mail I got when I "came out" against social media. It's nice to see some recent studies corroborating our experience.

"Wait, what?" you might be saying. "I still hear that talking to your customers on Facebook, doing videos to put on YouTube, and Twittering your latest office party pictures (and Instagramming, or Pinteresting, or whatever) is the way to have an authentic conversation with your prospects and create engaged brand ambassadors."

In short, no.

Sorry, guys. People are on Facebook to talk to friends. Not shills.

They're watching YouTube for funny cat videos, not smooth-talking tours of your factory set to some hip music.

They're on Twitter to get celebrity tweets.

Et cetera. If you want to talk to your prospects effectively:

- Clearly communicate the unique benefits of your products on a good, easy-to-use website

- Have a memorable brand

- Provide fast responses to any inquiries

- Take care of customer service before it spreads to Facebook

- Make sure the press (online and off) know when you have something new and cool, but otherwise stay out of their face

- Invest carefully in measurable marketing vehicles such as AdWords, reinvest in successful vehicles and revise or discontinue underperforming ones

- Continue improving your product so someone doesn't have a clear, unique benefit over you before you know it

And that is that. Social media will take care of itself, at that point.

"But wait, does that mean we can pretty much ignore social media?" you ask.

To be blunt: *yes.*

This "ignore social media" advice is even more relevant if you are a business-to-business company—that is, selling products or services to businesses. Do not spend a single second on social media. Concentrate on the seven points above. Don't dismiss one and two because you're B2B. And you're done.

Sure, there are gray area companies (such as audio companies like Schiit) which have rabid fans and may get some small benefit from social media, but your marketing dollars are better spent on

more conventional advertising and PR. And then there's microsocial (like head-fi.org), where there's a very concentrated niche
audience that is absolutely relevant to your products. Then, be
there. Yourself. Regularly. Don't leave it to an agency. Don't use
paid shills. And don't be a dick.

Still not convinced? Fine. Cool. You want to get into social media? Answer these questions:

- **Who's going to create the content?** Note: this is not just
  posting funny pictures on Facebook. This is about creating
  an article every week for a blog, or a video every month for
  YouTube, or doing cool imagery for Facebook. Are you
  going to do it? Or are you going to hire an agency to
  manage it for $200/hour? Yeah. There you go.

- **Who's going to respond to comments?** Social media is
  social. You'll get comments. You'll get hotheads. Someone
  has to manage it. Is it you? Or more $200/hour time?

- **Who's going to decide what's okay to say?** In larger
  companies, this is a HUGE problem, usually involving a
  team of lawyers. But even for smaller companies, this is no
  joke. What will reflect well on you? What will reveal
  competitive info you'd rather keep under wraps?

- **Who's going to measure and manage it all?** Social media is
  still evolving. Who's going to be the oversight to determine
  what to spend where, based on the sales you're making?
  What metrics software will you use, and what metrics will
  you track? What will you do when Facebook changes its
  algorithms yet again?

Yeah. Have fun. Unless you want to cheat. See below.

A Bold Prediction

Now, I haven't scratched the surface on social. Because it's a lot
more than companies posting contests on Facebook these days.
Social is, more and more, a bot-infested, paid-propagation-driven

exercise.

Which, in English, means:

- Much of the content you see on social media wasn't posted by a human at all, but by software—a bot

- Much more of the content you see on social media was posted by offshore shill accounts paid a pittance to say, well, pretty much anything

- And even more of the content was posted by people just like you who want to get something for cheap (or free) and are doing so to get referral credit towards their shiny new object of desire

So, social media is less and less about "an authentic conversation with real people," and more "prospect-powered advertising." Or, to be more topical, crowd-sourced advertising.

And in an environment where anyone can be a shill, and their financial motives aren't known, credibility disappears.

Which leads me to my bold prediction: that in the next decade, we're going to see paid, conventional advertising in big-name venues become the most credible source of information, and word-of-mouth the least credible.

"Wait, you're saying that we'll trust paid advertising more than our friends?" you say, aghast.

Yes.

Why? Paid advertising in big-name venues:

- Requires a large investment that the company wants to pay off, meaning the company is at least successful enough to make the investment.

- Subjects the company's claims to scrutiny by individuals and by regulators, which the company can be held accountable for.

- Has significant repercussions if those claims don't gel with the customers' experiences—as in, class-action lawsuits, etc.

With that on the line, paid advertising could very well be more accurate than the offshore shell account shilling the latest hot gadget, or even your friend, who may just be parroting fake claims in the hopes of getting something he wants.

Crazy? Perhaps.

But we'll see.

On to the Old Media

"So, after all this blathering, are you actually going to tell me what happened?" you ask. "I'm dying of suspense!"

Yep. Here's what went down.

In summer 2012, I was contacted by a writer for *The New York Times*, who asked if he could get a Bifrost to review for an upcoming story on DACs. And let's be clear: no matter how new-media biased you are, here's what you do when *The New York Times* asks for a review sample: you say, "Yes."

Same goes for if the national TV news wants to talk to you, or if *The Wall Street Journal* wants to have a phone chat, or *Wired* wants to do a profile on your company, or, hell, if *Ladies' Home Journal* wants to try some of your cables. It's big exposure. You say, "Yes," and make it happen.

Aside: well, actually, first you do a quick Google search on the writer's name and the publication title, to make sure he's really who he says he is. If it checks out, then get that product out the door.

So I sent out the Bifrost to our guy Roy at *NYT* and kinda forgot about it. Because sometimes these articles don't happen for a long time. Or ever. And that's fine. Editors have their own agendas. And you'll live through a missed opportunity or two.

I forgot about it, at least until early in September, when Roy gave me a call.

"Wow, this is a great DAC," he said. "Really, really good."

"Cool," I told him, or something lame like that. I'd probably forgotten who he was and was trying to put the pieces together.

"It was the crowd favorite," he enthused. "But I'm not sure if the *Times* editors will let me actually say that. I want to, but there's limited space, and, you know, stuff like this is a little controversial anyway."

Aha. *Times*. Everything clicked. "Stuff like this?"

"High-end audio. Subjective reviews. It's kind of, well…"

"Too much voodoo?" I prompted.

Roy laughed. "Voodoo. Yes. But it's real voodoo. It's just, well, we have to be careful not to go too over the top. But great gear really deserves more coverage."

"Roy, I spent twenty years in marketing. Believe me, I understand."

"No, it's not the advertisers or anything," he corrected. "It's just, well, everyone seems to have a price in mind for any piece of audio gear, and if something goes over that price, but the specs aren't any different, well, it's hard to explain how and why it's so much better. I don't understand why some companies can make great-sounding stuff, but so much gear out there just sounds, well, awful."

"But measures good," I added.

"Exactly."

I agreed it was unfortunate and let it go at that. But if I'd had a few drinks, I probably would have told him something like, *It's because nobody ever got fired for engineering a product that meets specs, but sounds bad. And it's because most people don't really care that much.* The first is understandable in a highly regimented, performance-review-oriented, hyper-corporate environment. The second is understandable too. Some people don't give a crap about cars. Some people don't give a crap about audio. Some people don't give a crap about cuisine. That's just the way it is.

Aside: And, while I'm absolutely for introducing everyone to great sound, we're going to meet plenty of people who don't care. And we have to be careful not to be tiresome proselytizers. Imagine if every Jehovah's Witness suddenly converted to the

> Church of the Perfect Sound and started going door to door with
> Audeze LCD-3s and a Mjolnir / Gungnir rig to spread the word.
> Yeah. Just as irritating.

In any case, Roy and I talked a bit more about audio, about what was different about Bifrost, and that was that. I kinda forgot about it in the craziness of the next week.

Then, suddenly, we got a huge explosion of Bifrost orders, and the email loaded up...not with our normal, relatively technical questions, or questions about "Is Asgard or Lyr better for my headphones?" but with a ton of super-noobie questions like "Can I hook up Bifrost to my flat panel TV?" and "How can I connect Bifrost to an AVR?" and "What's an optical cable?"

An email from Roy confirmed what I had suspected: the article—"A Sound System as Resonant as a Concert Hall," had gone live.

What I didn't expect was that it would hit the actual print version of the paper.

And I certainly didn't expect the response. No way. No how.

In fact, before the *Times* article, Alex and I were feeling rather smug. We'd preordered and scheduled a double run of Bifrosts in anticipation of the holiday rush. We were well-set to sell a ton of Bifrosts. There was no way we'd go into backorder on them.

Until that article. In the space of three weeks, our double run of Bifrosts was gone. Completely annihilated. Suddenly we were staring at a big, long backorder, right in the busy time of the year. I scrambled on orders for metal, boards, parts, etc., but there's only so much you can do when your metal lead time is six to eight weeks. You can beg a bit faster, but that's about it.

And that's how we ended up, not just with a single backorder that fall, but also a second backorder at the end of December, as the second double run we'd done also disappeared out the door. A good chunk of that was the *Times* article. The noobie questions continued well past the end of the year, and we continued to sell Bifrosts into homes that probably didn't even know what a DAC was before reading that article.

So, if someone says, "Old media is dead," laugh at them. They don't know what they're talking about.

Or, if someone says, "We can't convert new audiophiles," laugh louder. We absolutely can. We just need to get more attention in the mass media. And continue our inroads on sites where younger people discover stuff, like Reddit.

And that *can* be done.

But it *won't* be done with $40,000 preamps, $3,000 USB cables, and $500 magic pucks. It won't be done with Aspergers-like obsessive in-fighting about formats and provenance. It won't be done with religious fervor to spread the word about the One True Sound or the One Perfect Measurement.

And—this is the important one—it won't be done with magic name-branded processing tricks, or deceptively named mediocre technology, or the breathless hype of the Truly Established Big Names. Because that's one thing about marketing that's really changing…people today see through the BS much faster. And if they don't, their friends do, and they spread the word. That's the real power of social media, and, believe me, that's something the billion-dollar audio behemoths don't want to learn about.

So how do we break into the mainstream and introduce more neophytes to great sound? Well, call me biased, call me old-fashioned, but I believe it will be done in only one way: with quality product made at a price that's fair for its performance, construction, and looks.

And that's what we're focused on. It's astounding how many Magnis and Modis we sell to first-time audiophiles.

It's a small step, yes.

But just think: that person could have ended their journey with an iPod.

A Counterpoint

There's a counterpoint to the *Times* story.

This is a story about a review we got in a major audio magazine (which shall remain nameless.) This was a big deal for us, because they usually aren't so hot on direct-sale products, especially from relatively new manufacturers. And, outside the headphone community, we're not very well known.

It was a glowing review. We got our name on the cover.

And, remembering the *New York Times* review, we stocked up on Bifrost with another double run (actually quadruple, since we doubled the first run amount as a standard.)

But this time, the sales didn't materialize.

"What the heck?" you're probably asking.

Yeah. So were we. Sure, there was a minor bump—maybe 10% over our standard run rate—but nothing like the *Times* review. And there was another bump in emails—but this time they were 8000-word essays about how they got into audio, owned tons of very expensive equipment, and contained eighteen questions about tiny, tiny details about the product, usually regarding buzzword compliance with the latest press-propagated meaningless terms of the day.

Why? My best theory is the old marketing adage of "one ad does nothing." If two other reviews of Schiit products had followed the first one, maybe things would be very different. But that's not likely, given the focus of the magazine. They're more on the two-channel side of things, and we haven't yet made a big dent in that market.

But, in the *Times,* one review did a lot.

And that's a valuable lesson. That there are still huge opportunities out there...sometimes where you least expect them.

Stay open. To new things. And to old ones.

CHAPTER 26

Finally, the $99 Solution

BACK IN THE EARLY 1990S, while I was working at Sumo, if you told me I'd eventually be designing and selling audio products that retailed for $99, I would have told you that you were insane.

And, if you'd told me that I'd be designing and selling audio products that retailed for $63 (the 1991 equivalent to $99 today), I'd think you were even nuttier.

I suspect Mike Moffat would have had the same response. Which makes it all the crazier that he was the one who brought the idea for the $99 DAC to me first, and started the whole inexpensive-gear thing at Schiit.

Why would this be so unbelievable, you ask?

It's simple. Back then, it was a different world. Building a product for $31-37 in 1991 (which would allow the dealers to have their cut, in the dealer-dominant marketplace of the time) simply wasn't gonna happen. Selling direct was, to put it mildly, unfeasible in the pre-Iinternet world. And, back then, we'd probably have to make the products with thru-hole parts, rather than using surface-mount parts (which allow for efficient automated assembly), driving the production cost even higher.

And, early on in the Magni / Modi project, I had doubts that we could do it for $99, even direct.

So I was very, very thrilled when the original numbers came in for the chassis and wall wart, confirming that we could, indeed, sell gear with the near-unbelievable two-digit price tag.

Once the numbers were confirmed—this was in late August 2012—we started placing the biggest orders we'd ever done to date with our suppliers. We knew Magni and Modi would be big, and we knew how crazy things could get if we went out of stock. So we stocked up, in anticipation of being able to release it at CanJam, well-timed for the holiday rush that hits every year.*

> *Audio is a strongly seasonal business. October through March are hot. April, May, and June see falling sales, to a low in July / August. Then it picks back up again as people get into a stay-indoors or holiday-buying mood. This seasonality tracks very well with cold weather in much of the northern hemisphere, where people are more likely to stay at home and curl up with a nice glass of scotch...er, I mean wine...er, wait, warm milk or something is probably a little more PC, but whatever. As the days get warmer and vacation season hits, sales fall. This has been going on approximately since the earth cooled. If you're thinking of starting your own business, be aware if it's a seasonal one or not—planning in the fast season can leave you buried in unsold stock, and projecting forward from the slow season can put you in heavy backorder.

Of course, people who attended 2012 CanJam know there was no Magni and Modi there (well, not out on the table—there were under-the-table prototypes we shared with a few people.)

And, even more sharp-memoried readers will remember that Magni and Modi didn't ship "comfortably before the holiday season," and, in actuality, made their appearance on December 13— deep into the Christmas buying time.

Not ideal, right?

Yep. But much less ideal than setting an arbitrary deadline to be missed, or pushing a semifinished product out the door.

The Luxury (and Penalty) of Closed Doors

Magni and Modi were the first products we didn't announce beforehand. Indeed, they were the first products we didn't even hint about. This "closed door" approach is great in many ways. Namely:

- There's no chance of missing the deadline, because there isn't any
- If there are problems in production, you have the luxury to

take your time and sort them out

- Your competitors don't know what you're doing until you launch, which means it will take them longer to counter

Of course, closed doors have some disadvantages too:

- With no deadline, you may not work as hard as you need to in order to hold a schedule
- If you have cash-flow problems—that is, if you're running a business on a receivables-financing basis, or an assets-financing basis, or if you don't have shipping products to tide you over—the luxury of time is a cold comfort
- If there are significant delays, you may miss your first-mover advantage

The real danger to Schiit's launch of the Magni and Modi was the first point—with no deadline, you might not work as hard to get it out on time.

Now, this doesn't mean we sat around. But when metal was late, and when the board house was slow freeing up their surface mount line for us, we were probably less diligent than we should have been in being "in their face."**

> **Please note that "in their face" does not mean "being a total whiny bitchy ass at every opportunity." Running a business that doesn't do everything in-house requires great relationships with your vendors. They need to know when things aren't critical, and they need to know that you're not going to hold them to some insane algorithmic standard for to-the-minute delivery on every product. That means, when you do need fast delivery, or a quick change, they're going to be much, much more likely to get that done for you. Because you don't ride them on every little thing. So, "in their face," means "calling them more than once every three weeks to see how things are going."

So yeah, metal was a bit late. That killed showing Magni and Modi at CanJam. And boards were a little later. Which wouldn't have been as big a problem, except for two others:

- The pots (engineer-speak for "volume control") we planned

to use were late—even later than their six-week lead time would suggest. Which hung up delivery of the boards, since a headphone amp without volume control is, well, pretty much useless. Especially when there's a big hole in the chassis it was supposed to poke through.

• When we finally got the completed boards in, we had an engineering "oh schiit" moment when we realized the boards couldn't be inserted into the chassis. As in, at all. The big capacitors at the front of the board hung up between the pressed-in board standoff and the top inner chassis flange.

Aside: and, before you start saying, "3D CAD would have showed this clear as day," well, not really—not unless it showed articulating exploded views. And, these days, finally, everything we're doing is 3D—but not back then.

So, what did we do? Well, I knew at least one fix:

"We could send the chassis back to the metal guys and have them notch the front flange to clear the standoff."

Mike was less than convinced. "How long will that take?"

"A couple of weeks."

Mike looked pointedly up at the calendar. It was the first week of December.

"Yeah, I know, I know, we miss Christmas…"

"If it's really only two weeks," Mike said. "We could lay the capacitors down, couldn't we?"

"Yeah, but that looks awful." But then, I had an epiphany—the one I should have had in the first place. "But we can find shorter capacitors, I bet."

Aside: yeah, I know, obvious. But tell me you've never made any boneheaded mistakes. With a straight face.

"Can you get capacitors with the same value?" Mike asked.

"I'll find out. But even if we have to shrink the values a bit, it's pretty overkill already."

A quick Mouser search confirmed that we could, indeed, get the same value capacitors, at about half the height. Mocking it up with capacitors of that size proved that we could, indeed, just clear the chassis flange. Done.

Now, the above thing about capacitors of different sizes may seem strange to non-engineers, but it really isn't. Capacitors of the same value—for the sake of argument, let's say 1000uF at 16V—come in a huge array of sizes. Some are large for the sake of higher temperature ratings or lower ESR. Some are large because a lot of engineers think that large caps measure better than small caps. That's not always true, because a lot of manufacturers caught on to this little factoid and sometimes make electrolytic capacitors that are full of a whole lot of air. You need to look at the specs and make your decision based on that...and also consider that oddball sizes are the ones more frequently out of stock, and pricier.

So, after the capacitor debacle was resolved, we got some right-size caps in next day, and sent the first article boards back to the PCB house. Luckily, there were only ten first articles that needed reworked. The rest of them came to us with the new caps in-place.

And, in a few days, we had enough Magnis and Modis on the shelf to announce...

The Real Statement

On December 13, 2012, we announced Modi and Magni to the world. And, oh, what a crazy announcement that was—and a crazy last two weeks of December!

In terms of mechanics, it was a relatively uneventful launch. We had product in stock. We had enough labor to keep it in stock, and a big enough first run that we didn't hit backorder until January.

In terms of issues, it was also relatively uneventful. Some dead wall warts (which we tightened up by better vendor communication) and some out-of-spec pots with unacceptable tracking, even at relatively high levels (which we reworked, and re-spec'd the pots for the next run.)

But in terms of what it did to the company...suddenly we were all about $99 products. They were the vast majority of sales—easily outstripping all other products combined. We struggled to keep up with shipping and with inquiries, which led to fast changes on the shipping side and slower changes on the customer service side (until November 2013, I answered the vast majority of customer service questions.)

And, to this day, the best comment I think we ever got on the launch was amongst the chatter about the Schiit statement products (yeah, people were talking about them even back then, the as-yet-unnamed Ragnarok and Yggdrasil.)

The comment was:

"Now, this is the real statement."

Exactly. Thank you. Making another pricey product—no matter how advanced and innovative—is cool and all, and makes for good ego fodder (that is, at least when you can ship the darn things.) But making a good, solid product that almost anyone can afford, that's a whole 'nother thing entirely. It's wayyyy more important for the Magni and Modi to exist than Ragnarok and Yggdrasil.

And—you know what? It's a lot more fun too. Magni and Modi will always be special to me, because it proved that we could actually make, sell, and support a no-compromises, all-discrete amp, and a top-shelf asynchronous DAC in the USA for a two-figure price tag.

Nobody was expecting that.

Nobody was expecting that *from us.*

Magni and Modi were the first products that actually made me want to go to CES and do a press tour. To go in front of them and say, "You know, there once was a time in this country when we actually made things. Practical things, with top-notch technology and affordable price tags. Things without excuses about 'well, we can't really do that in a global economy,' or 'we don't have the supply chain here to do that,' or 'labor here costs so much we can't be competitive.'" And then hold up Magni and Modi and continue: "That stops today. Presenting the only fully discrete, no-excuses headphone amp made in the USA, from predominantly US-sourced parts, with a two-year warranty. No excuses. Ninety-nine bucks."

And, it's funny. After the launch, of course we got compared to the O2 and ODAC. And some people even opined that we brought these products out as a direct counter to those.

Actually, no. I was thinking bigger. I saw the headphone market growing. And I realized that, very soon, some large entity would wake up and say, "Hey, you know, we should have some of the accessories side of that. Like amps and DACs." Someone like Logitech. Someone like Harman. Someone *big*.

And, with a market fragmented amongst a bunch of smaller players, you know what? It could have happened. They could have gotten some engineers together, put together some of TI's textbook op-amp / headphone-driver solutions, built the whole thing in China, and sold it for a very attractive price. Maybe not $99 through distribution, but dang close.

But after Magni and Modi? A powerful, fully discrete US-built amp for $99? A USB 2 asynchronous DAC for $99? Well, then suddenly the market doesn't look so attractive.

And that's what I wanted to do—to set the value bar, and the barrier to entry, much, much higher. So that any of the big guys out there looking in would say, "Hmm, well, there's some very high-value, well-marketed stuff already established—considering the size of the market, let's take a flyer."

Hopefully, we have achieved a small fraction of that goal.

The Lasting Impact

At launch, I really was all about making an impact—but it took quite a while for me to realize what it really is. Chest-thumping about made-in-USA product is one thing. Setting the barrier to entry high is another. But the former doesn't really matter for much of the world, and the latter really doesn't matter much except to us and the competition.

No. The thing that really matters is that Magni and Modi are giving many, many first-timers their initial taste of very good sound. They're recommended on Head-Fi and on many other online communities, including the biggest first-timer venue out there: Reddit.

It's become almost a knee-jerk recommendation: "Oh, you're looking at getting into headphone amps and DACs? Well, there's the Magni / Modi…" (and others, of course), but Magni and Modi are usually amongst the first mentioned.

Why? Because they're inexpensive, and because they're good products.

I wasn't kidding when I wrote, "They may be the only amp and DAC you'll ever need." I was dead serious. Magni has a ton of power, and it's pretty open and neutral for many different headphones. It's easy to recommend. Same with Modi. It plugs into a whole lot of different sources, doesn't need drivers, and pretty much just works. Again, easy.

Sure, there are amps and DACs out there that scale up higher, or have more features, or serve the format du jour, or whatever, but for most people in today's largely 16/44.1 based world (and, dare we say it, AAC and MP3), they're just fine. And either can be had for the price of a good steak dinner.

So that's the real impact: bringing that first audiophile experience to a larger audience.

And *that* matters.

CHAPTER 27

Twilight of the Gods—the Ragnarok Saga from 2009 Until Today

AND...IT REALLY HAS BEEN a saga. Ragnarok was one of the first amps we discussed in Schiit's pre-launch days. I have sketches dating back to late 2009.

So why was it one of the earliest concepts? Because it was a direct outgrowth of driving headphones with Sumo speaker amps. I figured, well, if a Sumo 60W amp works with headphones, why not make a reealy reeeeallly ridiculous headphone amp. We could put a warning sticker over the headphone output, saying, "If you remove this, you realize that you can make the magic smoke come out of any headphone, and agree to hold Schiit harmless for any damage."

Yeah, silly. But an interesting concept for a publicity stunt for a then-unknown, unlaunched company.

Of course, reality soon set in—driving headphones with a speaker amp sometimes works out just fine, but most speaker amps are:

- Relatively noisy (forget your sensitive headphones and IEMs)
- Not headphone-friendly on turn-on (1V of DC is no big deal to a speaker, but a bad day for some headphones)
- Big, hot, heavy, and not desk-friendly

So, the idea got shelved, after I'd spent some time playing with the old Sumo Antares and came to the realization that, like duh, a speaker amp usually isn't a headphone amp—at least not without a whole lot more development work.

But the thought kept ticking over in my head. And, after our early experiences with planar headphones and the *moar power!!!* phenomenon, I decided that yes, it was something that we should pursue.

And, of course, I had to mention it. This was 2011.

Yes, I am an idiot.

The Ragnarok Saga: Post-Blab

Okay, so after I'd opened my mouth and told the world that we were working on a statement amp and DAC, I realized that we'd, well, actually have to deliver something eventually. But I didn't set any timeframe, because, well, I didn't figure there'd be many people interested in an unnamed, un-spec'd, unreleased super-power amp.

But they were. From the first mention that Schiit was going to do a statement amp, we started getting inquiries. When will it ship? What will it be like? What's the price?

Based on super-scientific complete-WAG BS, I started telling people it might be about a year, and it would be super-powerful, and probably about $1000.

Yes. Dig yourself deeper. This is a textbook example of what not to do. If you are silly enough to pre-announce a product, here's what you should do:

- Say nothing more, and hope the inquiries stop
- If pressed, say you got drunk and spoke out of turn, and the product doesn't actually exist
- If presented with documents you accidentally emailed someone confirming the existence of a project to develop said unreleased product, claim that you were either:
  - o Blue-skying it, but it has since been abandoned
  - o Developing a product for someone else

Or, in other words, *shut up until it dies.* Then, when it's ready, bring it out and let people buy it.

Yes, it really is that simple.

But no. I had to confirm its existence. I even had to opine that it would be a really, really cool product. Again: *don't do this.*

But...since the cat was out of the bag, I figured that I should at least get started on the design. People who know a thing or two about large power amp design know that you really start with two things:

- **Thermal design.** How do you get rid of the heat? Running speakers isn't like running headphones—there's going to be significant thermal load.

- **Transformer.** How big of a transformer do you need, and does it fit in the chassis you have in mind?

Once you've gotten those two things set, you can then proceed on to the rest.

So, the first calculations I did were for the chassis and transformer. Would our trick of using the chassis as a heatsink work? It turned out that the answer was yes—if we were looking at a standard 2U height rack-sized product. Which gelled with other 60W amps I'd designed in the past. Transformer? Sure, you could use a three-inch-high product with a thick stack. Done that before too.

But what about features? The first idea we had for Ragnarok was mighty conventional:

- 60W/8 ohms, 100W/4 ohms
- Three levels of gain switching
- Alps RK27 balanced volume pot
- Nice Grayhill input switch
- Five inputs, three SE and two balanced
- Circlotron topology
- 16" x 12" x 4" chassis

So really, nothing too nuts, except for the gain switching and circlotron topology.

We ran with that idea for a while, long enough to get some switch samples and order the balanced pots. But we never built a prototype of it.

No. Ego stepped in, and started us down the path to insanity.

Fun fact: one of the reasons we did Mjolnir was because the Ragnarok concept had already started to grow...and I wanted to use those balanced pots somewhere. So, Mjolnir was our shot at the simplest, most basic balanced amp we could do. Ragnarok had already been elevated, in our minds, to something that was quite a bit more.

It all started with the switches. Grayhill switches are very nice, but pricey. It really wouldn't cost any more for us to switch inputs with relays. And with relays, we could do the switching right at the back of the amp, where the inputs came in—which would save having to run a bunch of traces for each input up to the front switch. This would make things like crosstalk a whole lot better.

But then you have seven relays in the chassis (two each for the balanced inputs, one each for the other inputs.)

And, if you have that many relays, why not have a few more? Alps RK27 pots are nice. Sure. But a resistor-switched stepped attenuator is better. And another twelve relays would get us a sixty-four-step attenuator at 1-1.2dB steps—much better than you'd get with a front-panel switched attenuator...and tons of control with three different gain levels.

So now we're up to nineteen relays. Still not a huge deal.

But if we have nineteen relays, we should be switching gain with relays too, right. So add another four. And, of course, you have to have output muting. So that's another two.

Yep. Twenty-five relays in that first Ragnarok (there are actually twenty-nine in production, since we added a separate headphone / speaker mute, and changed the way the gain switching relays worked—but we'll get there.)

But twenty-five relays wasn't crazy enough. I also decided it might be fun to be able to run the amp with either a solid-state or tube input stage. So, that meant that the transformer would have to accommodate either one. Which meant a very large, complex transformer with like four Molex connectors hanging off of it, and a separate gain stage board (one for tubes, one for transistors).

And, of course, with twenty-five relays, we needed a microprocessor to run them—to handle switching, volume control, etc. So then we needed a shielded front control board…

…and, if we were going to all that trouble, then we might as well have a really cool volume control—that is, one that actually acted like a volume control, with stops at either end, rather than an endlessly spinning encoder. Which meant we needed a fairly beefy microprocessor, so we could A/D in a voltage and use that to set the output to the resistor ladder volume control.

Okay. So why do all this, you ask? For better sound. A better volume control and better switching is a big deal, when you're going all-out. Plus, we'd already begun to believe our own BS, with all the inquiries about the "statement products."

This is how you talk yourself into making something fairly insane.

The First Ragnarok

If the first Ragnarok had worked, it would have been a pretty damn good headphone amp, but a fairly crappy speaker amp. This is because I'd become used to doing headphone amps, and I wanted to do a super-simple single-gain-stage topology.

There's only one problem with that: single gain stages have low overall gain—which means you can't use much (if any) feedback to get the output impedance down.

Aside: Yes, Ragnarok is not a no-feedback amp. It is a no-overall-feedback amp, however…

Why is this important? It's important for control over the

speaker load. Speakers are physically large. They need a reasonable damping factor. As a single gain stage amp, Ragnarok would have had an output impedance of about 0.5 ohms in high gain—fine for a headphone amp, but equivalent to a damping factor of only 8 into 4-ohm loads. Not exactly ideal.

But, as it turned out, the first Ragnarok prototype was so problematic, we never got it fully operational. The tube stage didn't get enough power from the transformer. The solid-state stage had so many layout errors that it wasn't really worth fixing them all. And the board changes needed to accommodate both tube and solid-state really made it impractical to have it swappable—it would have to be built one way or the other.

(And, of course, this tube vs. solid-state realization came after I'd shot my mouth off about how Ragnarok would be configurable for either. Yeah. Again: *just shut up.*)

We hacked around with it a bit, blew up a few output stages, and never really heard music through it. So, finally, we did something sensible.

We went back to the drawing board.

The Second Ragnarok

The next Ragnarok was stripped down and simplified. We got a new transformer, only suitable for solid state use. We designed the main board only for solid state. We went to a two-stage amp with enough gain to give us the damping factor we needed.

This Ragnarok still used DC servos and trimpots to set the bias for the amp, as we do in Mjolnir. This worked, albeit with some difficulty. Unlike Mjolnir, Ragnarok wasn't thermally stable. You'd set the bias, and it would creep up, and up, and up…until bad things happened.

So what do you do in that case? Well, you either increase the source resistors (not a hot idea in a speaker amp), or you use something truly yucky, like a varistor, to try to compensate for the bias creep.

We didn't want to use varistors (which are resistors that change value depending on temperature, which is something you don't want—considering that resistors set gain and other operational parameters, varistors are usually pretty bad juju.)

So, it was back to some hacks...more board hacks to fix the servos, and a whole lot of parts tacked on to try to get it thermally stable...and once again, we found ourselves at an impasse.

And that's when I had my crazy, scary idea. The one that set back Ragnarok for over a year.

The Left Turn Into Hell

"Dave, if we have a microprocessor in Ragnarok, can't we use it to set the bias too?" I asked, one day when we were deep in the Ragnarok Second Prototype Fiasco.

Dave is our software guy. Well, he also does digital and analog design too, but since he's the only one around here who does software, he's our de facto "software guy."

"Well, yes, but—"

"And if we use it to set the bias, we could get around the thermal stability problem."

"Yes, but—"

I didn't hear him, though. I was getting excited now. "And, if we used it to set the operating point on both sides of the circlotron, we could throw out the DC servo too!"

Aside: this *is* very exciting. There are three ways to get rid of DC on the output of your products:

- **Coupling capacitor.** This blocks DC. DC gone. Done. Easy. But now you have a capacitor-coupled amp. And you get to try to choose the most sonically transparent capacitor you can find.

- **DC servo.** This is a feedback loop that only operates at very low frequencies (say, 0.1 Hz and below.) This is usually more sonically innocuous than a capacitor, but even the best servos feed back some audio-frequency stuff...and cause phase shift in the bass. Not ideal.

- **Trimpots.** And, if you're crazy, you can simply trim out the DC. And hope the operational point of the amplifier stays constant. And hope it doesn't drift. No thanks, I like certainty.

"Weeelll, yes, but—" Dave tried again.

"Then that's what we'll do!" I cried, envisioning the truly revolutionary amplifier that Ragnarok could be with full microprocessor control. It would always run at the same operating point...and we could get rid of the DC servo...and it would be insane! Nobody was making anything like this!

"We can do it," Dave said finally. "But the software will be pretty complicated, and I'm sure we'll run into some issues—"

"But we'll work them out!" I said, not hearing him.

In fact, I don't think I heard anything past the initial "yes."

But it didn't matter. I knew this was the way to go. Ragnarok would be the first truly fully managed amplifier, with a giant microprocessor brain overseeing everything it did. It would be amazing!

I got to laying out the new boards—which fundamentally changed almost everything about the Ragnarok. We had to add control lines from the DACs (yes, there are two DACs inside Ragnarok, but not for playing music...they take a 12-bit input from the microprocessor and use it to set the operational point of the amplifier.) We needed to add more sense lines so we could monitor what the amp was doing.

But I got it done, and we sent out for boards. This was it. I could feel it. We were going to have an incredible amp.

It was only later—a lot later—that I remembered Dave's, "Well, but..."

Releasing the Names

So what did I do after all these changes?

Well, I didn't do the sensible thing, which was to shut up. Instead, I believed we were far enough along that a six-month development cycle would wrap everything up. Which meant we could make some noise. We could claim the names of our statement products. And we could show off a little.

So, I released preliminary information on Ragnarok and Yggdrasil on Head-Fi, together with some product renderings and a very abbreviated spec sheet.

That was more than a year ago.

Yes. *Shut up.* That's all there is to do. Else, suffer the consequences.

The Trouble With Software—and Hardware

In the early summer of 2013, Ragnarok seemed pretty buttoned down. We got the boards back, stuffed them, verified basic things like DC operating points, and gave them to Dave to do the software. All that was left was to sit back and await the software, which would ensure the amp always operated the way we expected it, each and every time.

Yeah, and software never has problems. Never has bugs. It always works entirely as expected, from day one.

Uh-huh. Right. When you get into software, expect lots of fun—and the more fun, the more complex it is.

Actually, a primer on software should go here. Because, Ragnarok's software isn't really soft. Nor is it hard. So, it's what we call "firmware."

Smart readers are sitting back now, arms crossed, asking, *So how bad was the first firmware you got for Ragnarok?*

On first glance, not bad. The basic stuff—volume control, input switching, protection—all worked. The bias and DC nulling…well, not so much.

In fact, we only got it back after Dave admitted he blew up the outputs on the main board a couple of times. This isn't surprising in development, but Dave's efforts were hampered by his lack of experience with MOSFET-output amps. Which led to the Ragnarok main board running inconsistently, or not at all.

"But I replaced the parts that tested bad," he told me.

"Dave, Dave, Dave," I chided. Experience with thousands of MOSFET-output amps gives you a certain perspective. This perspective is: *complete and utter paranoia.*

MOSFETs are not BJTs. They are not tubes. When something goes wrong, it's entirely possible for them to test okay…for a while. It's also entirely possible they took out some other parts in the flames of their demise…which you might miss. When MOSFETs go bad, it's best to simply replace everything. And then start up the amp really slow, in case you missed something. Dave was following the procedure you'd use for a BJT or tube amp…which meant more failures, later. And, for Dave, these were mystifying failures.

And we had other problems too. The output stage oscillated and needed to be recompensated. Again, not a big deal for someone who is used to power amp development (hell, I get suspicious if it doesn't oscillate at some point before it's been properly compensated in-circuit.) Problem is, an oscillating amplifier doesn't exactly allow for accurate bias current measurement…which means even the best firmware is helpless.

And—to complicate matters—we had to have the microprocessor compensate for each of the gain stages, which required different voltages for each operational point. The problem was that at higher gains, the steps the DAC had to take were too large for good adjustment of the operating point.

This is where Dave stepped in and came up with a new feedback arrangement which allowed:

- The same operational point for all gain levels
- The same amount of feedback for all gain levels

This in itself is a huge breakthrough. As far as I know, Ragnarok is the only gain-switchable amp that uses the same overall feedback for all gain levels—which means that the sonic impact of switching gain is effectively nil.

Big win, right?

Right. I was very pleased with our solutions. Ragnarok was

finally running reliably…on speakers, on headphones, etc. Everything looked good. And we were still a couple of weeks away from RMAF 2013, which means we could bring an ugly prototype to the show, and ship shortly thereafter.

Except…a couple of days before the show, I turned on Ragnarok…and it smoked. No input, no load. Just smoke.

This, my friends, is not a good sign.

And that's how Dave, Mike, and I pulled a couple of all-nighters getting Ragnarok back together, right before RMAF.

Problem solved. Right?

Wrong.

Ragnarok's First Appearance

Ragnarok's first appearance was at RMAF 2013. This version sported a very ugly, unanodized, unscreened, unfinished chassis that definitely didn't show very well. We put a big sign on it saying, "This is a prototype!"

Which, of course, was ignored. People were so excited to see and hear Ragnarok that I don't think many of them saw the sign.

The good news? Ragnarok didn't blow up during the show.

The bad news? It didn't work very well. In fact, with the early software, the operating points were anything but stable. It was all over the place. It ran hot. It ran cold. It ran in-between. It sounded pretty good once in a while. It sounded pretty bad most of the time.

All in all, not an auspicious debut. But let's go back to that advice:

- Shut the hell up.
- Shutting up also means "don't show it before it's ready."

Yes. Seriously.

Do you wonder why we don't talk about products before release anymore?

Algorithmic Adventure

Once we were back from the show, Ragnarok smoked itself again.

All in all, probably a good thing. Because it was time for new boards to clear up some of the analog problems we'd encountered, and to fix some bonehead mistakes on the control board. So, we lost some time as I redid the boards and got them stuffed again.

Then it was time for firmware.

This time…this time, it did the same thing. Weird operating points. Unreliable operation. Random blowups. In other words, it was not yet a shippable product.

Which really sucked. Here we were, at the end of the year, and Ragnarok wasn't anywhere near ready. We were going to blow yet another deadline on it.

But why? It was a puzzle. At least to me. An enhancement-mode output stage will do exactly one thing, in the absence of bias: nothing. It will sit there all day long and not blow up. It can't. It's not on. And it won't be on, unless bias is applied.

And…there was no reason it should be unstable as far as operational points go. The microprocessor was setting that. It should be, well, set.

Which pointed at the software.

"Dave, how frequently are you adjusting the bias on Ragnarok?" I asked, trying to get to the bottom of our mysteries.

"Frequently?" Dave blinked, looking mystified.

"Yes. Once a second, once every tenth of a second?"

"Once," Dave said.

"Once? Once once?"

"Yeah, when you turn it on. Or when you switch gain modes."

"Once?" I cried. "And then you let it go?"

"Yes," Dave said. "But the operational point trends downward with temperature, so it's safe."

"Unless it gets so low the bias is turned off," I said. Suddenly the crap-sounding Ragnarok started to make a lot more sense.

Dave nodded. "Well, there is that."

Argh. "Dave, it has to adjust continuously, over time."

"But then you have to parse out the difference between output current into a load for a music signal, and quiescent operating point."

I nodded. "Exactly. But that's what we intended to do from the start."

Dave nodded, but fell silent. "That's a lot harder."

"Right."

"I need to do some more work."

"Right!"

A few more weeks went past, since I was tied up with other products, other problems. Eventually, Dave and I got together with new software...and a surprise from Dave.

"I also added debugging code so we can see the output current and the voltage out from the DACs at all times," Dave said.

And, sure enough, the Ragnarok control board sprouted a new connector: an ancient DB-9 computer port. This, Dave hooked up to a computer. Soon, numbers were scrolling on the screen, updated about once a second.

"This is the output current," Dave said. "This is the other channel. And this number is the DAC output, from 0-4096."

"Neat!" I said. Which is true. This was an insanely helpful tool to debug Ragnarok.

"But, uh, Dave," I added, pointing at the output current, which had risen from 250 mA to 300, then 400, then 550..."

"Oh," Dave said, switching it off. "It hasn't done that before. Did you change something? Maybe it's not adjusting fast enough."

I had changed something—the driver current. Which meant they were heating up at a different rate. Which the firmware couldn't compensate for.

"Can it adjust faster?" I asked.

"Sure," Dave said. He changed a few lines of code, and we restarted the Ragnarok. This time, the output current rose over 250mA, but more slowly. But it still wanted to run away.

"I can change it so that it adjusts faster, the farther it is away from the target," Dave said. A few lines of code later, and we had an amp that didn't overshoot the target by more than 10% before settling down to a nice, constant 250mA.

Holy moly, we really have something here, I thought.

Of course, that was before the next day, when Ragnarok smoked again.

"Dave," I said. "Why does this keep blowing up? I thought we put in a current limit that would shut it down."

"I was going to do that last," Dave said, a little sheepishly.

Argh, volume two. *Do you know how much time we would have saved if this damn thing didn't blow itself up as a failure mode?* I wanted to ask. But I restrained myself.

And, after another board rebuild and some new software, we finally had a safe, operational Ragnarok. This was a day before the San Francisco Head-Fi meet in February 2014. Satisfied, we packed off the Ragnarok to the show.

Where…it acted like a real product for the first time. No drama. No craziness. No too-hot, no too-cold.

We were done, I thought. *Now, all we needed was to order boards and parts, and get to shipping.*

Yeah, right.

Interfacing with the Real World

Back at the office, though, tests told a different story.

Ragnarok wasn't good at differentiating between music and bias, as Dave had solemnly predicted. Compressed, low-dynamic-range music into 4 ohm speakers could cause itself to de-bias the output stage.

Translation into English: very bad sound.

The DC offset wasn't all that hot, because Dave was only looking at bias, not DC offset, over time. At certain temperatures, it would go into a state where it wouldn't switch into high gain mode.

Yeah. More development. We had to work out an algorithm to help differentiate between bias and music. We had to improve the bias setting over time. We had to work out the non-switching-into-high-gain problem, which was due mainly to the way we were stepping up and down the bias (and never hitting the target, in some cases.)

Which meant, in reality, more months of software time.

And, when we were finally ready to ship the first prototypes (to Jude and a couple other NDA listeners), we still got bitten. Jude's first Ragnarok still had the "I don't want to switch into high gain" problem, which we thought we'd worked out.

In the end, we changed the entire bias algorithm. It's actually quite a neat bit of code…and something I'm not eager to get into. If someone else wants to do this insanity, let them have the pain too.

Which put us at about The Show Newport's timeframe. Ragnarok had been acting like a product for a while now. Everything seemed sorted. Which made us confident enough to bring it to the show and put up a sign that said, "Shipping in June."

Yeah. Right. *Shut up. Shut the hell up.*

The Final Gotchas

With all of our software problems, we were (ahem) somewhat distracted. Which meant that things we should have been paying attention to were passed by.

Things like:

- The entire first run of transformers being the wrong voltage. Scrapped. Our fault.
- The pots being the wrong length. Reordered.
- The control board tactile switches being the wrong length. Ditto.
- The board house stuffing a lot of the first boards wrong. Back for rework.
- Our production line being totally unprepared for a product with five boards, 700 components, wiring, chassis-mount switches, transformer connectors, specific mechanical decoupling requirements, etc. Training, training.
- Our production line literally running out of space. We've gotten more space.

And I've left out a ton of details in the saga above, details like:

- Six transformer changes, including splitting the circlotron output transformer and the input voltage gain transformer into two entities
- Adventures in circlotron summing circuits, and the multiple meltdowns that occurred while figuring out the right ones
- The insanity that is a circlotron, and the effects of nonsymmetrical loading on it
- The crazy software just for volume control—it actually mutes the input between levels, to eliminate any popping or big glitches
- Various blowups I'd rather forget

Suffice to say, the Ragnarok story isn't a story at all...it's a saga, befitting of the name. It is, by far, our most complex product to date, and it defines a number of firsts in the amplifier area—most notably as the first truly universal amplifier, using the same gain stage and output for speakers and headphones, and as the first completely managed amplifier, dispensing with DC servos and other Band-Aids that can affect sound.

As far as the whole saga goes—all the missteps, all the gotchas, all the surprises, well...this is the kind of pain it takes to make groundbreaking products.

If there's a lesson to be learned here, it's that blazing a new path isn't to be taken lightly. You should take a long, hard look at your capabilities and resources, and plan for how it will impact everything you do.

And, of course...keep your damn mouth shut until it's ready.

Welcome to Ragnarok. The end of the world.

Or the beginning?

CHAPTER 28

"You'll Never Do Any Upgrades Anyway."

WHEN WE FIRST INTRODUCED BIFROST as "the least expensive fully upgradable DAC on the planet" in 2011, we had some interesting responses.

Some of them went like this:

"Yeah, but it's not like there'll be any upgrades."

"Not that you're planning to do any upgrades."

"I'll believe it when I see it (with respect to the upgrades.)"

Why the doubt? Hell, I don't know. Audiophiles can be a morose bunch.

But, needless to say, I was shocked at the amount of negative sentiment we received. Sure, there was plenty of positive press, but the opinion of "the audiophile on the street" was less thrilled.

I didn't worry. I knew we'd have upgrades. It's in Mike's DNA to do upgrades.

I just didn't know when they'd come.

First, Let's Talk Theta

Mike's upgrade DNA was implanted at the inception of Theta Digital.

Why? When Mike started Theta, digital audio was in its infancy. Manufacturers were still trying to get the price of a good CD player under $500 (think $900+ in today's dollars.) There were no standalone DACs. Zero. None. SPDIF, as a transmission standard, was brand new.

And Mike wasn't just at the leading edge with Theta—he was bleeding edge. Literally. Before Theta, nobody had even considered making a standalone DAC. And nobody else would have started with a flagship $3000 product, using their own digital filter code running on megadollar Motorola DSP chips.

Aside: Think about that a bit. A flagship product that "only" cost about $5500 in today's dollars? Insanity! Add more CNC-machined parts and a fancier chassis and some custom dampers and heebie-jeebie clocks, until it's $100K+! Yeah, that's the only way to go! But that's a comment on how far we've fallen in the past thirty years.

But, back to the subject at hand: digital audio was new. And things were changing fast. In contrast to today's relatively stable market, new D/A converters and new digital filters appeared regularly—pushing from 16 bits to 18 to 20, from no oversampling to 2x and 4x and 8x.

And, manufacturers were learning as well. Mike was the first to measure jitter, opine that it might have something to do with the sonic deficiencies of early digital audio, and devise ways to minimize it. He experimented with the best interfaces for SPDIF, using transformer-coupled coaxial, and later adding AT&T ST-optical glass fiber as an option.

In this constantly changing environment, bringing a very pricey, first-of-its-kind product into this market with no ability to upgrade it would be stupid.

Which is why Theta Digital was built, from the start, around upgradability. Theta owners could pay a relatively nominal amount to upgrade their DS Pro Gen 1 to 2, 3, and 5 (there was no 4) as the years passed. Same with Theta's lesser gear. This way, they could keep pace with technology, without filling trash cans with their old DACs.

Fun fact: Theta's first non-upgradable product was the Cobalt 307, which I designed—their first "disposable" DAC, at "only"

$599 in 1992. Compare to today's $99 Modi. Yeah. There is such a thing as progress.

Today's "Stability" and Upgradability

"But...but today, digital audio isn't stable!" some of you are protesting right now. "USB changes quite a bit, and there's DSD, and standards for transmitting digital over WiFi and Bluetooth, and high-res music, and all that."

Yes. But it's still much more stable than the 1980s and early 1990s, when everything was changing. Today, most DACs have settled down into a comfortable model: inexpensive delta-sigma D/A conversion from AKM, Analog Devices, Crystal, ESS, TI, or Wolfson, coupled with a USB interface solution from C-Media, TI, Tenor, or XMOS, plus (perhaps) a SPDIF interface from AKM or Crystal...plus, of course, a power supply, analog output stage, and associated interface electronics. Sure, there are some outliers, but they're usually at the scary end of the price spectrum.

Beyond that, let's go through the sources of instability today:

- **USB.** Much more mature, but still improving. When Bifrost was introduced, things were a lot less stable. Today, we have robust, relatively good-sounding solutions. But, we suspect they will get better. So, yes, the ability to upgrade the USB input would be a plus.

- **DSD.** Yeah, it's there, but the floodgates have not opened. In our opinion, best to concentrate on the 99.99%—that is, PCM—rather than a possible dead-end excursion a la HDCD. Still, if it ever becomes more than 1% of the market, sure, it would be good to have upgradability that would allow DSD decoding.

- **WiFi Digital Audio.** Definitely changing, and may be promising in the future. The potential for uncompressed transmission is definitely there, but the challenge is in the interface (joining WiFi networks means a UI that is computerlike in its capability and configurability, unlike

Bluetooth.) In our opinion, best to sit this out while it matures a bit. Jumping in now would be kinda like backing a digital transmission method before SPDIF was established as a standard—with the downside of extreme software prowess and support requirements.

- **Bluetooth Digital Audio.** Definitely changing, but too compromised to jump into for the sake of convenience, in our opinion. None to date is uncompressed (not even aptX.) Much of this is highly integrated, single-chip solutions that deliver analog output (not a digital datastream). Some can get I2S out. New Bluetooth standards with higher speed may allow uncompressed transmission. Probably too early to build a standard "Bluetooth compatibility module" into a DAC, though.

So, what does this all mean?

When we started on the design of Bifrost, the latter three weren't really a concern. We were worried about the USB input changing over time, and, to a lesser extent, the DAC and analog section.

Which is what drove our decisions—and our caveat. When we introduced Bifrost, we told potential purchasers, "We're not going to have a DAC of the Month Club or anything like that. When real, meaningful changes come to USB or the DAC / analog stage, we'll release an upgrade."

Of course, we didn't know when those real, meaningful changes would happen.

But, after Gungnir development, Mike started wondering what the Gungnir analog stage would sound like in the Bifrost. That led to the first possible upgrade.

And, early in 2013, C-Media laid the second one on us: the CM6631A USB input receiver chip.

Which meant, as we went into 2013, we knew…upgrades would soon happen.

But First, Let's Talk About the Way To Do Upgrades, and The Way Not To

"Real, meaningful changes." That's an important phrase for any manufacturer thinking about doing upgrades. That's the phrase that keeps you from being the Burger King of audio.

For example, it would be relatively easy to offer Bifrost with a half-dozen different DAC/analog sections. Just pick the latest chip from AKM, Analog Devices, Crystal, ESS, and Wolfson, redo the analog section to meet their specific requirements, reprogram the motherboard, and you're off and running. Everyone could have the DAC of their choice! Have it your way!

Yeah, except:

- Everyone would also argue about which one was best
- If there was no consensus, nobody would have any idea what to buy
- If there was consensus, we'd be stuck with a ton of DAC boards that were impossible to move
- We'd have to stock twelve different versions of Bifrost (six D/A options, plus with or without USB), which is a logistics disaster
- We'd have to spend six times the engineering time in development, or shortchange one or more implementations
- We'd have to maintain records for all variations, so they'd be serviceable in the future

No. Upgrades are not "have it your way." They are a path. A path to a rational future where you're helping mitigate the cost of buying a whole new product.

Which means, quite simply: pick your upgrades carefully, and keep them to a minimum.

That is sanity. The other path, less so.

On USB and Mohammed's All-You-Can-Eat Sushi and Deli

When we got our first CM6631A USB receiver chips, we were both thrilled and cautious.

Thrilled, because there were some notable limitations with the older CM6631 that the original Bifrost USB board was based on—namely, lack of 24/176.4 support, and an extreme pickiness about the USB interface and cable quality. A tiny percentage of systems simply didn't like the CM6631 interface—on the order of 0.3%—but, in the time-honored tradition of Murphy's Law, of course 1500% of that 0.3% happened to be forum members who complained about the problem.

Cautious, because we knew that "new stuff" isn't always "better stuff." C-Media promised 24/176.4 support, as well as support for even higher bitrates (32/384, specifically), but were mum on the subject of there ever being a problem with the CM6631 with some USB interfaces.

So we sent a few out to our PCB assembly house to have built up on the current-generation USB board. The chips were almost entirely pin-compatible, so that was the easiest way to see what they'd do.

Or, more accurately, Mike and Dave did it. Dave may have even soldered some of those 100-pin QFNs himself. No thanks, not for me.

In any case, we soon had a handful of USB boards with the CM6631A on them, happily programmed and running away.

"Here you go," Mike said, handing me a little foil bag one day. "Try it out."

"What is it?"

"The new USB receiver."

"How's it sound?" I asked. The first-gen USB board was pretty darn good by USB standards, but it was never any great shakes by good SPDIF standards—hence all our trash-talking of USB when Bifrost first launched.

"You tell me," Mike deadpanned.

So, I went home, installed the board, and plugged it into my most notorious source—an older Apple MacBook that would sometimes not play nice with the older USB board. It fired right up, showed all the sampling rates, and played fine.

Pretty damn fine, actually, I thought, after a while.

And, it wasn't glitching like the earlier board.

Hmm. Maybe we had something here.

I tried it on a couple of different computer sources, and they all worked fine. I played it for Rina. Her face lit up. "This USB actually sounds good."

"I thought it sounded better," I told her. "But I was more worried about the functional side."

"No. This is good. Really good."

Still probably not as good as SPDIF, I thought.

But after switching the Bifrost back to optical input, I had to scratch that thought. It wasn't the same as SPDIF, but it was definitely not worse…black and white had been turned into shades of gray.

"So when will we be selling this?" I asked Mike, the next day.

"You liked it, huh?"

"Yeah, lots better!" I said. "I think it might be better than SPDIF in some ways."

Mike recoiled in mock horror. Or maybe real horror. "Have you started listening to techno? Savoring Mohammed's All-You-Can-Eat Barbecue Sushi and Deli? Drinking plastic-bottle Vons-brand tequila? Huffing Testors paint?"

"No, I'm serious."

Mike shook his head. "Ohh…kay. Remind me to pick the restaurant next time we go out."

"Mike!"

"And make sure there's some real music on the computer when we go to shows."

"Mike!"

"Hell, maybe I should just buy you some Beats right now. USB? Better? For audio?"

"It's shades of gray," I told Mike.

Mike shook his head again. I don't think he'll ever really like USB, but he's largely stopped complaining about it. And that says a lot.

On the Voodoo of Analog

At the same time as the USB Gen 2 board, we were investigating another upgrade…this one pulled straight from Gungnir. The idea was simple: if the Gungnir sounded better than Bifrost, what would a Gungnir analog stage sound like in Bifrost?

This wasn't as simple as dropping it in, however. Gungnir's stage was designed for the high +/- 24V rails in Gungnir. Not for the +/- 15V rails in Bifrost. I had to change every value on the board to get it optimized for its new home.

But beyond that, you guessed it—the Uber Analog board is, pretty much exactly a Gungnir board. It has a much more sophisticated discrete topology, and a DC servo to eliminate the coupling caps in the original Bifrost analog stage.

But it's the same DAC—the AK4399.

Why not a different DAC? Well, we hadn't found any we liked better than the 4399. It's that simple. And, to this day, we still like the AK4399 and AK4396 better than the newcomers—they are unique in their implementation of switched-capacitor filtering to lower high-frequency noise, which seems to give them a more natural quality than other DAC options.

(Or it could be all in our heads. The voices, the voices!)

If you'd told me that our first DAC/analog upgrade would use exactly the same DAC chip as our standard board, I would have laughed…

…until I heard the new Analog board.

It was a big step up. At least as big as the USB upgrade. Bifrost was no slouch in standard form, but with the new Uber board, it was in a different class.

From there, the hard part began.

The Logistics of Upgrades

You know how, when a new car model comes out, a whole bunch of people have to have it RIGHT NOW?

Yeah. That's the problem with upgrades. When you announce an upgrade, and you already have a significant number of products in the field, the first months are gonna be crazy. Everyone's going to want it, and want it RIGHT NOW. That could easily bring your service department to its knees—especially if everything all comes in at once. Then you'll also have the fun of trying to explain to customers why it's taking two weeks to turn it around.

Luckily, we already knew this from the Theta days. Unluckily, we also knew that our current systems would never survive the onslaught.

Which is one reason we completely rebuilt the website— throwing out its creaky old taped-together platform for a new, custom-from-the-ground-up development that was tailored exactly to our needs.

This change allowed us to put in place a queuing system to help manage the updates. With the Schiit Upgrade Queuing System, customers could buy the upgrades, and we could tell them when to send them in so we could guarantee fast turnaround. It also kept everyone in the loop—sending automated emails when the product was received, and when it was shipped out again.

But then, there was the question of self-upgrades.

So, a week or so before we announced the upgrades, we reached a compromise: purchasers could choose to self-install, but only if they said they were a "professional electronics technician." The copy is still in place to this day on the upgrade product pages.

"They're gonna break them," Alex said, before we launched.

"We'll see," I told him.

"They're gonna screw up their Bifrosts, and we'll have to fix them."

"Let's see how it goes," I reassured.

Alex shook his head, but agreed, yes, it was worth a try.

So how did it work?

Well, it was a damn good thing we had the queuing system in place—early orders could have easily swamped us, and even with the system in place, we were sometimes doing twenty upgrades a day.

And, as far as self-install goes, it turned out to be a non-problem. Maybe one or two boards were destroyed by careless individuals, or maybe they just died in transit—yes, even after testing, it could happen. But there wasn't a flood of bad boards, or bad Bifrosts. So, our compromise ended up being the right thing, in the end.

And those early comments about, "Well, you'll probably never do upgrades anyway?" Yeah, those ended.

Instead, some people said, "Wait, that's not fair! You mean you're gonna milk us every year, and have us rebuy the DAC we just bought?"

Yeah. As if throwing away an entire DAC is a better solution. And as if an upgrade suddenly makes their current Bifrost or Gungnir unusable.

What was I saying about some audiophiles being a morose bunch?

CHAPTER 29

Worst. Customer. Ever.

I'M ABOUT TO EMBARK ON something that's probably akin to a soldier mooning a sniper, a politician shaking a baby on national TV, or a sports coach making racist remarks on YouTube.

Because, well, you know, *The Customer Is Always Right.*

Yes. In title case and with italics for emphasis. Because this is what we're taught. The customer is god. The customer has all the power. The customer, no matter what, is always right. Always. Without exception. No debate allowed.

So, if I start talking about less-than-ideal customers, I'm grabbing a third rail. I can hear the shrill panic of politically correct sales managers everywhere, echoing around in the back of my mind: *Nooooo! Don't go there! Never insult the customers! You don't know who they know! It's Armageddon, end of days, the heat death of the universe!*

But this is an important discussion. Because, if you're going to get into business selling product direct to customers, you need to know two things:

- You're gonna get some buttheads.
- You're not gonna make everyone happy.

Note: the above two rules apply even if you are *giving away* free Ferraris with sales and use tax prepaid, or a free magic rejuvenation pill that takes twenty years off your age with no side effects, or free 6000 square foot homes in Malibu. It'll be too hard to drive to the store, or your young visage will make you less respected at work, or the home will be too ostentatious and the wrong color.

So what do you do? Well, I think the poster set above Alex's desk sums it up perfectly. It reads:

We bend over backwards for our customers.
But we won't be bent forwards.

Love (Most Of) The Customers

Okay, now, let's be clear, though: no business selling direct can be successful without loving and caring for their customers. Period. If you are so cynical that every interaction with a customer is a war, don't bother starting a business selling direct.

And we do really enjoy the vast majority of the customers that contact us. Many of them use the same humor we do—Schiit puns, jokes, etc. Many of them are very complimentary regarding pricing or performance, or the made-in-USA aspect. Many of them just need a simple question answered—something we may have forgotten to cover, or were unclear about.

Aside: if they're asking about something that's unclear, make sure you fix it right away. If they're confused, lots of other people are confused too. Remember Amazon's rule of customer service: *If you have to contact us, we've failed.*

And that brings us to some business-y stuff we should get into, before we go into the Worst Customer Ever. Business-y stuff like, "How do you maintain a high standard of customer service?"

Well, that's a bigger question. Because it gets into things like:

- How do you architect customer service to help ensure satisfaction?
- What do your customers consider a high standard of service?
- How will your customers contact you to get service?

Let's break these down:

Architecting Customer Service. *Wait, what?* Some of you are saying. How can you *architect* customer service? Isn't it just, people ask questions, and you answer them? They have problems, and you fix them?

In general, yes, but you can do a whole lot of things to architect your customer service so that you can offer much faster response—and minimize the personnel and time you need to give great customer service.

Note: Yeah, I know, "minimizing personnel and time," may seem like, well, not the most customer-centric thing you can do. But, in actuality, it is. The smaller the customer service team, the more consistent and high-level answers you can give. And the less time spent on each inquiry means that your response rate can get really, really small.

So what can you do to architect the customer service experience to make it better for both you and the customer? Several things:

- **Prohibit the "hard sell."** If your customer service team has a dual duty of solving problems and selling product—especially if they are measured and rewarded on their sales—you're in deep, deep trouble. This encourages the typical "audio fellatio" with promises that you're going to hear god without drugs—and, of course, the more you spend, the more magical it gets. This gets in the way of honest answers, it makes promises that may not be paid off, and it takes a ton of time to do, especially if you're talking about expensive gear.

- **Ban discussion of other manufacturers' products.** Same deal. If your customer service team is expected to give value judgments on other manufacturers' products, and upsell, wow…now, not only have you opened the gates to infinite time and unfulfillable promises, you now have started building a reputation for trash-talking other people's gear. Yes, I know, lots of companies do it, but it doesn't mean it's right.

- **Don't do promos, points, or sales.** Want to really open the floodgates on customer service? Start doing promos, customer loyalty points, or sales. Then you'll get to hear nonstop about things like, "Hey, I just bought this yesterday, now it's on sale," or "When's your next sale, I'm waiting for that," or "I can't figure out this points thing, how does it work?" This will absolutely eat your customer service alive—it will become all they do.

This is why, almost from the start, we put into place three policies that really, really simplify customer service. These are:

- No sales
- No hard-sell / audio fellatio
- No talking about other manufacturers' products

About 15% of our emails are of the "can I get a better price?" variety.

With no sales, no promos, no discounts, no loyalty program, the answer is easy.

In addition, we don't have to have any staff to manage the sales, promos, discounts, loyalty program, and the resulting refunds, exchanges, special deals, stacked offers, etc. that go with it. The result is simple: less complexity, less staff, and lower prices for everyone.

Wait a sec? Lower prices? You're asking. *What about the sale prices?*

Yeah, and what about the necessarily higher price you need as a baseline if you're going to do sales? Or the necessarily higher price you need for the staff you need to deal with sales, promos, and loyalty programs? Lowest complexity equals lowest price for everyone—and nobody thinking they got screwed because they missed the sale. That's a win-win—lower cost and higher customer satisfaction.

> **Aside:** with respect to sales, I can't say this more strongly: DON'T. EVER. Or you'll become addicted to them. They will never end.

We get more emails about "Will I hear a difference from my receiver / computer / etc.?" or "How does this compare with the Arglebargle XYZ?"

Again, our policies make the answer really simple. We don't know how you hear, or if you think the difference is meaningful. And we never discuss other manufacturers' products.

Which is really interesting. While we look at this being an honest, upstanding manufacturer, this policy really lights some people on fire. They really really really want to be sold, and they get majorly pissed when we won't engage in the usual circle-jerk about how our stuff is the greatest thing on the planet.

But…ask yourself two things:

- Do you really think we've heard everything on the planet?
- Do you really think we have the same sonic preferences you do?

Fact is, we probably can't make a lot of those comparisons you're so eager to hear our opinion on. Ask us about what amp we think best for, say, LCD-2s and K701s, sure—we can answer that. But comparing and contrasting our amps with products we've never heard before…um, no.

Maintaining a high standard of customer service. Okay, this is where we have to get subjective. Because we don't have all the answers. We haven't done extensive customer satisfaction studies, and we haven't tested a system architected from those studies.

But, we think that a "high standard" can be defined relatively simply.

Why? Because we have ample examples of what people hate. When was the last time you talked to your cable company? Or your cell service provider? Yeah. Endless trouble-trees going through all the stuff you already told them and email responses that stretch into days. Nobody likes that. It says, loud and clear: we don't care. You're not important. You're part of the little people.

So, a high standard of customer service starts by inverting their model.

Which is what we try to do. Here it is, in one sentence: *Put enough information up about the product so most people can make their own decisions, but when they contact us, make the answers fast and simple.*

Read that again. *Fast and simple.*

Read it again, stopping at the first word. *Fast.*

I can't stress this enough. Fast response to customer questions is key. Many businesses promise a one to two day response to email. This is woefully inadequate. There's no way someone can make a decision, much less troubleshoot a product with a one to two day response time. It's like getting customer support from Pluto.

During regular business days, one to two hours is more like it. Or even one to two minutes. We aim to keep this as snappy as possible. Which is why you're usually looking at minutes for an email reply during the week, and we check email at least two to four times over the weekend on nonbusiness days as well.

Is this the full answer? Probably not. But it seems to make most people very happy.

Choosing contact options. And, with this, it's a good time to talk about the kinds of customer contact options you have. Because, if you're starting a business, you have a ton of options these days. Which means that most companies start off by checking every box on the options list:

- Email
- Chat
- Phone
- Skype
- Facebook

- Twitter
- Mail

Congrats. You just screwed yourself. Who's going to be immediately available for chats? Who picks up the phone? Shouldn't they be making something? Skype rings on which computer? Why are you paying attention to Facebook if the rest of your customer service is working? Twitter, are you kidding? Mail? This is the 21st century, what are you going to do, send out brochures?

Here's what we chose to do as an experiment, when we started Schiit:

1. Be really fast at email
2. Never pick up the phone, but call back in a couple of days
3. Add additional services if this didn't work

We've never added additional services. Why? Because email response is so fast.

I was talking to the owner of another audio company when the subject of customer service came up.

"How many phone calls a day do you get?" he asked.

"Um…average?" I asked. "Maybe one. Maybe two."

"What the hell?" he exclaimed. "How do you keep it so low? I got three people working full-time on the phones."

I grinned. "Easy. We tell people not to call us."

The other audio company owner's eyes bugged out. "You…what?"

"It says right on the website: email us, we're really fast. Call us, and we may get to it eventually."

He shook his head. "And that works?"

"Apparently."

And it does work. It's called, in corp-speak, *setting expectations*. Expect fast email response. Expect really, really slow phone response. Which do you choose? There you go.

But I want to call, some people are saying now.

Yep. Got it. *Want to pay 25% more for your products?*

Thought not.

Fact is, phone support—that is, good phone support, from a real audio guy who can really help you with your question or problem—ain't cheap. It eats up pretty much a person's entire day, because the guy answering the phone doesn't know if he's going to get tied up on a one-hour call covering the life story and audio adventures of someone, say, interested in maybe buying a Magni.

Aside: even on email, it gets interesting. How about seventy-three emails with eighty-five questions from one person...on Magni and Modi. Not kidding.

If we invited phone calls...if we were *good* at phone service...we'd probably have at least two to three more salaried staff working full-time on it. Nick can handle all the email we get in a day—questions, support, etc.—while still being a tech.

Wait, wait, wait! some of you are crying. *Are you essentially saying your support options are pretty much email-only? How the hell do you get away with that?*

Simple. With fast answers. If we ran our email like Comcast, well...things would be very different.

So How Bad Was the Worst Customer?

Okay, so was the worst customer someone who didn't like our products?

No. There are plenty of people who don't like our stuff. That's perfectly fine. Send it back, get a refund, no harm, no foul.

Or someone who expected a ten-minute response on a holiday weekend, and sent twelve emails complete with onomatopoeic descriptions of what his product was doing?

Again, no. Maybe we should be more clear that we don't work weekends, nor on holidays, so our fast email response may be, er, a little slower during that time period.

Was it the guy who got a new Magni and Modi, threw a temper

tantrum when they didn't work (or he couldn't get them to work), so he beat the crap out of the product and sent an email photo of it in his trash can?

Again, no. Though perhaps some anger management is in order there.

Was it the guy who sent seventy-three emails with eighty-five questions asking about Magni and Modi?

Again, you guessed it, nope. He never bought them.

Aside: although we haven't done big customer satisfaction research, we have run some statistics that are very interesting. One of them is that anyone who emails us before purchasing is eight times more likely to return the order. Two plus emails takes it up to thirty times. But again, are these bad people? Not at all. Merely indecisive.

No. The worst customer ever wasn't just bad. He was criminally bad.

Here's what happened.

After work on Friday evening, I decided to check the customer service email. Until December 2013, I was the primary guy who answered customer service email, so this in itself wasn't an unusual event.

What I found was disturbing, though—an email from a very, very irate customer who had ordered a B-stock Mjolnir. Back in those days, we sold B-stock manually, by individual inquiry. If someone wanted B-stock, they had to email us, we told them the price, and if they were interested, we sent them a PayPal invoice.

Apparently I'd sent them an invoice, and they'd paid for it. However, we didn't ship the Mjolnir the same day, as requested. This also isn't unusual, since we quote a one to three business day shipping time on in-stock items that aren't ordered with expedited shipping.

But that didn't matter to this guy. He was livid. I mean, full-boat, cartoon-steam-whistle-out-the-ears, screaming red-faced rage. In acidic sentences strung in all-caps, he told us what a terrible company we were for not shipping it right away, expressed his extreme displeasure with our customer service, questioned our competence in an overall manner, and made various other personal assertions relating to our lack of professionalism and discipline.

And, to top it all off, he told me that Alex was the worst person in the universe, he didn't care about him as a customer, and had never returned the emails he'd sent earlier in the day.

In a perfect, algorithmic, Mr. Spock-driven world, I would have tweaked an eyebrow and said, "Curious," then investigated this incident in a dispassionate manner.

Humans don't work this way, though. I was pissed. I'd been called an incompetent idiot. Alex had been called much, much worse.

So, I bit back my first response and emailed Alex, asking if he'd replied to the guy's emails.

Alex sent me a long string of increasingly irate emails, beginning at ten that morning—all responded to in less than ten minutes by Alex.

Okay. That's all I needed to know. Screw Spock and dispassionate logic. This guy was a butthead of the first caliber. What could we do?

I called Alex. "What can we do about this guy?"

"If it were me, I'd give him a refund and invite him never to be a customer again."

"Can we do that?" I asked.

"I can have FedEx reroute his shipment back to us."

I only had to think for about a millisecond. "Do it. I'll refund his money, then he's a noncustomer."

"Done," Alex said, and went off to do what he does with shipping. He came back a few minutes later via email. "Done and done."

Cool. I went into PayPal and refunded all of his money. We'd be out the shipping and rerouting fees, of course, but that was a small price to pay to be rid of him.

> **Aside:** seriously, I am saving your mind by not posting the emails here. They were seriously, pathologically disturbed. This guy was, no crap, going to lose his mind because his amp shipped a day late.

There we go. Package rerouted, money refunded, done. Right? Wrong.

The guy came back to me about ten minutes later on email, even more livid than before. He'd noticed that we refunded his money, and wanted to know what was going on. (But with about 10000 times more expletives and rage.)

I sent him a pleasant email in return, saying something like:

Dear Butthead (actually his real name),

We have refunded your purchase in full and rerouted the shipment of your B-stock Mjolnir. We have done this because you are so disappointed with our service to date. If you are this unhappy now, we have no confidence that we will ever be able to make you happy. We believe this parting is for the best, and wish you luck in finding the perfect component to meet your needs.

Sincerely,

Jason, etc.

Oh, boy, was he ever pissed. After four or five more irate emails, Alex and I seriously wondered if we'd meet a guy with a lead pipe at the office on Monday morning.

But Saturday was quiet—no emails.

And Sunday was the same.

And nobody was waiting to jump us on Monday.

So, end of story, right?

Oh no.

About a week later, Alex starts wondering where that Mjolnir went. It had never come back to us. And it had only been shipping within California, so it should have come back already.

He checked the shipping record, and soon found the problem: the guy we'd shipped it to had called FedEx himself and rerouted it to a FedEx office, then picked it up.

Yes, the guy we refunded and finalized the transaction, so we couldn't charge against his card again.

"What do you want me to do?" Alex asked me, his eyes dark and murderous.

"Whatever you want," I said.

Luckily, Alex is very good at Internet forensics. Through this guy's multiple email addresses, he was able to track down his LinkedIn, his business website (yes, he had his own business), and his Facebook page. On his Facebook page, in plain view, was a photo of the Mjolnir.

Alex sent an email (and a registered letter) to the guy's main business address, demanding payment for the Mjolnir within seventy-two hours—or a visit from the sheriff's department.

He tried to play it off: "Thank you for the gift of the Mjolnir, in compensation for your poor customer service," the smug bastard emailed.

We reiterated that it was clearly not a gift, and repeated the timetable. Pay, or see how having a criminal record for grand theft felt.

Over the next few days, we endured various emails about what terrible people we were, our relationship with our mothers, how we had small body parts, etc. None were responded to, save to remind him of the time ticking away.

I really thought we'd have to get the police involved, but on the last day, he blinked. He paid for the Mjolnir.

And that, really, was that.

However—if he ever orders anything else, it won't be shipped. If that Mjolnir comes in for service, he will be getting a check for full value in return, and we're keeping the amp. We don't need customers like that. Ever. For any reason.

Starting a business? Working with customers? Repeat after me: *not every customer is worth having.*

Bonus: How to Get Great Customer Service From Humans

One of the problems with customer service these days is that most of it has become by-the-book and algorithmic. *Choose from these available options so we can route it to the right department. That problem wasn't found. I'm sorry you're having trouble, we value your business, your expected wait time is fifty minutes.*

Yep. Endless trouble-trees, backed by least-experienced customer service personnel who ignore the long list of troubleshooting you've already done. Four hundred words of boilerplate about what a special customer you are to them, and how they're truly so sorry they're going to self-immolate. Ticket systems that promise transparency and continuity, but don't deliver when shared by a team of 150 people.

The result? Everyone knows that when a big company says, "We value you as a customer," it's 195% BS.

Which means it's open season, guys. Get out the 12-gauge! Give them both barrels! Let 'em have it! Because they aren't really human, and they're not telling the truth!

Is it any wonder that yelling and screaming at large company customer support personnel is almost, well, accepted?

Because if you make enough noise, you might get somewhere. You might trigger the Rage.2.Uplift and get someone who knows more about what they're doing. Or you might trigger the PITA.Refund.1.1 and get your money back.

Big companies are making a very prickly bed with this combo. When nothing but anger works, they're going to get nothing but anger. And then it doesn't work.

Companies like Schiit are a little different. Hell, I bet most audio companies are a little different. Hell, most small companies, period.

Which means if you come in, guns blazing, things may end up very, very differently than you expected.

Why?

At Schiit (and companies like us), you're talking to humans.

And humans have emotions. They are not slaves to a script or to a corporate customer service code of What Can And Cannot Be

Done.

Not only that, at Schiit, you're talking to fully empowered humans. Nick, Laura, and Alex all have carte blanche to give you anything they want—or nothing at all.

Now, this doesn't mean that you need to suck up to them. In fact, that can be just as irritating, or more so, than anger. But you should be aware that you are talking to humans that can—and do—bend over backwards. But if you come in hot, that willingness to bend over backwards diminishes.

Instead, if you come to us:

- In a concise manner (we do not need Your Life Story With Audio)
- With clear questions (you'd be amazed how many emails we get where we ask, "Was there a question here?")
- Using complete sentences at least some of the time (no kidding—and phone autocorrect is the worst)

You'd be surprised at the fast, helpful answers you'll get. And you'll be shocked at how much we'll bend over backwards to make you happy.

Aaaanddd...I'll bet any other company with human-powered customer service will work exactly the same way.

Remember, you're talking to people, not machines.

Don't be the next *Worst. Customer. Ever.*

CHAPTER 30

Death of a Product

THIS CHAPTER COVERS SOMETHING THAT any business will have to face at one point or another: the death of a product.

Of course, most product deaths aren't usually deaths, per se—they're more a phoenix-like event, where a new and even shinier product rises from the ashes of the previous one. At least hopefully.

But...that leads us into the first question. When a product gets long in the tooth, do you update it, or give it the full Kevorkian treatment?

Good question. And, with that, let's talk about product life cycles, and product life cycle management. Yeah, good boring corporate stuff. But I'll try not to make this too tiresome.

Product Life Cycles, AKA the Game of Update, Assassinate, or Cannibalize

Okay, let's start with the basics:

- No product is fresh or competitive forever, especially a technology product; the competition, and the market, can and will change—sometimes in new and unpredictable ways.

- Because of this, you have to think in terms of product life cycles—or, in regular English, how long a product will be a good, solid competitor in its market.

- You should determine (at least) a guess as to how long your product life cycle is, so you can be working on updates or replacements before the end of its life.

And, the bonus stuff that most companies ignore:

- Killing your babies is perfectly okay, if updating won't make them a good product for new market realities—you have to be ready and willing to do this.
- It's better for you to cannibalize your own product lines, rather than waiting for someone else to do it.

The above is why you typically see an iPhone every year. It's why most other flagship phones are on the same life cycle—the technology, software, and market have changed enough in a year that a new, fresh product is required to stay competitive.

It's also why you see new laptops and such on time frames dictated largely by the release dates of new chipsets from major manufacturers like Intel—the introduction of the new chipset changes the game enough so that new products need to be introduced.

Cars? They have longer life cycles, typically two years between minor refreshes, four years between "making it look new on the same platform" and eight years between moderate to major platform changes.

Same goes for a lot of less techy stuff—appliances, etc. Their product life cycles can be much longer than a year.

Audio? Hmm, now that's a conundrum.

On the mass-market side, the major manufacturers of "bulk" gear like receivers and such have been chasing a one-year product life cycle for a very long time—but the new products that come out frequently aren't anything more than re-badged and slightly de-contented versions of their predecessors.

Aside: My theory is that the ongoing de-contenting allows them to maintain arbitrary price points (determined by copying their competition). After all, it's much easier to follow somebody else's rules than make your own. The latter might require intelligent marketing to show how your products are, well, *actually* different from, and better than, the competition.

In high-end, product life cycles are all over the place. Some companies make essentially the same products for nearly a decade. Some make changes every couple of years.

What's right?

- **Some use the old metric of "when sales slow down, it's probably time to update."** But this is an astoundingly bad metric. When sales slow down, it's probably too late. When sales slow down, you're under pressure to come out with something, fast. And when you're under pressure, you may miss a critical feature—or not do your best work.

- **Some use a fixed schedule:** "We have decided our product life cycle is three years, so we will begin working on significant updates twenty-four months after launch." This is better, but what happens when the market undergoes rapid changes and your sales fall off a cliff at eighteen months in? Do you simply sit and wait the remaining eighteen months to launch a new product?

When we started Schiit in 2010, if you'd asked me what I thought our product life cycle would be, I probably would have shaken my head and said, "I don't know. Two years, three years? Let's see how it goes."

And, to this day, I can't really put a number on it. We've decided to set our product life cycle on a more flexible metric than falling sales or dates on a calendar. If I had to put it in words, it would be something like this:

Our products are updated or discontinued when significant positive changes can be made, or need to be made, at a time not disruptive to customers.

Note the specificity: updated *or discontinued* (it's okay not to keep a zombie product alive), significant *positive* changes (not just a small tweak, and not de-contenting), at a time *not disruptive* to customers (updating a product three months after release, for example.)

In the case of Asgard, early in 2013, those significant positive changes *needed* to be made.

Why? One word: Magni.

The Death and Rebirth of Asgard

Before Magni, we never really thought about updating Asgard. It was a great amp, a strong seller, and sales continued to pick up. By the "wait until it slows down" metric, Asgard was doing fine.

But as soon as we heard Magni, we all looked at each other, and said, almost in unison: "What about Asgard?"

Magni was just too close in performance to Asgard. In fact, it was more powerful than Asgard. It was quieter. It ran cooler. About the only thing Asgard had going for it, objectively, was a much better volume pot—better tracking, better taper—you can't beat large pots for that, no way, no how. Aesthetically, it was a much more elegant-looking piece, but elegance only gets you so much. Sonically, we believed it was still ahead of Magni—but not by enough.

So it was time to look at the end of Asgard.

But did we kill it, or did we update it? That was the first question.

Deciding to update it was really easy:

- Asgard was still selling well after Magni—in fact, sales continued to increase until it was discontinued—so there was clearly still a demand for a step-up amplifier.

- Magni had taught us a lot about surface-mount parts. Surface-mount parts, applied to Asgard, would actually reduce its manufacturing cost due to robotic assembly. This would open up putting the money into other areas.

- We regularly got requests for two features Asgard didn't have: gain switching and preamp outputs. Adding these made a lot of sense.

- Assembling Asgard was a real pain, with four separate

MOSFETs, plus thermal pads, screws, lock washers, and electrically insulating bushings for each—I'd been thinking about a new way to do it with one simple bracket, two screws, and a single custom thermal pad. We were now of a size where we could do the large custom orders that made the switch viable.

- Asgard's gain stage was pretty basic—it didn't even have a current-sourced front end, and it had coupling capacitors at the output. Mjolnir had taught us a lot about how good a high-voltage, cascoded, current-sourced front end could be—and going to surface mount meant we could afford to do it—together with a trick DC servo that connected to a sonically innocuous (as in, non-amplified) terminal to eliminate the coupling caps.

- And while we were at it, we put the rest of the money saved by surface-mount to change the transformer and power supply from unipolar to bipolar on the output, plus added an 80V rail for the HV front-end like Mjolnir.

That's a big list of updates, guys. Different board, different topology, different power supply, different chassis, different transformer, different feature set—the only thing that our proposed Asgard 2 had in common with the first generation was the same chassis styling, the same pot, and the same basic connections.

So how did development go on this radically updated Asgard?

Almost comically boring.

I built a perfboard proto one evening and verified that the basic concept worked—including delivering measured distortion performance that was almost ten times better than the original Asgard. Total time: a couple of hours.

From there, the first boards we got fired right up and worked. They even fit the revised chassis just fine. All the pain of your typical product development—all the tiny little nits and problems— were conspicuously absent. I changed a couple of resistor values from the initial calculations, but that's about it. Total time: maybe four to five hours.

From there, we took the first in-chassis prototype inside to the listening area where I had Mjolnir and Gungnir set up. I plugged it in, put on some headphones—most likely HD800s, because they're great at revealing what's wrong with an amp—and sat back.

Crap, I'm still running the Mjolnir, I thought, as soon as I heard it.

But I looked over...and the headphones were plugged into Asgard 2.

Asgard 2—sounding like a Mjolnir? *No way.* Not believing it, I switched the gain to Low, and the volume decreased, as expected.

Holy moly, I *was* listening to the Asgard 2.

Still not really believing it, I swapped back to Mjolnir—and, yeah, Mjolnir was a step up, but it wasn't leaps and bounds like the original Asgard. Of course, Asgard 2 didn't have the raw power for, like, HE6s, but it was *very* good—much, much better than the original.

Next, IEMs. Dead silent on low gain. I grinned. This was gonna be a winner.

I decided to call in Rina and demo it for her.

"I want to hear the Asgard 2, not the Mjolnir," she said.

"You are."

She went through the same rigamarole as I had—switching gain, unplugging headphones, comparing to Mjolnir—before believing it.

"This ain't no Asgard," she finally pronounced.

Mike? Pretty much the same reaction. We had a winner.

And, you know, sometimes things just work out. And sometimes, things work even better than you expected. In product development, this is known as a "gimme." Also known as, "oh crap, watch your back."

I should have watched my back.

The Asgard 2 Launch Debacle

The run-up to Asgard 2 launching was filled with the same little delays that happen with every new product—waiting for parts, waiting on chassis, etc.—so, in that respect, there was no clue that we had any nasty surprises waiting in compensation.

But when we launched the product, word quickly came back—some of the Asgard 2s hummed like a refrigerator. Mechanically. As in, you could hear the transformer humming with headphones on. Closed headphones.

But that made no sense—none at all. The prototype hadn't hummed. And we hadn't heard any hum in production.

"But we wouldn't necessarily hear it," Alex said, as a big train went by outside, shaking the paper-thin stucco of the Schiithole.

"Crap," I said, realizing for the first time just how loud it was in our building. It wasn't just the trains—it was the constant traffic noise from cars passing on the four-lane road outside.

Late at night, we confirmed it. Many of the transformers did hum. And the prototype didn't.

Why?

This is known as a "production surprise." As in, "Surprise...although the transformer meets specs, we decided to make them a little differently...and that difference transformed your product from a headphone amp into a combo headphone amp / massager."

The transformer manufacturer was apologetic, and promised new samples posthaste. But that didn't fix the humming Asgard 2s in the field—now the entire first run. We'd been so deep in backorder, we'd sold out in just a few days.

So what did we do? The only thing we could do: accept the returns on the Asgard 2s that hummed, or swap them out as we got the new transformers in.

Aside: gimmes are dangerous, guys...be suspicious, be very suspicious, of something that is too easy.

And that's why we started a new policy after Asgard 2: multiple prototypes, multiple listeners...and multiple locations, some of which we knew were quiet.

Yeah. There you go. But that's also why the launch of Valhalla 2 and Lyr 2 were, well, relatively uneventful. Almost boring.

And, in terms of "production surprises," that's exactly where you want to be.

CHAPTER 31

R&D Sometimes Means,
"Try It, See If It Works"

SOMETIMES R&D IS EXTREMELY FOCUSED. You know exactly what you're shooting for, and you apply the collective smarts you have in a concerted effort to hit—or exceed—the mark.

This was certainly the case with the previous two products I talked about (Ragnarok and Asgard 2.) We knew (pretty much) what we wanted, and set about to achieve it. In the case of Ragnarok, it was an all-in deal with me, Mike, and Dave all contributing—and a long and winding road to the endgame. In the case of Asgard 2, it was just me—and, as I said before, R&D-wise, the product was a gimme.

But I strongly believe that R&D shouldn't always be so focused. There's value in making sure your engineering staff has time to play with crazy ideas.

How much value? Consider this:

Without playtime, Mike would have never put together the micro-DAC that became the first Modi. Which also would have meant:

- There'd be no reason to develop Magni, ever

- We may never have investigated low-cost products at all

- We may never have discovered how cost efficient all-steel chassis could be

- Which would mean that we also wouldn't have Vali, Sys, Loki, or Wyrd

- Our lowest-cost product today might still be Asgard (because why bother updating Asgard in the face of rising sales?)
- Valhalla 2 and Lyr 2 might not exist, either, for the same reason

So what would Schiit look like today, if Mike hadn't had the wild butthair to develop a DAC orders of magnitude less expensive than any he'd ever done?

Well, we'd certainly be a lot smaller. Magni, Modi, and the sub-$150 products are the majority of our sales.

But at the same time, ironically, we probably wouldn't be much farther along, if any, on Ragnarok and Yggdrasil—the low-cost product line barely impacted Dave's software development time at all.

So, it would easily be possible for us to be, say, half the size. Maybe still at the Schiithole in Newhall. And still not have Ragnarok and Yggdrasil out.

Give your engineers some playtime. It pays off.

Those Tempting Tubes

Sometimes it's funny what sets off those "I wanna play" moments. In the case of what would become Vali, it was eBay.

Yes, eBay.

In this case, it was my fault. I keep an eye open for bulk tube deals. We kinda have to. Valhalla 2 and Lyr 2 production chew through an incredible amount of tubes. And good tubes are getting scarcer.

Why? Simply because they aren't making any more 6N1P or 6BZ7 tubes, just to name a couple of NOS tubes we use. And, while there are some good new-production tubes, they tend to be eye-wateringly expensive. So, we prefer to work with NOS tubes, at least as long as we can.

Anyway, my search for bulk tubes sometimes takes me to tube resellers in Russia, sometimes to surplus warehouses where piles of tubes are forgotten for decades, and sometimes, yes, to eBay.

And what came up—what started the whole Vali thing—was an incredible bulk of NOS Jan Raytheon 6088 tubes, at a very attractive price. I mean, so many tubes that it would take us through half a decade of production, even if the amp sold like Magni. Truly crazy numbers.

And those numbers—and that attractive price—got the wheels turning. What could we do with this? Could we make an amp with them?

An amp, maybe, at a near-Magni price?

There was only a whole buttload of problems with this scenario:

- 6088s were pentodes. Using pentodes in pentode mode for gain is pretty barfy. And you don't know what the triode-strapped curves will look like until you run them on a curve tracer. Would they be linear enough to use?

- We'd never used subminiature tubes, so we had no idea how best to use them, nor any specifics of their care and feeding.

- Even if the thing worked, how would we run the high-voltage supply (because, as Mike says, running a tube from a low-voltage supply is for "children and amateurs.")

- And, what about the output stage? What exactly could we bolt this tube to?

And it's doubts like that which kept me from simply clicking "buy it now." Because if I just jumped on it, we might end up with a whole bunch of useless tubes.

But I kept coming back to *all those tubes*, at *that price*.

After a couple of weeks, nobody else had jumped on them, probably because they had the same doubts.

I did some research—had anyone used the 6088 for audio? A couple of DIY projects popped up, but they were the most basic and simplistic things imaginable—nothing that would be able to drive a wide range of headphones, nothing that could be sold as a commercial product.

But still, those tubes...

Screw it. I contacted the seller and purchased a few tubes just to play around with. In the process, they confirmed that they had five times the amount of tubes they had listed on eBay actually available—a truly eye-popping number.

Which meant if I could do something with them, then we could have a real winner on our hands.

The Road to Vali

The tubes came in a couple of days, and I set up a quick breadboard circuit to see how they performed. I was just interested in the basics:

- What plate voltage did they run best at?
- What plate load did they like for lowest distortion?
- What was the distortion like in triode mode?
- What did the operating current and heater current look like?

Why these basics? Because, based on these measurements, I could make a go / no-go decision on purchasing the tubes. Or so I thought.

It was interesting, running the early tests on those tubes. They were different than any others we had ever worked with. How so?

- Maximum plate voltage was only 60V—most tubes are in the hundreds of volts
- Plate current was 750uA-1.5mA for typical loads—much lower than most tubes
- The cathode was directly heated, rather than indirectly, like most tubes we've worked with
- It only needed 1.25V heater voltage and 20mA heater current—again, far lower than the 6V and hundreds or thousands of mA for most tubes (wonder why tubes run hot? Simple—they have a heater in them that usually

dissipates a few watts of power.)

So, how'd they do?

Not so hot, at first. Nearly 1.5% distortion at the first plate voltage and load I tried. But, by tweaking the plate voltage and load, I was able to chart where the tube was the happiest. THD was still high, by our current standards—0.3% or so—but it was mainly second-harmonic distortion, and the distortion profile was nice, with 3rd 20dB down and 4th almost at the noise floor.

But—0.3% was still pretty high. How would it do, with an output stage bolted to it? What would it actually sound like?

That was beyond what the breadboard would tell me. I needed to lay out a board, and see how the amp really would do.

Laying it out on a Magni-sized board would be easy...except for the fact that it was a totally different amplifier, with radically different voltage requirements. (Remember I mentioned those high voltages for the tube? 60V is pretty low in the tube world, but it's still a far cry from the +/-15V we were running in Magni.)

At the same time, I wouldn't want to run a solid-state output stage at 60V. That's pretty, ah, adventurous, especially since the standard TRS headphone jack shorts the output every time it's connected or disconnected.

And, we needed a regulated heater voltage too, at 1.25V.

Oh yeah, and 5V for the relay.

And it would be ideal if we could get all those voltages from Magni's standard 16VAC wall wart.

Sounds impossible, right? Actually, far from it. With AC input, you can run a voltage-quadrupler and easily get 60V after regulation for the tube. Half of that circuit gives you DC voltages that can be regulated to 30V. And the 1.25V and 5V requirements are low enough that you can bring them down from the standard rectified output.

But (you knew this was coming, right?)...

But there's always a but. Voltage quaduplers also aren't very good for high-current output, and have significant ripple. But the half-wave rectification we'd used in Magni (effectively a voltage doubler) worked well enough. For a couple of mA going to tubes, run through a voltage regulator, it should be fine. Or at least that's what I told myself.

I laid out the board in a couple of evenings. Everything fit really easily, including the tubes and an output stage that kinda started as something out of a Magni, but morphed into a pretty cool design that used a phase flipper to level-shift the output of the tube for DC coupling from the front-end, plus LED biasing for the output devices, which ran in Class AB.

Then it was just…send out the boards, and wait a week.

Two Big Surprises

The first Vali boards that came back weren't perfect, but they weren't bad. They needed a couple of hacks to smooth the input to the 30V regulator, and additional bypassing for the 1.25V regulator, but that was about it. After a couple of small tweaks, they were up and running, with the LED biasing simulating the glow of a traditional tube heater.*

*Subminiature tubes with 1.25V heaters don't glow. They hardly run hotter than room temperature, in fact.

What was even better was the fact that it was running on the standard Magni wall wart, without any signs of strain. Vali does draw a bit more current than Magni, so this was a welcome sign.**

**Thermal design really is the starting point for any amp. Get that wrong, and you're in a world of hurt.

So, what did it sound like?

I took the prototype from the garage (where I still did most of the design and tweaking) back to the listening couch, where I kept Mjolnir and Gungnir.

Okay, I'll admit it—I used Gungnir for those early first listens. Overkill, yes…

On first listen, I was a little surprised. Vali didn't sound like I expected it to. I thought it'd be more tube-y, with the more typical euphonic colorations of an inexpensive tube design (rolled off highs, syrupy midrange, tubby bass—that kind of thing.) I had every reason to expect it to sound this way. The distortion profile suggested it. The single-supply output stage suggested it. The fact we were using (horrors!) coupling capacitors for the output suggested it.

But it didn't.

In fact, it sounded pretty neutral and transparent. Maybe even a little bright. And, it sounded pretty darn good. I sat there for a while and just listened, which is usually a very good sign.

But was I hearing reality? Or was I just full of it? That's always the designer's dilemma—being too close to something and losing perspective.

I gave it to Rina to have a listen. Her eyes widened. "Wow," she said. "When do I get one?"

I also gave it to Mike. He listened for, like, five seconds in the shop, then picked up the prototype and put it in his bag.

"Hey!" I cried. "That's the only one!"

"So build another," Mike said.

"I will, but…I was listening to it!"

"Don't be lazy," Mike said, and left the building with it.

A few days later, he called me. "How many of these tubes are there?"

"A metric buttload," I told him.

"Get them all. This is good. Really good."

That's what I'd thought, but it is good to have some confirmation. I contacted the eBay seller and cleaned up on the tubes.

Now, the only problem would be telling Alex he had to find more space—again—for the pallets of tubes that would be coming in. He was a lot more happy about it when I gave him a prototype Vali to play with.

And the early accolades kept coming. At a big head-fi meet, several of our golden-eared friends (including some who have given us, well, brutally honest feedback) proclaimed that it was better than 95% of the tube amps there. And people really flipped when we showed it at CanJam.

So, everyone's happy, right?

The Catch

Nope. Of course not. There's always a catch. And in Vali's case, the catch is directly related to those great-sounding tubes: tube microphonics.

What are tube microphonics? They're noise that's generated from tapping or jarring a tube. Some tubes are pretty non-microphonic (especially the 6N1P we use in Valhalla 2), and some are very microphonic (like the tubes we use in Vali.)

In the case of Vali, microphonics sound like a little "ting" sound that takes a long time to decay. It's like a delicate silver bell. It's actually a neat sound…

…that is, if it isn't interfering with your music.

And these tubes were microphonic enough to ring when you first turned the amp on, and when you plugged or unplugged headphones. We warned everyone about this, of course, but it wasn't enough. It turned out that some amps were microphonic enough to be set off by typing on a keyboard, or simply rang all the time.

So what did we do? We started doing an extended burn-in on the Valis, and checking them when they were still warm, to weed out the self-ringers and over-ringers. We also had input from a very helpful customer, who came up with one idea we hadn't thought of for reducing microphonics (specifically, damping the PC board itself, as well as using Sorbothane pads under the tubes.) Those two changes have brought down Vali failures to fractions of a percent.

So What Did We Learn?

Take time to play. Even if that play comes from seeing a pile of tubes, and wondering, "What can we do with these?"

CHAPTER 32

Name Me One Non-Standard Format That's Succeeded, Ever, Or, A Trickster Cometh

THE DSD SURGE STARTED IN 2013, shortly after the announcement of the DOP (DSD over PCM) USB protocol.

It began pretty innocuously. In early 2013, we started receiving a few emails asking if we were planning to add DSD decoding to our products. It was a literal handful to start, but as we got into spring, the inquiries started coming faster, as a number of companies introduced DSD-compatible DACs.

As the company's marketer, I wondered if this surge in inquiries would become a movement, so I asked Mike about the possibility of adding DSD to the existing Bifrost and Gungnir.

Mike groaned. "DSD. Argh. No." I waited for him to explain, but he didn't go any further.

"Why not?" I asked. I actually knew some of the technical reasons, but I wanted to hear it from Mike.

"DSD requires completely different filtering," Mike said. "It's essentially wideband noise. You want that going to your amps?"

I shook my head. Running ultrasonic noise into an amp is a good way to test it to destruction.

"So, we need way more aggressive filters to get the noise out," Mike said.

"But, technically, the AKM DACs do DSD, right?"

Mike shook his head. "Technically, yeah. But *doing DSD*, versus *doing it right*, are two different things. If we put in the DSD-appropriate filtering, we'd be compromising our analog stage performance for PCM. And it's not as simple as switching it in and out, because that would require more space on the analog board, and I don't even know if we have the hooks on the analog board input, anyway."

"So no DSD," I said.

"Not without a lot of changes. For Bifrost, we'd need a new USB input board, a new main board, and a new analog board. Technically, yeah, that's just upgrades—"

"—but it's essentially a whole new product," I finished for him. Mike nodded.

"So what if DSD gets big enough to matter?"

Mike laughed and waved a hand. "Remember HDCD?"

I nodded. HDCD was a technology of the early 90s that was supposed to be the One True Savior of digital, allowing more dynamic range to be encoded on special disks that could only be decoded by a specific digital filter.

"HDCD almost took down Theta," Mike said. "We got in screaming arguments about it. My marketing guy said the same thing you did: 'What if it gets big? Everyone else is doing it. We're going to lose sales if we don't have it.'"

"I didn't say those last two things," I told Mike.

"Yeah, but just asking about DSD implied it," Mike said. "You're worried that we'll lose sales, or we'll miss out."

I shook my head. Though Mike was right, in a sense. If DSD became big, we'd be vulnerable to other products that offered DSD playback.

"Stop worrying," Mike said. "Where did reel to reel go? Nowhere. Where did quadraphonic go? Nowhere. Where did Elcaset go? Nowhere. Where did DAT go? Nowhere. Where did minidisk go? Nowhere. Where did HDCD go? Nowhere. Where did SACD go? Pretty much nowhere. I expect DSD will pretty much go the same exact place."

"But what if it doesn't?"

Mike groaned. "These special formats all end up the same place, because there's no software for them. When there are more DSD downloads available than SACDs, let me know. Then I'll start worrying."

But the Inquiries Kept Coming

In fact, they intensified. As the press flogged the new shiny thing known as DSD, we began to get several inquiries a day—on slow days.

"Mike, we should do something about DSD," I told him, finally.

"Ignore it," he said. "It'll go away. It's just the press. They're so monumentally bored, they'll talk about anything, including a nonstarter like DSD."

"But what about, just, you know, as a CYA."

Mike sighed, and was silent for a long time. He knew we were getting inquiries. He knew some people really wanted DSD. And here he was, between his partner's paranoia and his experience with dozens of nonstandard formats that have come and gone.

"You want me and Dave to divert time from Yggdrasil to work on this?"

I crossed my arms. That was the ultimate threat—taking time away from a product that was literally the antithesis of DSD, and which we believed would help redefine the digital market in toto, to work on something that could be a passing fad.

Mike laughed. "You do."

"I just think it would be safer—"

"To do what everyone else is doing," Mike finished. "To jump off the cliff, just because everyone else is doing it."

"Can we really not afford to take a look at it?"

Mike looked thoughtful. "Okay. Fine. I'll think about it. That's all I'll say right now."

Mike's Thoughts

Time went on. DSD inquiries continued. I watched our sales cautiously, but they kept increasing for all the DACs—definitely not an indication that DSD was a gotta-have thing.

But the press kept flogging it, the articles kept coming out, and rumblings of lower-cost DSD DACs started to surface (prior to this, DSD DACs were all stooopidly expensive.)

Eventually, Mike came back to me, grinning like a fool.

"Okay. Here's what we do. We make the least-expensive DSD DAC on the market."

I blinked. "What?"

"If they want this format to succeed, they need wide adoption. And you ain't gonna get wide adoption for a grand and a half."

"So it replaces Modi?"

Mike shook his head. "No. It's a standalone DSD-only DAC. That's why, even though it's gonna be the cheapest DSD DAC out there, it's still going to sound insanely good. We'll do the filtering right. Just for DSD, and only for DSD."

"But what if you want to play both PCM and DSD?"

"If you're so into DSD, convert it on the fly," Mike sniped.

"Seriously."

Mike looked thoughtful. "Put a switch on it. Then you can run the output of your current PCM DAC through it."

I sat straight up. "So you can use it to add DSD capability to any DAC!" I cried.

Mike nodded, looking very pleased with himself. "Exactly."

I nodded. That was a perfect fit with Schiit's ethos. *Keep your existing DAC, add DSD, see if you like it, then go from there if you do.* Instead of throwing your existing DAC away to get a DSD-compatible one.

"How cheap are we talking?" I asked Mike.

Mike grinned. "Not much more than Modi."

Okay. Now this was getting good.

Tech Challenges

There were just a few problems with this plan—starting with the fact that we didn't have any DSD-capable USB receivers. The CM6631A we were using didn't accept DSD streaming or DSD over PCM. C-Media was planning a CM6632 for later in the year, which would be DSD-compatible, but late in the year was too late for our plans.

Enter Dave.

Dave's plan was simple, but somewhat insane: use a 32-bit Microchip microcontroller to do our own unpacking of the DSD-Over-PCM standard, and then send that along to the DAC. Yeah, quite a programming feat. But he did it, and soon we had a prototype that could play native DSD, using a Crystal Semiconductor DAC.

There was only one problem: it sounded like crap. Dynamically compressed, soft, boring, and lifeless. Yeah, I know, it measured fine, so it should sound fine, right? Not in this case.

"Why'd you do Crystal?" I asked Mike, one day when Mike, Dave, and I were together at the Schiithole.

"Crystal will do 2X DSD," Mike said.

"But the Microchip controller would have to be faster to unpack it," Dave said.

"So we can't do 2X DSD right now?"

Dave nodded. "But with a faster processor, we could."

"But not now," I confirmed.

"Right."

I frowned. "Why don't we just use AKM, then? We know they sound good."

Mike shook his head. "We have no idea what they sound like when they're fed DSD."

"Isn't it worth a shot?"

Mike and Dave looked at each other. Dave shrugged. Mike sighed.

And a few weeks later, we had another prototype—this one with an AKM DAC. And it sounded worlds better. It still measured pretty much the same, but it had a lot more life and energy. It had dynamics and pace. Both Mike and Dave smiled when they heard it.

"But AKM doesn't do 2X?" I asked.

Dave shrugged. "It might do it undocumented, but—"

"—but we don't know," Mike finished for him.

I sat silent. Should we wait to add 2X capability, for the literally twenty to thirty recordings that were out there done in 2X? It would mean another prototype cycle, and maybe different code, and maybe some unforeseen problems.

"And it would take different filtering," Mike said. "This is as good as it gets for 1X DSD. Throw 2X in there and we start having to make some different decisions."

Still, I sighed.

"Let me propose a solution," Mike said, as he usually does when I'm hesitant about something. "Let's bring this to market, see how it does, and if DSD really takes off, we can work on a 2X solution, or whatever we need."

I nodded. That made sense.

"Good." Mike said. "Though I doubt if we'll ever have to do any more work…"

Loki Cometh

We introduced Loki under the banner of "Add DSD to any DAC for $149." At the time, the least-expensive DSD-capable DAC was $849, so this was quite a coup.

Or so we thought. It turned out that the idea of a DSD-only DAC and switching system was a little more challenging than we thought. Some people thought we were converting DSD to PCM and running it to the main PCM DAC (why, when you can simply do it in software?). Some people thought we were taking the analog output of their DAC and converting it to DSD (fat chance on that one.) Some people really, genuinely wanted to throw out their old DAC, rather than run DSD through it.

And lots and lots of people didn't like having to run two USB cables (one to their main DAC, and one to Loki), and switch between the two on their playback software. For a main DAC fed by SPDIF, the switchover was easier (and seamless if they were using a different player, like a CD player, for their PCM content), but it still wasn't something that most people wanted to do.

That, combined with the appearance of new, inexpensive DSD / PCM DACs, quickly cooled Loki's sales. Mike will still argue that doing PCM and DSD in the same DAC is a compromise, and the math (and measurements) are on his side, but convenience usually wins out over sonics when you're playing at the lower end of the market.

Still, these wouldn't be insurmountable problems if we wanted to do, say, a Loki 2 with automatic interface switching. It could then interface seamlessly with a PCM DAC. But it would be significantly more expensive, especially if we added DSD 2X (or 4X, or 1000X, or whatever the latest unicorn format is today.)

And I suspect that's the way we'd end up going if we were to continue pursuing DSD—not adding it to our current DACs, but making a seamless, dedicated DSD DAC with interface switching.

But as of the time of this writing, I don't think it'll happen.

DSD Today

Today, Mike has crossed his arms and declared, "No more DSD development, unless something really big happens."

Why?

Because, from our point of view, it looks like we're past the peak. Despite dire pronouncements from other manufacturers saying, "You can't move a non-DSD DAC with a boxcar full of Ex-Lax," we haven't seen it. Cases in point:

- Sales of our DACs continue to increase—and to accelerate
- Inquiries at TheShow 2014 included literally two (that is, two) half-hearted questions about whether or not we were going to support DSD, in stark contrast to the literally 200 questions the year before
- Sony's presence at TheShow (featuring DSD prominently) was a ghost town
- Email inquiries have fallen from a dozen a day to maybe one or two per week
- The predicted "opening of the vaults of DSD" hasn't happened—there are still only a few hundred recordings available, many of which have questionable provenance

(more on that later—and even SuperHires's announcement about Warner probably won't answer even a tiny fraction of the questions on provenance, and prices remain TBD)

Sure, there are plenty of DSD-capable DACs out there, including some that do 4X and 8X DSD...but where's the software?

So What About the Future

Okay. Let's say the next Sony reorganization (they ain't exactly healthy these days) doesn't kill DSD, but results in them releasing 20,000 DSD recordings of popular artists, all with DSD-guaranteed-from-the-start provenance, for, say, $5.99 an album.

Would this result in a whole lot of DSD out there? You bet.

Would it be a game-changer? Absolutely.

Would it have us dusting off plans for a Loki 2, or working on ways to include DSD decoding in our DACs without compromise? Yeppers.

But I think that scenario is about as likely as the disembodied head of Steve Jobs giving the next Apple Keynote.

What's more likely is this:

- DSD recordings will continue to be a small part of the market
- DSD recordings that actually start as DSD, or were converted direct to DSD from master tapes, will be an even tinier part of the market
- High-rate DSD with the same provenance will be even smaller
- DSD recordings will continue to be very expensive
- Some people will continue to really like DSD, and will flip us off as they pass us at shows
- More people won't care, as long as the music sounds good and doesn't cost a fortune
- Even more people won't care if it's DSD, PCM, or compressed, as long as it's available to download at a good

price

- And the vast majority of people will never have any idea what the hell us crazy audiophiles are talking about, as they happily stream compressed music for a small monthly fee (or free)

- About ten years from now, a new quantum-based encoding format will come out so that everyone can buy their music again…

How about we deal with the elephant in the room—recording quality—before worrying about formats, hmm?

CHAPTER 33

No Sample Left Unchanged: Digital Today

OKAY. LET'S FOLLOW DIGITAL WITH more digital.

That's cool, though Mike is also doing his own "story of the Yggdrasil." This chapter was originally going to cover Yggy, but I'll let Mike do that now in detail.

Instead, let's talk business. As in, business cases, business philosophies...and, yeah, Digital Today (and yesterday).

Business Cases, Standards, Licensing, and Assorted Fun

Here's where we go back to being a business book. Because Yggdrasil is an interesting case that illuminates some of the problems that manufacturers have to deal with, in the arena of standards. With standards, you have a choice of "going along and getting along," or "forging your own way."

"Standards, what the hell are you talking about?" you might ask.

Okay, let's take an extreme case: surround sound processors, AV preamps, and AV receivers. Today, these types of gear are on the bleeding edge of standards compliance. A typical AV preamp today must:

- Decode all the Dolby surround standards
- Decode all the DTS surround standards
- Decode any other bizarre surround standards that are en vogue at the time
- Be compliant with the current, and changing, HDMI standard

- Probably also accept SPDIF and USB standard audio inputs
- Maybe accept Bluetooth audio standard
- Maybe accept Apple Airplay standard

"Well, who cares," you might scoff. "Meet the standards, and you're golden."

Yes. Except that the ongoing turf war between DTS and Dolby means that there's a bazillion surround standards out there. I've stopped counting, but I have been told that the standard test disk for surround modes is now up to 1200+ tracks. You run that disk, connect your system to an 8-channel Audio Precision, and cross your fingers. The surround standards guys will tell you if you failed. Then it's back to the drawing board if you did.

Plus, new standards pop up all the time. The new one is Dolby Atmos now. Oh, it's not Atmos compatible? Say bye-bye to sales. You don't control when the new standards appear, so you're always playing catch-up.

Same thing with HDMI. HDMI 2.0 is here. Kinda. Sorta. Well, not really. Because you can be compliant with one part of HDMI 2.0, but not another. And, by the way, 2.1 is coming. Will it work with your current system? Maybe, maybe not.

Same with Apple Airplay. First step to become an Apple hardware licensee is, literally, "Have your lawyers contact our lawyers." Being of the opinion that lawyers are kinda like raw plutonium—very useful in some specific applications, but not something you want to get near very often—you can see how we feel about this.

Same with Bluetooth. We're on Bluetooth 4.0, and it still can't do uncompressed audio. Want to bet on 5.0, and when it comes out?

Fun fact: the HDMI consortium has meetups called "Plugfests" so that manufacturers can see what they're compatible with, or not. Yes, even they don't fully know. It's up to you as a manufacturer to figure it out. You can't make this crap up.

And, to make all of the above even more fun, guess what? You get to pay some exceedingly non-trivial licensing fees for the privilege of putting those standards' logos on your box.

Bottom line, if you're going to be standards-compliant, you're always going to be at the whim of the standards-setters. You're not fully in control of your own destiny.

So why do they keep changing these surround-sound standards? Three reasons:

- To improve performance (higher bit rates and sample depths, more / optimized speaker placements, new algorithms, etc.)
- To increase revenue from the licensees' additional licensing costs.
- To drive a continuous upgrade cycle—buying newer gear to unlock new capabilities, upgrading cables for the latest HDMI standards, and re-buying content mastered to these standards.

If you were cynical, you could say that 2 and 3 combine to form a perfect "devil's bargain," where, if you keep spending on licensing, they'll continue changing the standards to keep your market coming back for the latest and greatest. Of course, that's a very cynical viewpoint. And, it only works for so long. When a true home theater enthusiast doesn't know what the latest Dolby Super HD Wowiematic Ultra Extra Fine And The Kitchen Sink standard is (and doesn't care), the whole thing comes crashing down.

So, why do I bring up these "standards?"

One, as a thought experiment. Imagine a surround processor that didn't have any Dolby Digital or DTS logos on it, running its own non-standards-compliant decoding algorithms...and sounded good with most surround-encoded materials. Is this something that would sell? It's an unknown, because nobody has done it yet, probably due to the threat of possible infringement suits from

Dolby and DTS (and maybe HDMI, if you don't pay their license fees as well.)

Before you start the heavy breathing, we are not working on this. It is simply a thought experiment. Would potential buyers be OK with a product that didn't have 73 logos on the front of it, and the comfort of the Dolby and DTS stamp of approval? I don't know. But it's fun to think about.

The second reason is more pointed. In audio, we have few standards, and virtually none of them are licensed. USB Audio Class 1 and 2 are standards, SPDIF is a standard, PCM is a standard, and DSD is a standard. Okay, you can also throw in fringe stuff like I2S over HDMI, as long as you're OK with paying the HDMI licensing fee...but then you're getting into licensing...and technically, Plugfests. Shudder.

So, in audio, why would you change standards?

#2 from the surround example is out (to increase licensee revenue), but seeking to improve performance, and to drive upgrade cycles, are both relevant. We don't get many new standards in audio, so the excitement around something new and shiny is much higher than it is in surround.

So, let's do another thought experiment.

Let's say DSD wins as the next audio standard—it's recognized as a significant upgrade from PCM, and it is embraced by enough users that every manufacturer has to support it, and support it well. What happens?

- Recording studios have to convert to DSD workflows. Manufacturers of pro gear celebrate.
- Every listener must go out and buy a new DAC. Manufacturers of consumer gear rejoice.
- Every listener must go out and buy new DSD recordings. The record industry throws a huge party.

On the other hand, let's say DSD fades away, and PCM continues as the reigning audio standard. What happens?

- Recording studios continue to do what they do. No impact on manufacturers.
- Listeners don't have to buy new DACs. No impact on manufacturers.
- Listeners don't have to buy any new recordings. Big sad face for the recording industry.

Something to think about, hmm?

Digital Yesterday: Steady Progression

When digital audio was new, you could pretty much chart the steady, linear progression of the technology for about a decade. From the first 14-bit multiplexed non-oversampling DACs in CD players in 1982, to the fully realized, 8x oversampling, 20 bit ladder DACs in the top DACs of the early 90s, there was clear and steady progress:

- 14 bit multiplexed D/A converters in CD players, no oversampling, brickwall filtering
- The first 16 bit converters, still with no oversampling and brickwalled
- 16 bit converters with 4x oversampling, to eliminate the brickwall filter
- Standalone DACs with 18 bit converters and 4x/8x upsampling
- Standalone DACs with custom DSP filtering, 20 bit converters and 8x upsampling

And, along the way, you could chart the course in measurements. D/A converters got more linear, less noisy, and achieved higher performance by every measure. New versions of the old products performed better, because the multibit technology behind them was improving. Publications like Stereophile started measuring jitter, which raised awareness of its importance and led to jitter numbers steadily decreasing.

The result? By the early 1990s, it was possible to get 19+ bits of linearity out of multibit converters—a huge leap forward from the 13 or so bits of early CD players.

Progress wasn't only made on the playback side, either. Mobile Fidelity contracted Mike Moffat (yes, our Mike Moffat) and Nelson Pass to create their GAIN system, an insane recording chain with a real 16-bit oven-controlled multibit DAC that output linear PCM with no missing codes up to 500kHz rates. This multi-chassis product took up almost a full equipment rack…but it was what was necessary to do good 16-bit ladder analog to digital conversion. Arguably, it still is.

Now, of course, there was only one problem with all of this progress: price.

Check the historic price of a PCM63 D/A converter, and you'll quickly realize that it's something that will never appear in an iPhone (nor would it fit.)

So, what to do? D/A chip manufacturers came to the rescue with products based on 1-bit sigma-delta modulation. These products were less expensive, easier to use, and more highly integrated. And they measured pretty well.

Another leap forward? In one way, yes. Without sigma-delta D/A converters, we wouldn't have the wide range of DACs and ADCs we have today. Your smartphone has a DAC in it with specs we would have killed for in 1990. The analog to digital converter inside it may even output 24 bit samples, at higher sample rates than we would have ever imagined.

And we can't underemphasize the impact of sigma-delta technology. It has allowed us to create more DACs (and ADCs) more inexpensively, with higher performance than we would have guessed, 20 years ago.

But we did lose something in all of this progress.

Digital Today: The Lost Decades

Today, it's largely a sigma-delta world.

- **Recording.** Most recording studios use analog to digital converters that employ A/D chips that use an intermediary multibit sigma-delta format before their PCM output. Note that this isn't DSD. And note that even sigma-delta can have shades—single bit, multibit, etc.

- **Mixing.** From there, the PCM output is mixed / mastered in PCM (pretty much all mixing and mastering is in PCM...yes, even recordings that end up as DSD.)

- **Playback.** From there, it's typically going to be compressed and downloaded or streamed to a player using a multibit sigma-delta D/A converter.

Or, in the case of some crazy audiophiles like us, it's stored uncompressed, maybe even in high-res, before going to a DAC with a fancy multibit sigma-delta D/A converter.

Or, in a literal handful of cases, it might go to a true multibit R-2R converter, just like the old days. But that's a fraction of a fraction of a percent.

"So, who cares what it is, I just want good sound!" you say.

And we agree! We're far too wrapped up in formats. Take that format-proselytizing energy and aim it at the studios. Lobby them to produce better recordings. That will produce greater benefit than any format "regime change."

But...here's the deal (and here's where we get philosophical.) In today's sigma-delta world, we've lost something that *we* consider important: the original samples.

They're destroyed by upsampling, they are destroyed by asynchronous sample rate conversion, they're destroyed by sigma-delta D/A ICs. What you hear is an interpretation, a *guess,* at what the original content was (they don't call them successive-*approximation* converters for nothing.)

"But this can't possibly matter, it's hard to measure the distortion of your typical ASRC, for example," some will say.

Hard to measure doesn't mean *it isn't there*, we say.

Bottom line, it's a mathematical fact that samples that have passed through a digital filter, an asynchronous sample rate converter, or a sigma-delta modulator *are not retained.* There is no closed-form solution to the math.

"And why should that matter to me?" you ask.

Maybe it doesn't. Maybe the approximation is good enough.

But maybe it isn't.

And this is where we get to the core of what Yggdrasil is about: *what if we haven't been hearing everything PCM is capable of, because we've been hearing it on delta-sigma technology that throws away the original samples?*

Yeah. We know. We're crazy.

And perhaps we are. Perhaps it will make no difference at all. Perhaps it won't be important to anyone other than us. But the fact is: we have a solution to retain the reproduce the original samples, without the drawbacks of a non-oversampling design. It is in Yggdrasil. And we'll see what you think, very, very soon.

And that is the absolute core of our digital philosophy: retaining the original samples, all the way through to the output.

"But, It Doesn't Matter, Because..."

Because this position, this philosophy, is so counter to the currently accepted wisdom, I've prepared a quick discussion of possible objections to it, for your convenience.

"It doesn't matter anyway, because everything comes from a delta-sigma ADC these days. Do you have any original bits at all?"

Actually, this isn't entirely accurate. There are still multibit ADCs out there, though they are probably thin on the ground. There are also plenty of recordings made with multibit ADCs, including Mike's GAIN system. They don't disappear when new technology appears. And, you know what? Instead of being fatalistic and negative, we'd like to consider the best-case scenario: that we actually push PCM's capabilities forward to the point where new multibit ADCs appear.

"But how can those old DACs possibly perform better than the best of today? They're only 20/48. We have 32/768."

Going from 16/44 to 20/44 actually makes more difference than anything else, when it comes to digital. Why? Although the Nyquist theorem says you can perfectly reconstruct a waveform from digital with 2X the sample rate, it assumes an infinite-bit ADC with no quantization error. The more levels, the less the quantization error. 16 bit = 65536 levels, 20 bit = 1048576 levels. 24 bits is 16 million+ levels, but nobody has ever achieved 24 bit linearity, period. The best DACs are about 19.5-20 bits, even after 20 years of "progress." (Hence, "the lost decades.") Higher sample rates are nice for analog filtering, but limit the amount of horsepower a digital filter can bring to bear...and it takes up more storage space. So that's a tradeoff. And "32 bit?" LOLOLROFLCOPTER. There will never be any 32 bit music. Because physics.

"It doesn't matter anyway, I'll buy whatever sounds best."

Yep, absolutely. That's what everyone should do. No argument there. Have a listen, and decide for yourself.

"But I really like the sound of DSD, I want it to win."

That's totally cool as well. Just don't make it out to be anything "magic." It is simply different. As is analog. Which can be very, very good as well. Treat us like the crazy uncle who's a little touched in the head, and continue enjoying your DSD. After all, even if it "loses" as a format, it's not like the files will disappear.

The Summation

Here's what we propose: let's see what we can do with the huge amount of music we have in PCM format.

Can we make it better by retaining the original samples? Can we get out of the performance we've been in the past 20 years? Can we bring this technology down to lower price levels? Can we change the future by picking up where multibit left off, 20 years ago?

Maybe. Maybe not.

We'll see...

CHAPTER 34

Black Friday

THERE'S BEEN A LOT OF technology and philosophy in the chapters above, and that's fine, because in a tech company, there's gonna be a lot of tech, and in any company, there should be a defined philosophy (or mission, or whatever other corporatese you'd like to call it) to define *why* the company does something, because otherwise you'll just be a reactionary company, and that usually doesn't work out to well. Companies without focus, who respond by trying to please everyone, will usually find that they end up pleasing nobody.

So, this chapter is about choices. Let's start with the title subject, specifically two business choices centered around the new American "tradition" of Black Friday.

Setting the Scene

Okay, at the time of these choices, it's October-November 2013. We're still in the Schiithole, but we won't be there for long (that's the next chapter.) Vali is getting ready to launch. We're deep into Ragnarok, and beginning to realize that it will be a lot more difficult than we first thought, after a not-stellar showing of a rough prototype at Rocky Mountain Audio Fest. Yggdrasil is still going through questions about D/A architecture, and we're beginning to realize that there may be some deeper questions we have to answer before we get that product into prototype form. At the same time, several other products are in the hopper.

It's a busy, even somewhat insane time, and it's the first time that Alex decided to load up on ordering for the holidays, so we'd be able to avoid the Schiit "completely out of stock before the end of the year" syndrome. Alex threw away our predicted numbers and ordered what he thought would truly reflect sales—and, in the end, he was very close to keeping us in stock on everything.

The Schiithole, at this time, is insanely overstuffed. We'd brought in a container so we could store a lot of packaging and other bulky stuff outside in the beautiful patio area, but one container only went so far. Metal, packaging, boards, and finished products were stacked to the rafters, and more was coming in.

And, in the middle of all of this, we got a shipment of Valhalla, Lyr, and Bifrost chassis. Cool.

Except they're painted black, not brushed clear-anodized aluminum.

Black Schiit?

So what were we going to do with a whole bunch of black chassis—especially since we'd always told prospective customers, "Nope, only available in silver?"

So what do we do?

"Sell 'em," Alex said. "They look good."

And they did. The black powder was very nice—completely unlike what you'd expect to see on a painted product. It wasn't grained and anodized, but it had a very finely pebbled and consistent texture that looked nice.

"And charge more," Tony quipped.

I groaned. "And then what happens when we have to stock black and silver forever, into infinity?" I asked Alex.

"Make it clear it's just a one-time special," he told me.

"If that works," I said. Visions of Theta, where everyone ordered silver when we had black in stock, or vice versa, came back to me.

"I don't want to stock it as an ongoing thing, either," Alex said. "But we have it. Why not sell it? The guys who have been asking for black will be thrilled."

Alex was right. We should just sell it and go from there. It would make some people very happy. *And*, I thought, *it'll give us a better idea of what demand is like for black products.*

Which is how, in mid-November 2013, I ended up announcing a limited run of black Schiit products on Head-Fi.org.

And We Waited

When I made the announcement, I also made it clear that this was a limited run, and when they were gone, they were gone. For all the emails we'd gotten asking for black products, I thought I'd have to sit over the website admin, ready to turn off ordering in very short order.

And I waited.

And waited some more.

A few orders trickled in. But not the anticipated flood. I went on Head-Fi to answer a few questions about whether the black products were going to be an ongoing thing, and made it clear that, with the current response, they certainly weren't going to be.

A few more orders trickled in. But again, no gigantic wave.

I was really surprised. For all the emails we'd gotten, the insistence that black was "make or break," the people who'd actually taken our products and anodized them black themselves, sales were slow.

How slow? It easily took three times longer than our normal sales cycle to sell out a very limited run of black products. Now, this isn't to say that some customers weren't delighted with their black products. And I'm thrilled we were able to make them happy.

But, in the end, the noise around "gotta have black" eclipsed the reality of the demand. And that's a learning experience (AKA, "you got boned, remember not to do this again".)

And that lesson, I think, is one of the most important ones for any company, start-up or not: *the clamor doesn't always equal the demand.*

Why is this? Well, I think for stuff that's mainly cosmetic, the reality is that if you have a great product at a great price, people are going to buy it anyway. If you like, say, Jura espresso machines, you may want one with the red side panels, but if it's only available in black, that probably won't break the order. Or vice versa.

Same thing goes for stuff that is very niche. Niche features or functionality can evoke a lot of passion—and, while that passion may translate into many emails, it may not translate into sales.

If we had simply said, "Yes," to all the requests we get (or tried to accommodate them), it's quite possible that, say, Lyr 2 would be:

- A DAC/amp rather than an amp
- Available with an external power supply that costs more
- A balanced amp as well, and have balanced inputs too
- Available with several tube options, some costing +$300 over the stock ones
- Capable of all kinds of data rates that you can't buy content for
- Orderable with fancy power cords and fuses
- Delivered in at least two functional levels, one more expensive than the "standard"
- Available in at least four colors

It would also:

- Cost a lot more
- Make the possibility of shipping screw-ups much higher (oh, you wanted black / uber / power supply / etc.)
- Be much more difficult to service (need to maintain docs for all variations)
- Be more confusing to buy, possibly leading to paralysis by analysis

And so on.

So, after our brief black experiment, we made another choice: that we weren't going to add black to the line as a standard option. Nor would we speculate on whether or not we'd have black again.

Now, this doesn't mean we won't have it again in the future (black, we realized, is a great way to refinish chassis that cannot be re-grained). But, as before, we won't speculate when it may be.

So, What's This Got To Do With Black Friday?

Well, other than the fact that the black chassis were introduced shortly before Black Friday, it's all about choices. Yes, more choices.

Many companies, both retailers and manufacturers, choose to participate in Black Friday through special deals that start the day after Thanksgiving. Some do a lot more than participate—they actively flog the upcoming deals and whip people up into a buying frenzy so people can ruin a good chunk of the spare time they might otherwise be spending with their family, or simply dozing in a good turkey coma.

Of course, this is US-centric, and perhaps other countries around the world don't have this yearly buying orgy. If so, you're fortunate.

Because it wasn't always like this. The stampeding, deal-crazed, sometimes murderous customers-trampling-customers thing is really recent. As in, last decade recent. And each year, it seems to get whipped up more and more.

Why? I suppose the theory is that "if ya ain't got customers right away, y'aint gonna do well this season." Or something like that, translated into corp-speak.

The real reason why? Because companies *choose* to participate.

That's a choice.

Companies (like Schiit) can also choose not to participate. And we don't. But one company did us even better in 2013. And because of this, they have my ultimate respect.

What company? Cards Against Humanity. Instead of offering discounts, or remaining neutral, they actually *raised prices* on Black Friday.

Nicely done.

Sometimes the hardest thing to do in business is to not just opt out, but stand against a trend. Kudos to them. It's a choice—a powerful choice.

So what am I going to do this Black Friday? I don't know. Turning off ordering is tempting, but I'm thinking of simply doing a banner like this:

Really? Shopping today?
How about spending some time with the people you care about?
After all, the prices will be the same tomorrow.

Coda: More Choices

It's funny. I just came back from Rocky Mountain Audio Fest. It was a great show. But I'm simple. Any show is a good show when we remembered to get our hotel rooms, ship all the right products, and our products performed as expected and no smoke came out of the latest prototypes we were showing.

But it was a great show, because I noticed a trend with some of the visitors who stopped by our booth. Over and over, I heard, "Wow, there are actually prices in the brochure," and "Wow, this is actually affordable!"

And, during the course of the show, we had some pretty big-time visitors, including a prominent audio technology blogger, a very big-name audio design engineer, and a high-level TI engineer, amongst others. The audio design engineer and the TI engineer seemed very taken with my straight answers on our products, how we achieved the performance levels we did, and the overall look, feel, and construction. That was part of a trend where I noticed that the people closest to the design and manufacturing side were most impressed—from product design and engineering to the DIY community.

"How do you do this…for this price?" they asked.

"Well, we're simple," I explained. "We don't do fancy chassis, because that would dominate the cost." I showed them how we do all the punching, machining, and finish work, then fold the metal.

They nodded, understanding.

"And we don't have a dealer network, because we're not living in the 1980s anymore," I said. "As soon as you choose distribution, prices will—"

"Double!" one of them finished for me.

"Or more," his friend added.

"And we don't have to advertise very much, because the value is clear," I said. "If we were doing a bunch of products that were very similar to other stuff at the same price point, we'd have to do a lot more advertising."

"Or you could just make mega-price gear," the friend said. "Though that's getting crowded as well."

"And then we'd have to deal with the audiophile nervosa," I said. "We're not really set up to convince people to buy our stuff. I need to do a shirt that says, 'Schiit sales department org chart' on it, with an empty box below."

They laughed. "Yeah, upstairs is about $130,000 turntables with no arms, $30,000 players that are computers in billet chassis, and $50,000 amplifiers that would have cost $3K a couple of decades ago," the first opined.

"That's a choice," I said. "They chose beauty, fine finish, and distribution. We're a lot more functional."

They laughed. "And that's why everyone's down here in this room!"

We talked for a while longer, they had a listen to Ragnarok and Yggdrasil, and listened to Mike Moffat say, well, whatever he says at shows (sometimes I don't want to know.)

And in the end, they nodded and grinned, clearly understanding.

"Good choices," they said.

CHAPTER 35

You Want to Pay How Much?
Or, How We Moved Again

THIS IS PROBABLY HOW A "real" company decides to move their operations:

- Based on future plans and internal feedback, decides they need to have more space / less space / different space / different location (more tax favorable, etc.).
- Gets input from key management on the kind of space they need.
- Surveys the available space in their target area with the help of an industrial lessor / realtor.
- Weighs the options available and decides on one.
- Plans well in advance for the business disruption of a move.
- Has any buildout done, and a floor schematic ready, at the new office before the move commences.
- Moves in to the new built-out, planned office space with minimum fuss and muss.

Here's how we moved, late in 2013:

- The landlord came to us and said, "Hey, we have someone who wants to buy the building you're in. Can you move?"
- I laughed and said, "Sure, have them pay us a year's rent for the business disruption," expecting them to laugh in return.
- Unexpectedly, they paid, and we moved. Total time elapsed:

about two months.

Yeah. There you go. We don't do anything by the book.

Except there's more to the story than that, which I'll get into. But I want to riff on trusting your employees, rewarding them well, and thereby ending up with a highly motivated, self-policing team. Which plays into the move as well.

Condensed Employee Advice

Okay, you can take any number of shill courses on how best to motivate your employees—the bottom line of most being that "they want to be recognized and appreciated, more than just paid well."

This is 100% total bullschiit.

Exactly two things motivate high-performing people:

- Money
- Freedom

That's it. If you meet someone who really, truly believes their "employee of the month" cake is a big deal, or who thinks the free soft drinks are a sign that the company really loves you, or who's a head cheerleader at the company's monthly corporate pride rallies, or who says, "whatever they want to pay me is okay with me," do this: *run*. Fast. This is not a person you want in a high-functioning company.

High-performing people know they're good. They expect to be paid well. Period.

High-performing people also value freedom, such as flexible work hours. Sometimes this can be traded off against overall salary.

This tradeoff works very well in the agency world. Many creative directors would be happy with, say 75% of a top salary and truly flexible hours (work from home four days, come in one day, for example), rather than a top salary and the twelve-hour / seven-day grind of a typical agency.

This tradeoff works less well in a business that has to run during typical business hours, but, truth be told, there are no expected times of arrival or number of hours per day for anyone at Schiit. Our assembly team usually works nights, because they want to. Alex and tech usually work during the day, because they're motivated to. And not vampires. Unlike our assemblers, who I sometimes wonder about.

So, how do you pay good salaries when you're just starting up and money is tight? Great question. Tricky answers too. Because the first temptation usually is to give away a percentage of the business. Which is exactly the worst thing you can do.

"What?" some of you are yelling now. "Why wouldn't I show my trust in who I bring on by making them a partner? That way, both rewards and risks are shared."

It also makes running the business much more complicated. Co-owners may be on a high for a while—until they find out the business isn't going to do as well as they thought, and their portion of the profits is small...or nonexistent. Co-owners also may share with each other their percentage...and it's gonna be a bad day if the guy who got 2.5% thinks he's more important than the lady who got 5%. And when the majority owner (or owners) have to outvote the minority owners on something, buckle up for a significant productivity hit...or even discord that could end up with partners exiting.

And when they exit, remember, you have to buy back their shares—either per your buy-sell agreement (you have this, right?) or by some kind of entrail-reading known as "professional business valuation." Oh hey, the partner doesn't agree with your valuator's figures? Buckle down for a lawyer orgy, featuring painful forensic accounting, and "expert witness" tea-leaf prognostication of the company's future value.

Bottom line: you'll both pay lawyers, you'll both lose, the lawyers have a party.

And I haven't even gotten into the tax ramifications of giving away shares. It's complex, painful, not pretty...and can be costly, for both you and the awardee.

And yes, having an agency for twenty years, and making this

give-away-the-farm mistake more than once…it is, as they say, a "learning experience."

Effective Motivation—Without Giving Away the Farm

Okay, so how do you create a high-functioning team without giving away parts of the company?

First, by realizing the extreme worth and intelligence of a motivated, engaged person. Don't minimize their worth, and don't insult their intelligence. If you don't literally want to create everything by hand, yourself, you *need* great people.

Repeat after me:

- Don't minimize their worth
- Don't insult their intelligence

Now, say it again.

I had a boss in a former life who loved to do #1: go around saying, "Nobody is irreplaceable!" Usually after I offered an unpopular opinion or asked for more money. I had a business partner on the agency side who loved to do #2: "We're doing this for you, we all have to make sacrifices."

Riiiiigghhhhttt.

"Anyone can be replaced," should be amended to "Anyone can be replaced, but there are people worth keeping, and be very, very scared of who might come after."

"We're doing this for you, we all have to make sacrifices," should just be banned from ever being said. Any person with more than a few active neurons knows you're doing it for the company, and that people who are laid off are making a much bigger sacrifice than you are. Just say it like it is, do what needs to be done, and treat everyone like an adult, not a child.

So what do you do?

- **Tell the truth and keep your promises.** Okay, you're just getting started. You can't pay someone what they're worth on the open market. But if they believe in your company and its potential, they may start for less and bet on the promise of future rewards. But let them know exactly how it is, and set some dates and measurements on when they can begin seeing the rewards. If you don't meet goals, let them know, and don't sugarcoat it. But, always, always, always keep your promises. Because it's gonna get really ugly if you forget about them and buy a new Mercedes first. Remember: good people aren't dumb.

- **Provide personal motivation.** And by "motivation," I mean *money*. This is the better way. Start with a livable salary, and add bonuses that are based on visible personal or company metrics. Number of products shipped. Number of products built. A bonus on experimenting with and getting the company into a new channel. Royalties for products developed on the side. Stuff that can be translated into dollars, without having to reconcile profit, and without having to resort to nebulous proclamations like, "If we're doing well." This is really the best way to do things—and it is the best way to get your company running at a five to ten times productivity advantage, relative to the "norm."

Schiit has done both of the above. The result? A recent meeting with the city economic development manager revealed our sales, etc. (we're going for becoming a duty-free export zone). He said, "Oh, you must have about forty to fifty employees, then."

"We have six," I told him.

The guy nearly fell on the floor. "How do you do it?"

I told him (pretty much the same as above.) He shook his head. "That would never work in most companies."

I disagreed. It has worked everywhere I've applied it, without exception. The key is getting smart, motivated people to start with. And that, as I've explained in previous chapters, is less of a "checking off things on a resume" thing, and more of a "gut reaction" thing. Every time I've ignored my gut, I've screwed myself.

So, how weird are we, besides breaking the productivity / employee ratio really badly? Let's look at two other figures.

- **We *don't have a sales department* at all** (something I realized when writing last week's chapter.) There's not one single "salesperson" here. Nobody to pimp us out to dealers or distributors, either. Nor anyone on contract.

- **We spend only about *0.2% of our revenue on marketing.*** That's ten times less than the smallest figure advised for start-ups, and fifty times less than what's considered "typical" for a sustaining company.

So much for us being "just a marketing and sales company."

Bottom line: your people matter, *and* your customers matter. Treat them both right. Don't insult their intelligence, and know their value. Do that (for real), and you don't have to do the normal BS babysitting / micromanaging / spoon-feeding / infighting / sales / shilling / promo / hype thing.

And, I think, your life will be a lot more sane.

So, On This Move Thing?

Why is the above employee motivational blather important? Well, beyond the productivity advantage outlined above, it also made for a smooth, uneventful transition into the new space. Because Mike and I don't have to babysit anyone, we were involved at only two points:

- Looking at the available space (with Alex)
- Showing up when the move was complete

That's it. Fully empowered employees take care of everything else—including finding and booking the movers, packing things up, unpacking and getting set back up, arranging things once we were there, buying things we didn't have, etc.

And...they were ready to move. The place was packed and

overflowing. We wouldn't have been there much longer if there'd been no buyer. It just moved up the timeline about three months.

Looking at the space was fun. We were in the market for, as I told our real estate guy, "Something 3000 to 5000 square feet," which would give us one and a half to two and a half times as much space as the old place. I expected to see a long list of candidates, since Valencia Industrial Center is the largest industrial development in Southern California, and 3K to 5K is above the starter spaces and below the 20K-100K foot boxes.

And the list was pretty long…until we got to particulars.

The one particular that broke the back of most of the candidates was "air conditioned throughout." Most industrial spaces have AC only in the office section, while the warehouse remains uncooled (and, in some cases, unheated.) This is less than great in 110 degree summer days.

So our list of about forty candidate spaces was reduced a bit. And by, "A bit," I mean, it went down to two.

Yes, two.

Both spaces were in the same building, and right next to each other. I went through both of them with Alex and the realtor. One was just over 3000 square feet, one was about 5300. The 3000 SF space looked pretty much like the ideal place for us, except for one thing: a lot of these concrete tilt-up boxes have office built out in two levels up front, so you have upstairs and downstairs offices. Upstairs is useless to us (imagine carting products up and down stairs all day.) So, the 3K space really didn't net us as big an increase in usable floor area as it seemed.

The 5.3K space? It looked stupidly huge. I mean, ridiculously, cavernously huge. Bigger than Theta was at its peak. Bigger than Sumo. (Though not bigger than Centric during the dot com boom, which was in a converted 7200 SF industrial building. How I wish we'd have stayed there.)

But 5.3K? That was silly. Even with the office buildout upstairs, there was no way we'd ever use all that space. I mean, really, we were a small manufacturer, right?

But it definitely had the floor area we needed, and more. It also had a glassed-off area that would be perfect for tech.

So, after another visit with Mike, we made them a lowball offer, and got it.

And yeah, I've said before that you shouldn't haggle, etc., but this was more in line with bringing the price down to reality. It's a 1980s building, not super well-kept, and the landlords were loathe to do anything at all to it—not even the usual new-paint-and-carpet deal you get when you sign a lease. So I said, "We'll take it, no tenant improvement, at this rate."

They jumped on it, and the rest was history.

The actual move took place as Mike and I were at RMAF 2013. We left for CanJam, and came back to a different building.

And that's when the reality started setting in. This "huge" space turned out not to be so huge at all. With all the stuff we'd packed into the old building on the floor, there was a lot less space than I thought. It wasn't disturbing, as in "having to look at moving immediately" disturbing, but we definitely didn't have as much space to grow as I'd expected.

So what to do? Alex suggested racking the place out, so we could stack chassis and packaging up three levels high. Shortly before the end of the year, that's exactly what we did—and that's when we started to look like a real company.

And what would we do with all of that space upstairs? Sure, I could take an office up there, but Mike hated the heat, and didn't want one. The bullpen area would be essentially useless as a listening room.

Rina came to our rescue. Her own business, Twilight's Fancy, was growing too big for our house (now, we can claim two businesses launched there—one in a garage, and one in a spare bedroom...).

"I'll take the upstairs," she said. "I'll sublease from you."

"How much of it?" I asked, remembering the adage that "a turtle always grows to the size of its tank."

"As much as you'll let me have."

Hmm. That saying really had me sweating now. Rina's business is space-intensive, and she is, ah, well, apt to, um, disarray. And piles.

"Let me think about it."

After some discussion, we came to an agreement where she took one of the upstairs offices, and much of the bullpen. So now we share our building with a seller of jewelry findings and ribbon chokers. Makes perfect sense, in a way.

What We Didn't Do

Our new home, or "The Schiitbox," as we call it (appropriate for a concrete tilt-up) was big, but it wasn't opulent. The upstairs is carpeted with somewhat-worn, medium-blue industrial carpet that may have been the cat's pajamas in the early 1990s. The downstairs is pure concrete floor, concrete walls, and sheetrock. The windows don't open, there are no balconies, walls are painted utilitarian white.

In the peak agency days, this wouldn't have stood. We would have ripped out walls, done new carpets, gotten rid of the drop ceilings, bought new desks, and generally gone on a remodeling spree to make it something we could be proud of.

At Schiit, we did none of that. The same ugly carpet, concrete walls, and white paint remain. We did put up some pictures, but that's about it. Alex's "office" is a desk downstairs by the side door (we don't use the front door, that's Mike's office now.) We pulled the brand-new, nice carpet out of the tech area so it wouldn't be a static threat, and left the bare concrete with glue marks.

We did, however, finally buy a full-sized refrigerator.

And racks. And desks. And more racks, as we expanded. And more test equipment. And shipping tables.

Why the focus on utility? Because we're not a listening room, a lounge, or anywhere you would want to hang out (well, unless you're super-geeky.)

And...because, when you have smart, engaged, motivated employees, it doesn't really matter. They think it's funny. They're thrilled to help us grow. And growth doesn't come from Hermann Miller chairs and Steelcase desks and faux-finish paint and $600 LED lamps.

It comes from, as Mike said, *Giving a schiit.*

Coda: *We recently took the space next to ours, bringing us up to about 8300 square feet. The landlord was as cheap as ever. The carpet is as ugly as it's always been. We needed the space for the Ragnarok / Yggdrasil lines, and some other future plans...*

CHAPTER 36

A Real Company?

SO HERE WE ARE IN December 2013: in the Schiitbox, busy racking the place out, and looking upon a company that was no longer a scrappy garage start-up, but well and truly *real*.

We were also supposed to be looking from a point of view of having been shipping Ragnaroks for eight to nine months and Yggys for five to six months, and you all know how that worked out.

(Cue evil, polite, or disgusted laughter, depending on your own POV.)

Let's look at December 2013, and take a look at just how well we did on the "real company" front.

By Our Own Rules

When I started this whole thing, I tried to condense down the business rules up front for people who just want to cut to the chase. These were:

- Shooting to be the next billion-dollar mass-market company is insane—you might as well buy lottery tickets.

- Niche is where it's at—specifically a niche where people can get in fistfights over the color of a knob.

- Pick a niche you know and love and do something nobody else can do—"me-too" never works.

- Be memorable—this isn't about getting *everyone* to *like* you, this is about getting *some* people to *love* you.

- Go direct—distribution is a poisonous remnant of 19th century economics in a disintermediated world.

- Run from both conventional marketing wisdom and the social media mavens—both of them are geared towards the mass market with eight-digit ad budgets and multiple decades to build a brand.

- Don't think this'll be easy—this is hard work, but you'll also be having a whole lot of fun if you're doing it right!

So, how did we do?

- **Not being the next billion-dollar business.** Yep. Check. Schiit will likely hit eight figures sooner than later, but ten is really, really beyond the pale. If someone gave us $100 million of VC to come out with the broad range of products needed to get there, I think I'd rather leave than continue. Because, to hit that kind of revenue, you're looking at $99 headphones and $79 Bluetooth speakers and $199 soundbars and $149 powered speakers with Class D amps…true mass products. And don't dare think about trying to take a creative approach with something—the path to success would be in low-dollar, high-volume products that are absolutely guaranteed to find buyers. Which means you want them in established product categories. Which means no swinging for the fences, no trying to break the mold…and, in turn, that means that we'd more than likely fail. Billion-dollar audio companies got there either through decades of product development and marketing (and a bit of luck)—think Bose and Harman—or through 100% sheer luck, by creating a new product category—think Beats, though they never cracked more than $0.5B a year in sales. The Apple acquisition is what sent them over the top.

- **Niche is where it's at, and fistfights.** Yep, check. We are a dominant player in a niche market (what they're now calling "personal audio.") We also play in the larger two-channel realm, mainly with DACs, and now with Mani and some other products. But we're definitely a niche—and a niche so narrow that it's smaller than the audiophile market as a whole. We're not trying to be another Bryston. And fistfights? Yep. All the action is in personal audio. Traditional two-channel audio has the "Buick disease." It's moribund, almost literally. Over seventy, you lose 10% of your customers a year. Over sixty, 5%. That's basic actuarial table stuff. And you can't make up for the loss by increasing your product costs forever. Eventually, the last 200 people who think a $120,000 DAC is a good idea will die off, and you're done.

- **A niche you love, doing unique, non-"me-too" products.** Check again. I got back into this because I've always loved music, and I found a new and exciting way to express it in the headphone space. It was everything that two-channel wasn't. Mike, who'd checked out at the end of the golden era of multibit DACs, felt exactly the same way. This isn't a field you can get into based on spreadsheets and margins and feature analysis. This is something you have to love. And unique? Yes. We have a unique place—not the cheapest made-in-China gear, and not the eye-wateringly expensive audio jewelry stuff, either. With unique topologies, unique value, unique sound. It's a great place to be, because I don't think everything should be about price, nor should everything be about bling. I think we've struck a good balance. Others disagree. See below.

- **Be memorable, it's about some people loving you, not everyone liking you.** Check, check, check. There are some people who have literally bought everything we make, and think we can do no (or very little) wrong. There are people who go out of their way to help us. And, at the same time, there are some people who dislike, or actively hate us. Dislike because of the name, dislike because of some perceived slight, dislike because they got a dead product (hey, it happens), irritation because we stood up for our policies, hate because of some imagined agenda pushing crappy products on an unsuspecting public, dislike because we don't toe the line to being 100% subjectivist, distaste because we don't toe the line to being 100% objectivist, irritation because we skewer some sacred cows, hate because we say what we believe, even if it's wrong and goes against the "accepted wisdom." But, you know what? It's the dialogue between the unabashed fans and the skeptics and the outright hostile that keep the discussions going—and that's what helps more people find out about us...and make their own decisions.

- **Go direct, avoid distribution.** Almost completely check. We made the mistake of putting on some dealers in the early days, and some distribution that didn't do us any favors. Chalk it up to a learning curve. Now, with our quasi-direct pricing coming into play in Europe through Electromod, and the clear non-necessity of any dealers in North America, we're 100% committed to staying direct. Asia is still a conundrum...but we'll see what we can do next year.

- **Run from both conventional advertising and social media both.** Check and check. I mentioned our marketing budget as being a tiny fraction of what would be normal for any other company. Part of this is due to the fact of heeding our own advice. Yes, some advertising is necessary, but we've stuck to just a couple of online venues that are completely measurable and trackable as to their actual results. If they don't pay off, the plug is pulled and the funds reallocated. We have yet to take print pages in any magazine (and the way magazines are going, I suspect we may never have to— except for one stunt for a new product I'm thinking about...hmm). At the same time, we have spent exactly zero time on Facebook or Twitter. Of course, this isn't entirely fair, because we (meaning I) have spent significant time on microsocial like here at Head-Fi. But this isn't just marketing…I enjoy writing, and I enjoy the various arguments…er, I mean *discussions*…that we get into. No ad agency would have proposed this. And most corporate lawyers would go pale at the thought of their CEO going online and, say, calling out things like "the worst customer, ever."

- **Hard work, but fun.** Yes, hell yes, and yes again. In some ways, this is the hardest thing I've ever done, but I'm having a whole lot more fun actually *making things* than I did on the agency side. But it hasn't exactly been smooth and easy, or all dancing-through-the-sprinklers. In fact, probably not a day goes by without a minor problem (out-of-stock parts, for example) and not a week goes by without something more moderate (new shipment of boards acting weird, for example.) Nothing is insurmountable, but this isn't a hands-off business, especially when we're rolling out many new products.

The Perspective of December 2013

December 2013 was the first time I could look around Schiit and legitimately say, "This feels like a real company." Of course, we were still just a handful of people, rattling around in a messy, not-yet-organized big box with ugly carpet and scuffed walls. But Theta was just a handful of people too, and the facility was never a looker. For the first time, we had a real tech area, a real assembly area, enough space for parts, an office for R&D, a listening area…and, more importantly, things were running smoothly. The team had gelled. Nobody there was perfect, but everyone did their jobs—and believed in the overall direction.

For the first time, it seemed like we'd *arrived.*

But at the same time, there was still a ton of work to do. Ragnarok still wasn't working right, after many, many firmware revisions. We were still going back and forth on DACs for the Yggdrasil, instead of moving into production. The Valhalla 2 and Lyr 2 prototypes had their own niggling problems.

And, worse...I'd gone off on some tangential stuff that looked like it might never become a product. We had one product just sitting on a desk because we were too busy working other things out. And at the same time, Mike was playing with phono stages, Dave was designing Wyrd, and I had a bunch of crazy ideas that I figured we could launch in 2014, as soon as Ragnarok and Yggdrasil were put to bed.

But without the freedom to experiment, without the ability to dream about what might be...many of our products would never have come to market. As I told Mike recently, "It says something that our only truly conventional design is Magni."

Mike laughed. "And it's essentially a small speaker amp, which is insane for a ninety-nine dollar product."

Remember: *be unique.*

So Where Do We Go From Here?

Now, 2014 didn't solve all the problems we were facing at the end of 2013. But we never expected it to. That's not how business challenges work. When you knock the current ones down, you find new ones.

But, in 2014, we were in a new position: that of being part of "the establishment." This in itself is a challenge. We've noticed a recent increase in threads that go like this: "DAC recommendation (besides Bifrost)," or "Headphone amp (not Magni or Asgard 2)." Simply by being part of the perceived "establishment" means that we can be dismissed.

Why? Plenty of reasons:

- **When "everyone else" has one, it may be enough to simply be different.** I know lots of people who don't want a Camry (or a Corvette) simply because they're "too popular," not based on any objective criteria.

- **Something new and shiny is new and shiny, period.** There's excitement in being one of the first to discover something new and good. We know this. We also know there's inevitable backlash against a perceived "flavor of the month." People were calling us the "flavor of the month" for years. Some flavors last longer than others. Only time will tell.

- **We don't make what they want.** Whether it's black gear, or DSD, or power switches on the front. And that's perfectly cool. We can't please everyone all the time.

- **They heard we're crap.** Yep, that still hangs out there. It'll never go away. We have to just keep on keeping on.

- **They had a bad experience.** This usually means they got something that didn't work out for them (like, say, an original Valhalla and LCD-2s) or we shipped them the wrong thing (it happens—and even if we fix it right away, sometimes bad feelings linger), or they got a DOA / defective product. And even though our DOA / defectives are less than 0.05% now, that still adds up when you're moving tons of products. Again, all valid reasons (though really, if you aren't sure if one of our headphone amps is ideal for your products, ask us…we'll tell you honestly, and it won't be "just buy the more expensive amp.")

But, bottom line, we aren't the new shiny anymore. We aren't the One True Challenger who will Redefine Everything, Forever.

So what do we do with this?

Well, the first step to overcoming a problem is to recognize it. We can't dismiss it out of hand. Nor do we think it's right to respond in the manner of many companies—which is to throw marketing money at it. Nor can we simply reinvent ourselves as a company making expensive audio jewelry, because, well, that's not us. Nor is it fair to our customers.

So here's what we're doing:

- **Staying where we are, and getting even better at it.** This means staying affordable, and putting the bulk of our effort towards creating truly amazing, groundbreaking, and inexpensive products. This may also entail "killing our babies," as I've said in another chapter. Because the only thing worse than bringing out a product that might cannibalize sales of your main product line is to have someone else do it first.

- **Exploring new vistas.** This doesn't mean $20,000 DACs or $15,000 amplifiers. This doesn't mean a full line of two-channel products, like conventional preamps and power amps. Nor does it mean crowdfunding or "co-creation" or any of those fancy new models that essentially say, "We have no ideas." But it *does* mean we'll be looking at how we can make a difference in the two-channel world—including in some very, very surprising new directions. But all on the affordable side. And all with some significant advantage. No me-too products.

- **Less product introductions in 2015...but with more significance.** There are some real surprises on the horizon, no kidding. At least one product...no, well, two products on the horizon for 2015 are real eye-openers. It pains me that I can't really talk about them, because the best thing besides introducing a new product is talking about it. And many of these are really far along. In fact, I'm listening to one now. Another I've been listening to for months (but it is going in for some changes to bring in some very cool trickle-down tech.)

- **Continuing this conversation, and listening to your input.** Yes, we do listen to your input, and it does help when we're developing new products. You'll see some of your own ideas reflected in the coming year. But...and here's the real but...it's just that we also have our own point of view. Call us old-fashioned, but we think that if we can't add something of our own to the product development, why are we here? Why not form a coalition and go to a contract manufacturer to realize your perfect crowdsourced dream product? If we're right, we'll do well, and if we're wrong, we'll take our lumps.

- **Continuing to challenge the established wisdom.** Whether it's product design, buzzword compliance, unicorn formats, en-vogue branded power supplies, fancy capacitor types, or any other of a dozen different things, we have a unique point of view. It's far too easy for someone to wade through a forum, look at some product websites, and decide that "well, everyone's talking about ABC, and it's gotta have XYZ, and of course it has to be isolated with SuperWowie technology, and of course it has to support rates up to 64/3472…" without knowing that everyone's talking about ABC because a big name is putting big money behind a proprietary technology, and one person said it had to have XYZ, and SuperWowie technology doesn't work at the rates that high-res is available at, and 64/3472 doesn't even have any demo tracks available, much less any music you can buy. We call out this marketing-based "common wisdom" and skewer these sacred cows. Some people like it. Some people disagree politely. And we rub some people completely the wrong way.

Because…(you know it's coming) it's not about getting *everyone* to *like* you. It's about getting *some* people to *love* you.

And that, in a nutshell, is what we're going to continue doing. It's up to you to decide if we're completely insane.

Or not.

Bonus

Mike's Yggy Backstory

Yggdrasil: The Back-Back Saga, Part 1
Pre-Digital Years

It was spring 1976.

I was back from Peru, working for Texas Instruments, wondering what I was going to do when I grew up. I sank hopelessly back into my audio habit, a mental neighborhood I hadn't visited since before Vietnam.

My best audio buddies were Mike, John, and Paul. Mike ran a janitorial business, John and Paul were mechanical geeks—they specialized in making engines for model airplanes that weighed twenty pounds or so that were still legal to fly back then. When they crashed, they killed people and occasionally started forest fires.

We'd just finished Bruno Walter's Beethoven 9th on my Quad 1956 ESLs, homebrew / modified Dyna all tube pre/poweramps, and Sony TTS-3000 Rabco arm with Decca 4RC cartridge tracking at 4 grams. I was in a goose-stepping, excited-about-audio mood.

John looked at me and said, "Let's start a company building audio electronics—you know how to make it sound incredible. It just looks like shit, and I can help you there."

Just then Paul raised a leg and anally sang a thirty-second, ten-note, atonal melody. Despite my audio reverie, I instantly sensed why he had no girlfriend.

Mike, who actually had a modicum of sensibility, offered, "At least you'll be able to hang out with civilized people," before we adjourned to the garage to escape the stench.

Thus was conceived Theta Electronics. (Not Theta Digital—that was almost ten years later.)

I was terrified. I had a wife and stepdaughter to support. I thought about what Mike said about hanging with the civilized. I was still naive; I didn't realize that audio geeks were little different from mechanical geeks and I was therefore condemned. What the hell, I'd take the plunge, but what would I build?

In the time before digital audio, audio sources were usually turntables, which meant reputation was won by the builder of the best electronics designed for turntables. So the first product was a preamp which, unlike power amps, was a product suitable for all systems, regardless of speaker.

At the time, solid-state gear had almost universally replaced older vacuum tube based hi-fi systems. (hi-fi = high fidelity = legacy speak for good sounding audio gear). This was just about the moment that most audiophiles were beginning to realize that they had been conned. Early germanium-based transistor gear made deafening noise like stuck toilets. Low bandwidth solid-state power devices sounded grainy and strained, when they weren't setting fire to your speaker or stinking up the house. To quote the Japanese, the soul of the music had been destroyed with solid state. The biggest market for the better used tube equipment was, indeed, Japan. That bid up the price of used tube gear, and there was little to no new tube gear available.

Almost all tube preamps used a variation of the same-old, same-old, two section 12AX7 active feedback EQ circuit. 12AX7 tubes were designed for table radios and those shitty phonographs like schools used to use in the 60s-80s because they were cheap. (The only cool thing about older schools were the mimeograph machines that made copies that all of the future audiophiles and drug addicts used to sniff.)

Not only were the 12AX7s cheap, but they were also designed with high gain so you don't have to use so many of them. They have terrible curves (read distortion), require lots of feedback to partially correct, and are noisy to boot. I hadn't and wouldn't use these in any of my beloved gear!

So there was this tube called a 6DJ8. It turned out that the intellectual badasses at Tektronix and Hewlett Packard used a lot of them in their oscilloscope amplifiers. They also had good curves, low distortion, and are 12db quieter than 12AX7s. I also lost the active EQ, switching to passive, which allowed my Theta Preamp to be the first 6DJ8, passive equalization, NO feedback design.

Before I was done with this company, I designed the first hi-fi hardware app for a 6BZ7 (in a power amp), and the first WE417A tube design in a head-amp (moving coil pre-pre amp) which was, indeed, the first tube head amp.

Why did I do these designs? Because they sounded better!

Now did I get rich doing this? Nope.

Did I go bankrupt? Nope.

Did I learn? You bet.

I also picked up two characteristics, neither of which I realized at the time. The first was an addiction to build audio stuff. The second was a reputation amongst audiophiles for building against-the-grain, maverick audio equipment, even if it appeared to be traditional in nature.

There were many other valuable experiences: I met Dave (Yes! *The* Dave who I still work with today that Jason mentions in his writing). I learned how to do tradeshows with hangovers and too little sleep five out of the four nights. I learned that a huge percentage of the high-end audio exhibitors were playing to their competitors and their dealers rather than their customers. Most tellingly, I learned that a loaded dealer was a loyal dealer, which often did not bode well for their customers.

Be all that as it may, I told myself I was done with audio—another grand adventure awaited me in Japan. So off I went.

The trouble was that wherever I went, my audio junkie self was there as well. So I very excitedly bought the first available compact disk player—a full year before they were available in the US! It was a cool-looking thing that played the disk vertically behind a plexiglass door.

The first CDs were Japanese pop songs—not exactly my style, but WTH, I cued it up and listened.

Just then a painful edge distracted me from the music. I wondered if one of those old-fashioned supersonic burglar alarms was in the vicinity. Slowly, it dawned on me that this system really did sound like bats with clothespins on their testicles.

The digital audio event horizon deflated with a flatulent roar.

Wow, it was as if I'd just found out that there was no tooth fairy, no more Twinkies, and no more LPs or vinyl available because Warren Buffet or whoever cornered the market all at the same time.

Stubbornly I took this player home with me and took it apart in an attempt to discover why it was so excruciatingly bad. Little did I know that this would begin the Yggdrasil back saga, which will be continued soon.

Yggdrasil: The Back-Saga, Part 2
Why Does Digital Suck?

Here I was, all dedicated to finding out why the CD player I bought in Japan sounded so terrifying. There was at that time only one problem—I didn't know shit about digital audio as applied to hi-fi.

Okay, okay, I had worked with *the* first digital-audio recorders in Peru; they were sixteen channels of 8 bit log encoding, 5 Hz sample rate machines used for oil exploration. They were for measuring ground motion as a function of increasing distance from a subterranean explosion. As far as I knew, digital audio worked great for finding pockets of oil for which to drill. So it would seem to be reasonable that it oughta sound right for hi-fi, no?

So I studied and researched what I could in a pre-Internet era. There were a few things that I accepted as creed, chiefly that the more technology changes, the more the requirements stay the same; this explains the syndrome where new doodads promising ever better performance often disappoint; the technology takes precedence over the application.

I learned that the vacuum tube, the transistor, the speaker, and the cartridge, was either invented or perfected by Bell Telephone Labs. The way that it used to be back in the day was that Bell

Telephone Labs had a monopoly on all home phone service in the US. In today's dollars, a month's worth of phone service where you had a calling radius of twenty miles cost about one hundred dollars or so. What that did was subsidize one hell of a think tank that was dedicated to developing electronics goodies; computers, TVs, radios, etc. They made it possible, among many other nifty hardware apps, to hear announcers at baseball games, not only in the ballpark but at home!

Turns out they also developed and propounded information theory and digital audio well before there was hardware to implement the same: papers date from 1912 to 1916. This even before the US got sucked into World War 1!

But I get ahead of myself. After all, you have to crawl before you can walk. I had to look at current CD players. There had to be some things one could do to make digital audio palatable.

It turns out that the D/A converter chips are the most expensive chips in the whole CD player. The first CD players in Japan cost 380,000 yen, or north of a kilobuck!

A great way to save money was to use only one DAC chip function for both channels—one stereo channel converted and then the other; no kiddin'! No way for the two channels to ever be in proper phase.

That had to be it! So I bought another DAC, duplicated everything else, and fed the DACs (now two) at the same time to fix the coherence problem. It got coherent! There was an incremental change. I was excited!

Mike came by, listened a bit, and curled his lip. I put the turntable back on—he was right.

Next I got rid of sample and hold amps and replaced them with brick-walled amps. Another improvement!

Mike came by again, curled his lip again.

Paul showed up, listened for about ten seconds. He then opined to no one in particular: "The corn kernels are gone, but it's still a turd."

Mike, his sensibilities temporarily abandoned, nodded approvingly.

The solution had to be simple, I told myself. By this time, 2nd generation CD players were out. I settled on a Toshiba Model with 1 DAC chip per channel, did my usual mods, and hooked up my scope to the digital end of the DAC.

I thought, "What are those just awful-looking fuzzy edges on the digital waveforms?" No one was calling it jitter yet, but it occurred to me that that would convert to some really random wow and flutter (a forgotten analog turntable and tape recorder spec that really is not obsolete in the digital audio era).

So I re-clocked the whole deal from the DAC chip back with crystals and PLLs. The digital waveforms were far less fuzzy. I hooked it up yet again. I listened for two or three evenings before I convened the cast of usual judges.

Mike listened quietly, while Paul picked his nose. Both were quiet, requesting more music, inscrutable faces. After an eternity, Mike exclaimed, "There's actually an image."

Paul grunted in agreement. "Violins still kinda suck," Paul said, "but it's kinda ballsy for rock."

That was fine with me. Progress, I thought.

I began to recommend and modify these players for an ever-widening group of audiophiles. One of them, Dick Olsher, wrote for *Stereophile* and gave me some kind words. Everyone basically said the same thing: "Not bad for digital."

Another one of the early adopters was a math professor at the University of Iowa named John Lediaev. Classical music geek and true TWAD (Tree Worshiping Analog Druid). He got interested in the whole digital audio sojourn and gave great input.

Meanwhile, Phillips came out with a multi-rate 4x chipset and CD player! (Multi-rate=different input and output digital frequencies, in this case 4x up or oversampling.) This meant that the signal rate to the DAC was 176.4KHz instead of 44.1KHz, allowing a much gentler analog filter than the brickwall filters required before which by comparison rang like old telephones.

So I rushed to buy one of these new boxes, hooked it up and

listened in amazement at the total lack of consistency in any property at all: image, tonal balance, etc. The only saving grace was a less harsh / edgy top end—logical for the much softer filter. The oversampling approach used a Phillips provided DSP chip. In those days, it was called a digital filter chip.

Reverse engineering of the Phillips digital filter chip, (as well as virtually all other subsequent ones by other manufacturers—up to this day) all utilize a frequency domain (read flat) algorithm, which has no mathematical solution, only a succession of approximations. (Read close—horseshoes.) Worse yet, it does not keep the original samples—it throws them away and *approximates* new ones. Ugh.

I wondered why all of these filters used this method of derivation. In a flash of brilliance reserved for the obvious, it came to me that this algorithm is efficient (cheap) and gives good measurement (very flat).

There were also a variety of tool kits and developmental software available to buy devoted to this algorithm only. This simplified things—making it relatively easy for anyone to develop such a filter. There was no need to hire and babysit socially handicapped genius savants who needed cages as well as food and water pushed under the door from time to time in order to develop a proper filter.

I decided to consult my old Bell Telephone Labs seventy-year-old-at-the-time references.

Wow, not only did they discuss the common-frequency-domain one, but a time-domain one as well! Now here we go!

Well, the problem was the time-domain one was that the frequency-response curve looked like an anthill. (It turned out later that a competitor actually used this very algorithm.)

Out of this knowledge two new conclusions arose. The first was that oversampling digital filters were important—to keep the decoded audio from ultrasonically cleaning windows and loosening tooth fillings. The second was that whatever audio information remained in the original audio samples could *not* be lost.

I called John Lediaev back and told him we had to combine time and frequency domain optimization for digital filters.

He told me it couldn't be done because it required a divide by zero, and by the way, why did I want to do it anyway. So I told him I wanted to beat the sound of analog with digital audio. Instantly he said, "There's **no** way—it can't be done."

A stubborn kernel of determination blew up in me like an air bag. "Hell with him!" I thought, "I'll show him!" One of the manifestations of my audio insanity is that if anybody ever tells me I can't do something, I will move heaven and earth to get it done.

But there was a problem: intuitively I knew I couldn't get it done without the combination of the two algorithms with the original samples preserved. If there were anyone on the planet sufficiently motivated and capable, it was him. A bonus was I really liked and admired the guy and wanted to work with him.

Sooooooooooooooo I told him, "I bet *you* can't friggin' combine the two optimizations **and** keep the original samples."

Silence… More silence. I had him!

He finally said, "Give me some time."

But I was still overburdened; I knew a DSP engine of some kind had to be built and programmed. This was a big deal in the mid 1980s. It was a lot of research and hardware.

So a week or so later I was reading all about TI DSP processors, when I heard a noise that sounded like a combination of a twenty-year-old power lawnmower and a coffee can full of nuts and bolts slowly rolling down a steel staircase. The turquoise 1964 Toyota Corona out back with white smoke coming out of its exhaust and black smoke coming out from under the hood confirmed it. There was only one person I knew who drove cars that were so f'ed-up that cops, reluctant to deal with crazies, balked at stopping them. I used to wonder how he got so broke, but later came to realize he was just cheap. I mean, this car was such a loser that you couldn't actually give it to a charity, even if you hauled it to them.

In any event, out stepped a grinning Dave, and I knew the team was complete.

Yggdrasil: The Back-Saga, Part 3
Frankenstein Cometh

So here I was, at home in Sherman Oaks, occasionally modifying a Toshiba CD player, struggling with the necessary space to not only continue modding CD players, but to actually begin prototype manufacturing with eccentric personalities who were either total night owls used to eating lunch at midnight (Dave and myself), or wannabe farmers who got up at 4:00 a.m. (John).

The bottom line was that I needed an office / workspace where any and all had access. At the time, I had some bucks saved, but with little money coming in, I was interested in cheap.

I found a quaint, windowless, 400 square foot office in Van Nuys for $160 per month. It was two blocks from the regional courthouse and cop headquarters, free parking, and was surrounded by a wide variety of interesting businesses, both in and out of the building! We had bail bondsmen, VD clinics, criminal lawyers, and travel agents with "send money back home" windows in the back. (All of my time in South America had paid off—I could actually read all of the business signage!) We had a variety of some of the best Mexican food anywhere, offered by dozens of competing restaurants.

The neighbors in the building were ambulance-chasing lawyers upstairs, sports equipment and computer vendors on the ground floor, and a low-budget movie studio in the basement. The neighborhood, although a blatant dump, was quite safe, because of the proximity of the court and supporting police. The local economy was cash based on the transactions of those without proper US documentation—robberies were nearly unknown.

Oh, and did I say? It was CHEAP!

One of our local characters was Russ, the local trash raider / recycler / hoarder guy who lived in the driver's seat of his 1964 Pontiac Bonneville. The car was filled up to the window line with trash, except for a hollowed-out area, which was the driver's seat and floor. This car was incredibly degraded, but no worse than the average car driven by other Van Nuys denizens. The cops tolerated him because he helped clean up the neighborhood. Besides, he was prone to loud, incoherent babbling and was probably too much hassle to mess with. Now, he would grab anything lying the alley. He was a skinny guy, so much so that I was impressed when I saw him pick up a huge drunken lady who was passed out next to a dumpster. When he was trying to gently place her in his trunk to recycle her, she awoke and took great umbrage at his rescue attempt, running for her orphaned bottle of Night Train Express Wine.

Please pardon the nostalgia.

The neighborhood was also a learning experience for me. For example, I never knew what a "fluffer" was until I toured the movie studio in the basement. What is even more of a riot is that they are considered part of the costume department!

But I digress.

Dave got a day job at this company who sealed together leak-proof plastic liners together that were 1/8' thick. They lined landfills, copper mine work areas, and small nations. This was to make the products or services offered at the sites environmentally and legally compliant.

So, to seal the plastic together, they used RF power proper to megawatt international radio stations. The voltages on the power tubes were so high that you could literally pull arcs off the sealing machine that were six feet long. It was better than a 1950's science fiction movie set! The place smelled like the immediate aftermath of hundreds of simultaneous thunderstorms. Trouble was, all of the cold drinks in the building would heat up. Dave was fearless.

Meanwhile, back in Van Nuys, we started working on this contraption we would eventually call a "Frankenstein."

The power supply was a collection of surplus power supplies on a rack panel that weighed just slightly less than a refrigerator with the added bonus of sharp edges that could rip huge gashes in your hands.

The next thing we needed was a DSP engine to implement the John Lediaev-derived filter. The circuit board was laid out by

Dave—right after the earth cooled the boards were laid out on transparent plastic sheets with black tape of various widths for the traces. They also used "donuts" of various sizes and different holes specced with "C" holes, "B" holes, and of course "A" holes for the pads. There was a time when we cut the layout all of the way through about ¾ of the way to the top, cut out another huge section, and taped it back together with transparent tape. Try that with modern CAD systems!

In those days, they still sold blank boards that you could expose to light, soak in radioactive-toxic-waste-looking 40W chemicals, which left permanent stains on your trays and fingers, and drill all of the holes by hand. We did just that with the prototype Frankenstein DSP 2 layer boards! We drilled our own holes and put jumpers through the boards to simulate plated through holes—the hardware apparently worked!

We had only three remaining problems: the first was that we had no one foolhardy enough to program the Texas Instruments 16-bit DSP processors in direct machine language. Neither could we afford the thousands of dollars to buy the TI proprietary software compilers and assemblers to do it. We were stumped.

Well, my dad used to say that when the student was ready, the teacher will appear.

It turns out I had this Toshiba modified CD player local customer named Tom who worked at a think tank in Santa Monica. He had more graduate degrees than I had fingers and was the type who would try any mental exercise at least once. He was blind as a bat, walked around squinting, and smoked like a chimney.

I gave him the datasheets and programmer's guide. A few weeks later—voila! We had a working implementation of the filter that we could look at on the scope.

The second remaining problem was I needed to convert the DSP output to analog—we needed to make another circuit board with the toxic waste chemicals. We did, it got stuffed with parts (multi-bit DACs, the only kind available then), and we were ready to listen to audio—except for the third problem: there were no digital outputs on any CD players back then. (This was still the early eighties.)

What I had to do was hack up the Toshiba Player with the bit, word, and data digital signals, and graft them into the DSP board to make it all work.

The contraption was complete!

Contraption it was—you needed a wheelbarrow to carry it around. It was a CD player hard-wired to a DSP / converter box, both of which were in turn hard-wired to the huge power supply.

In a rare moment of genius, I installed connectors in the wire harnesses between all of the boxes—all of the connectors were actually different so that it was impossible to screw up plugging it together. The device became portable and shippable! The true Frankenstein was born!

So I hooked it up to the rest of the system, and invited all of the usual suspects by to listen.

Mike was silent, very silent…a faint nod of approval.

Paul also said very little, no disgusting utterances.

Dave, who was usually silent unless asked a question, responded with his usual "Weigh-ulllllllllllllllll…"

Tom was mumbling something about fixed versus floating point math implementation in DSP processors.

I did NOT hook up the turntable.

It was time to build another unit and send it to John Lediaev.

A couple of weeks later John had the opportunity to listen to his brand-new Frankenstein. He opined what eventually became the four dreaded words: "Pretty good for digital."

At that moment I realized I needed to listen to my analog system again. He was right.

Notwithstanding, I built probably fifteen to twenty or so Frankensteins and sold them by word of mouth to my Toshiba CD Player customers. Dick Olsher at Stereophile even mentioned them. It was very meager income, in spite of the fact that the team had a lot of time invested in this thing. We'd endured a small office with a freak show in the basement in a dumpy neighborhood for years.

I was frustrated—there was no way to mass produce them. They had to be hacked in to whatever CD player the user had. I was at an impasse, until Sony and Phillips actually got together and announced S/PDIF! The Sony/Phillips Digital Interface. Within a few months, CD players from both companies appeared on the market with coaxial digital outputs!

Excitedly, I added an S/PDIF interface to a Frankenstein. I now had the basis to build not only a prototype, but a salable product.

The notion of a D/A converter that could be added to any digital audio device with S/PDIF connectivity was born! A new product category!

However, I couldn't sell tacos to starving millionaires—I knew I needed a marketer.

So I called an old acquaintance who I knew could sell ice to eskimos, and even better than that, loved audio. I told him what I was doing and could we work together. He said that he had just agreed to get involved with a company who was going to make CD players with tube analog. I explained that that was like putting makeup on a really ugly person, they remain ugly, just less so, but he was unswayed.

In those days, the audiophile scene was really emotionally polarized between analog and digital. Ana-philes and digi-philes were like Democrats and Republicans. The analog guys knew that their stuff really sounded better, but that digital was on the upswing. The digital guys knew time was on their side, and the digital sound could only improve. Kinda like Miley Cyrus and Merle Haggard at the same show at the same time.

So I called another audio/lover marketer who was starting a tube audio electronics company in his garage. He took the audio-as-a-religion approach with me, preaching that how could a former tube audio product maker like me descend into digital, after all that was why I was located in a shitty neighborhood. I took the high road and avoided telling him that I may be in a shitty neighborhood, but you're in a friggin' garage.

I went down the list, but could not find a taker.

I felt like the high school senior who couldn't get a prom date no matter what. I knew I had the best working digital product concept, but couldn't move it even with bran.

What to do?

Yggdrasil: The Back-Saga, Part 4
The Theta Digital Years

So a year or so later, the marketer I had originally approached, Neil, had once again become available from the Tube CD Player Company and gave me a call. I was thrilled! He was the kind of a guy who could get away (in the days before Internet and email) a phone campaign to put our product in every dealer in the country that mattered.

You see, back in those days, it was a different world. There was no acceptable infrastructure to launch a direct sales audio company.

The systems were more fiddly (think turntable), larger (think big listening room, not surrounding a computer), and far more expensive in 1980's dollars. Also, a dealer served up necessary functions in an era when there were no bloggers. The only data available on audio were in the magazines. There was no convenient way for the ordinary user to contribute opinion except by hanging out at dealers, a few clubs / users groups, and inviting each other over for the equivalent of what has now become mini-meets.

Also, since the users were then as odd as they are today (look around you at any meet), the dealer provided not just the heavy lifting in terms of turntable setup and system install, but also functioned as the therapist / counselor, albeit with biases according to which lines he carried. Even though the very presence of dealers nearly doubled the prices, they were a very necessary component of sales at the time.

My duties then were as they are today: produce and design a line of digital products with proper familial integration.

If I were to design the aesthetics, the products would have been as ugly as the original Theta Electronics products, so then Neil (and today Jason) made them suitably aesthetic.

But before we built anything, we had to name the company, so Neil suggested that we call it Theta Digital to link my earlier company to the new one.

That was simple. Then was the agony of the first product.

Neil lobbied we go from the top down in terms of products. The tricky part was to figure out how to configure the first product, difficult since there were no other D/A converter product models. Do we integrate it into a preamp with digital inputs as well as analog ones? Or do we configure it as a digital-in, analog-out box required to be hooked up to another preamp. Not being sure, I built both, the Theta DSPre and the Theta DSPro.

The DSPro outsold the DSPre significantly, but we were committed—we had to keep both in the line. Further, the norm at the time was everybody building electronics offered both black and silver (clear anodize) finishes. So we started out with four SKUs, which needless to say increased our cost and decreased our inventory velocity significantly.

Of course, this made our products more expensive, but still far less than that of our eventual fellow DAC makers: Wadia within a year, Krell a year or so later, eventually the high-end ROW (rest of the world).

And so we continued. Neil relaxed, seldom leaving his house, running his phone campaign to put us together a first-class dealer network at just the right pace to keep me permanently backordered. It was my job not just to design the line, but to produce the products; to run the factory / operations of the whole deal.

Along the way, I learned quite a few things.

The best way to learn them is to screw up. The first run of Theta DSPros had a 30% failure rate. I learned all about eutectic solder, rigid static procedures, and selecting good assembly houses, which Schiit still uses today.

I learned about component crib deaths, the benefits of burning-in my products. I learned about the tragedy of even one failure of any Theta Product and how much that really costs us. I improved our reliability to the point where we offered free FedEx two-day both-way shipping for repairs. (FedEx was a very big deal back then—exclusive and expensive).

I learned that service needs to be instant; that it also needs to be friendly; and this was the best way to build goodwill. By this time we were shipping hundreds of units per month.

I learned that the biggest mistake I could possibly make was to hire a manger to deal with my assemblers, tech, front office people, and inventory / shipping people. It just insulates me from the people I need the most and causes resentment all around.

I put in a bonus system tied to production, reliability, and on-time shipping equal to the manager's salary and learned some more.

I learned if you treat a crew like imbeciles, you get the same. If you treat them as self-supporting adults, guess what you get! They correct problems they see and in one case, even push out those who will not pull their own weight.

I learned what employees really care about. It's not platitudes or company rah-rah cheerleading or fucking turkeys or cards.

It's money… What a shock.

When we gave employees a multi-thousand dollar Christmas bonus (a big deal twenty-five years ago), they will follow you anywhere, be self-policing, and require little of your remedial time. Moreover, they cared about what we were doing and were proud to be a part of it.

I also learned that there was a very small percentage of customers who were abusive; they were the 2% of our users who were 98% of our trouble. They would call and have our secretaries in tears.

I learned that it was far better to refund them and tell them it was on the condition they never buy anything from us again. We have to be at work a significant percentage of our lives, and it should be as pleasant as possible, even with a goal of being fun. The better we do, the better the morale; all I had to do most of the time once the self-policing workforce was set up was stay out of the way.

Speaking of staying out of the way, Neil, who we seldom saw, was marketing us into continued prosperity and never-ending back orders. He was amazing!

Oh, and lest I forget, all during this time of Theta's growth there was another audio company in a neighboring building run in a much more corporate manner.

In their employ was a young engineer (late twenties). He was intelligent, street smart, and nearly as irreverent as I am. He hadn't yet learned to take a look around at his audio peers and stop taking himself so seriously, but he's improving at that today. He was still trying to figure out what he wanted to do when he grew up, but then again, so am I as of now. He was a great engineer, but kept babbling about marketing. We began to hang out a lot, and he was just like a blotter, sucking up every Theta experience I had.

He had a sardonic sense of humor—but, before I get there, there is a backstory. At Theta we worked with a recovered cocaine addict named Fred Caccione (name changed). So one day, I walked into the Theta production men's room and looked up on the wall to see a new poster: "The Fred Caccione Cocaine Weight Loss Program" then something about white powder, no fussy diets, appetite reduction, and send $50,000 for your first ninety days supply."

I laughed my ass off, and Fred thought it was just as funny as I did.

By the way, if you haven't figured it out, that engineer was none other than Jason Stoddard. This was the first of a series of posters from my current Schiit co-founder. He was starting to loosen up!

There were some good times there. We were like a big family, with enough dysfunction to make it terribly interesting. I had a secretary named Ann (again not the real name). She was one I had rescued from an abusive customer by firing and refunding him. She was in her early twenties, amazingly cute, and had an aura of innocence. I always followed the never schiit where you eat rule, and as a result was always well trusted by my female staff.

One day she walked into my office, closed the door, and said to me very seriously, "I have to show this to somebody."

She then began to unfasten her pants. My eyes were enlarging as she turned around and revealed a bare rear end so perfect that da Vinci himself could not have done it justice. There was a still-healing tattoo of a rose on her upper right ass cheek.

Turning around, she asked me what I thought. I told her that the tattoo was beautiful. Relieved, she pulled her pants back up and thanked me. I could tell she really meant it.

So one day Jason comes over to my house for a batch of Mike's famous margaritas. He mentions that Theta, (which now was a multimillion-dollar company with three lines of DACs and a couple lines of transports, as well as accessories) needed a cheaper series of DACs. He already has a name (Cobalt), an industrial design, and a price. Even though we were probably drunk (we only got drunk once—it just lasted about ten or twenty years), we worked the electronic design out quick, even with jitter reduction to fit the projected $600 price. ($360 direct equivalent.)

The outcome was that Theta sold not thousands, but tens of thousands, of those. Lots of money. He was really right.

Even in my mid forties, I still had the idealistic high-end attitude, kick all of the other high-end, pretentious companies selling jewel-encrusted, over-machined, arbitrary-industro, neo-art, angular-looking, waaaaaay overpriced crap. I was all about making high-performing products with money sunk into performance, not sculpture.

Further, in the early 1990s, the DAC chip technology had peaked with the PCM63, IMHO the best fuckin' audio-branded DAC ever made.

The new marketing direction was delta-sigma DACs, which I have flamed many times before, as being bit non-perfect, full of bad math, and noise glare, etc. These were proliferating, with cookbook spec sheets and reference designs published so that even non-engineers could design them.

This meant that anyone could build a DAC, and with the fall in prices on the new "audio-branded, shitty-sounding parts, that everybody and his brother were coming out with me-too DACs with no value other than cheapest. Even big audio corporations that never had built digital products were hiring dishwashers and landfill workers to design DACs.

What was worse was all of the good DACs were disappearing. Even the new multi-bit PCM1704 DAC sounded like ass compared to the PCM63.

It was time to get out of the DAC business. So I sold my portion of Theta to Neil. I decided once again what to do when I grew up—only to set myself down the most excruciating path I had traveled since Viet Nam...

Yggdrasil, the Back-Saga Part 5
A Home Theater Detour

So, in the early nineties, I was trying to figure out what I wanted to be when I grew up again. DAC design had become unrewarding as the good building blocks were disappearing from the chip makers, new DACs were beginning to appear as elementary school science projects, due to the cookbook approach of the new "audio DACs", and I was looking for a virgin territory for the high-end.

Home theater—perfect!

The competition was produced from companies whose priorities were to produce equipment which adhered to Dolby technical standards—not to sound priorities which I had been honing over the last fifteen years or so at that time.

At that time, videophiles had laser disc-based systems (DVDs had not yet appeared). Dolby Pro-Logic was the encode / decode standard of the day. The competing products were principally analog designs, and all had terrible UIs that required considerable attention to learn.

So, I produced the Angstrom 200 HED (Home Entertainment Director) all digital surround sound decoder / stereo D/A converter.

It had such an easy-to-use UI that you could set up the unit intuitively, all digital pro-logic decoding, and was by far and away the best-sounding unit on the market. It won design awards, was amazingly well reviewed, and was ready for sale.

The problem was that even though I had ponied my licensing

fees, I had to await the appropriate licensor test and blessing. I was in a queue and it took a while to get through it.

Lesson #1 was that licensed products are never released on my time, regardless of how much I have invested in the parts and how soon I need to turn my inventory. Not to mention how much my customers want it.

Lesson #2 was that high-end audio dealers were almost never equipped to handle home theater customer support issues, other than take the equipment to the house, hook it up whether set up properly or not, collect the money, and leave. That left us to do the customer support. Bummer.

Lesson #3 was that there was a whole new crop of installers who had their own trade show who were really the main players in home theater. The customers would give a budget to the installer, and the installer would select and install the equipment. Totally changed the to whom marketing vector. The show was CEDIA, by the way, and I was the first of the old high-end guard exhibiting there.

So, AC-3 laser discs began to appear—the laser disc solution was to RF modulate a carrier—the first step of the Dolby Digital process was to demodulate the signal. There was a special purpose demodulator chip available to do just that. The problem was that there was no channel through which to buy them in the US. The only way was to develop our own grey market channel for the parts (Japan or Hong Kong), which was quite an endeavor in the pre-Internet era of telexes, and pre-phone deregulation era of very expensive overseas phone calls.

Lesson #4 was that this whole home theater deal is really a big corporation's arena. I got the parts (some six months after all of the giants)—and came out with an AC-3 (Now Dolby Digital) adapter for the Angstrom 200—then waited for Dolby to approve the product (Repeat Lesson #1) I was a year late, and my customers were pissed. Lesson #4 again.

Somewhere along the way, DTS capability was added to the Angstrom 200—I still cared about industry firsts.

About that time, DVDs and DVD players appeared. No more need for demodulators. Cheaper software. Time to come out with a cheaper model. The Angstrom 100 HED appeared, based on a Crystal Semiconductor Codec and a Zoran DSP engine. I now had a big HED and a little HED.

("So I got a little HED and it totally changed my perspective on home theater." He'll never admit it but that was totally Jason's idea.)

Months later, Dolby approved the Angstrom 100, and it was released to a user base that largely already purchased other gear.

Shortly after that, the sold Angstrom 100s began to return, with blown-up Crystal Semiconductor codecs. I called their engineering support. They insisted that my power supplies were improperly designed. I countered that they were the same power supplies I had used in several other Crystal Semiconductor designs.

The returns continued to pile up. I continued to replace the parts until they called me admitting that the codecs they had already shipped me did not work well with my improperly designed power supplies, and they were going to replace them with a different date code of parts. I kept on going with the new parts, finally fixing the failing in the field units.

Lesson #5 – If you can't afford a lawsuit, you are screwed.

Lesson #6 – If you can afford a lawsuit, you are still screwed.

It was too late—I was doomed. I shut it down. I lost a lot of money, but along the way I had still made more.

Let me count the ways why manufacturing to someone's licensed technologies suck.

a. You are doing all of the heavy lifting and taking all of the risk for your licensor.

b. You are entering into a crony-based association where the licensor will always do what is best for him in his time.

c. You surrender certain freedoms—inability to ship pending licensor's approval, subject to licensor's priorities and other relationships.

Not to mention lessons #1 through 6 above.
So is Schiit going to do home theater?
Over my dead body.
When hell freezes over.
When shrimps learn to whistle.
I know, but just in case I was vague, NO.

Coda: One Year Later

The Perspective of December 2014

OKAY. LET ME GET THIS off my chest now: introducing twelve products in one year is too much. Yes, even when half of them were updates, and two of them variations on the updates.

Twelve? Yes, twelve.

A nice, familiar, comfortable dozen (well, unless you like that easy metric-system stuff, where 10 is a better number.)

Let's count:

- Wyrd
- Optical Modi
- Sys
- Valhalla 2
- Lyr 2
- Mani
- Ragnarok
- Fulla
- Magni 2
- Magni 2 Uber
- Modi 2
- Modi 2 Uber

When we introduce this many products in a year, it naturally lights people up with a lot of questions. Why did we go bonkers and introduce so many new products in 2014? Will we do this again?

I'll answer all of these—and get into the whole whys and

wherefores of the Magni / Modi 2 / Ubers a bit later. First, let's start with what we learned.

Hard Business Lessons

If you're thinking of starting your own business, or running one right now, this is probably the most important part—something that can be boiled down to heeding our own advice about "keeping it simple, stupid."

Because we end 2014 as our most successful year ever—and, at the same time, asking ourselves pointed questions about the future.

Here's what we learned.

12 intros in a year is too many with our engineering resources. And probably even with additional resources. We have nobody to blame for this except ourselves. Early in the year, I put up a whiteboard in my office and outlined all of our possible / planned products and numbered them. I came up with 16. Three died in the Valkyrie experimentation, and one missed (Yggdrasil.) Even at that point in time, I knew that an average intro of over one product per month was logistically painful—or perhaps even impossible. We are lucky that only one product had significant issues, and that only one product missed its intro date. So how many products makes sense? I'll get to that.

12 intros is also probably too much for good marketing impact. If you're hitting the press with a dozen new products—especially when they are concurrent—it makes it hard to digest. The intro of the second-gen Magni and Modi coming right after Fulla was not ideal, but our hands were forced by production delays. The initial plan was Fulla in August / September and Magni / Modi 2 in mid November. Yeah. There you go. Fewer products, more widely spaced, allows the press to absorb, digest, and comment on the new stuff, before you hit them again. What's the ideal timing? I'll get to that, too.

Each product has many more complexities than you expect. Yeah, it's one thing to have a working PC board, and it's another thing to be shipping. Even getting to a fully working board can be challenging. But, to get to shipping, you need to:

- Have that fully working PC board—in our case, we will go through 2-5 revisions of the initial proto to make it right

- Have the firmware fully functional, tested, and busted—and, in some cases, this means multiple firmwares, as with Modi 2 Uber, which has both a microprocessor and a USB input that need to be programmed. And by "busted," we mean, "hand it to some people and have them do everything crazy they can think of, including pushing all the buttons simultaneously, pushing the buttons on power-up or down, etc.

- Have a working, fitting, cosmetically perfect chassis in large quantities, ready to go—again, we usually go through a couple of revisions on this, though some of our chassis are at "Revision J" by the time they're released to production...but then you're waiting for production to arrive, and crossing your fingers that it's perfect.

- Have any knobs / buttons in large quantities—see above, though it's usually just one rev and we're done

- Have all the fasteners for that chassis in large quantities—surprisingly nontrivial, especially in the case of complex products like Ragnarok and custom stuff like we use with Fulla...Ragnarok uses literally two dozen different screws / nuts / standoffs / washers / spacers / etc.

- Have any custom insulators / etc. for that chassis in large quantities—see the two products above, which use either custom Sorbothane parts, or custom electrical insulation parts

- Have all the parts for the PC boards (and we can be talking hundreds to thousands of parts, each and every one of which might make finishing the product impossible—talk to Alex about this...)

- Have complete documentation necessary for the PC board assembly house, including any special test procedures—or what you get back from them might not be, well, what you expect

- Have your team ready for any new assembly challenges—especially with complex products like Ragnarok

- Have a shipping box that will protect the product tested, busted, and ready to go—sounds simple, but a cheap, sturdy box is not as trivial as you think…put a prototype in it and ship it across the country a few times to check

- Have a manual for the product fully written and ready to go in the box—no manual, no time? Then you'd better at least have online instructions. But really, a manual. Seriously.

- Have the technicians and final sound-check guys ready to test the product—if they don't know what to expect, again, brace yourself for the unexpected

- Have at least one staff member ready to answer questions about the product, based on actually having used it—again, sounds simple, but this really isn't trivial

And this is in addition to all the marketing stuff:

- Product description—what is it, what does it do, why is it special, how is it different? Yes, I know lots of people don't read, but you do need this.

- Product photography—and I'm not talking photos with your iPhone. Even if it is an iPhone 6. Get some professional work done.

- Specifications. Testing, retesting, confirmation, and more testing, decisions on claims (even if your products measure 0.0004% THD, are you comfortable claiming this, in all systems, on all analyzers?)

- Press release—an email release in PR-speak that tells the press you are serious, and covers all the basics about the product, including price and availability

- Community announcements—like on head-fi.org
- Facebook, if you're crazy enough to do that
- Product FAQ—it really does help. You should do one. And sit back the first day and watch the online feedback so you can add to it.
- Excerpts and links to any early reviews—if you have them
- Anything else—stunts, videos, laser-etching your logo on the moon, skydivers, rockets, soda dispensers in bathrooms, whatever, yeah, marketing is stupid, but cover the first stuff before "anything else"

This giant-ass list above applies to updated products as well. Yes, it does. Don't tell yourself it doesn't. Updates, real updates, give you a shortcut in only one place: chassis. You may be able to use something very similar, and cut down on the rev cycle. But that's about it. A revised product is a new product, unless you are so stunningly cynical you're gonna reprogram it a bit and slap a "2" on it.

The line may now be too large. When you look at it, we have a hell of a lot of options. Which is really cool, because not everyone likes the same thing. But we are getting into "confusion by profusion," so this is something we'll have to look at. Don't panic—we're not thinking of killing off anything, but we will be trying to make it more clear how the different options stack up...and, of course, we're going to weigh any additions to the product line very carefully in the future. Again, don't panic—I think we have a pretty good grasp of where the shortcomings are...and this does not preclude moving into different markets (more "traditional" preamps and power amps...though our evolving ideas are very much non-traditional...)

Harsh? No, realistic. Again, want to start a business? You're gonna have to be realistic. You need to step back, look at what you've done, and evaluate it as Spock-like and dispassionately as possible.

Am I down on Schiit? No, not at all. It's the most exciting thing I've done, ever…and the stuff we do have coming is, well, pretty darn wowie. Looking at it dispassionately, even.

Would I have done things differently, introduced less products this year? Maybe. Not sure. Get back to me on that one later.

The Ideal Scenario

"Okay, so what would be an ideal number of products for the year?" you ask.

Cool. Let me preface this by the fact that I'm not a trained, professional product manager, and I never spent any time at a big company that introduces dozens, or hundreds of products a year. So this applies to niche businesses…maybe only niche audio businesses…or maybe only Schiit.

I think it's about 4 products per year.

Why?

Engineering-wise, it's a comfortable rate. At least for us. Our engineering cycles usually start with "what ifs" more than a year before the product is a reality. But once we've decided we have a product to do, 3 months between releases allows engineering to concentrate fully on the product, rather than pinballing between several different ones.

Production-wise, it fits very well with typical cycles. Metal has a cycle of 6-8 weeks, and finding all the other parts can take another few weeks, and dealing with out-of-stock parts, first articles, and production ramp-up is another few weeks. Releasing every three months allows you to work through the issues on one product at a time, which is much more sanity-inducing than several.

Marketing-wise, it's ideal. Think about it. You introduce a new product, and everyone's talking about it for a month. Another month, and you get the inevitable "it ain't that great" people coming out of the woodwork. Another month, and it's settled down into the line well, and the press who were excited about it have moved on to different products...so when you introduce a new product, they're ready to hear about it again.

"So you're not going to introduce more than 4 products per year from now on?" you ask. "If you go over that, the world will implode?"

No. Not at all. I'm just saying that from a technical and marketing standpoint, it seems like 4 per year is ideal. The number might even be lower.

So Where Do We Go From Here?

Well, we are definitely going to be keeping to our same basic philosophy. You won't see much change there. If you're into this whole "vision" thing, you could say that our vision is *completely upending the value—and the values—of high-end audio.*

In other words, let's make affordable stuff and have some fun. Sounds simple? You haven't been around high-end audio much, have you?

In any case, again, you'll be the judge of whether we're crazy or not.

Let us know. And don't be shy about sharing your own stories...about your own improbable start-ups.

www.ingramcontent.com/pod-product-compliance
Lightning Source LLC
Chambersburg PA
CBHW070849180526
45168CB00005B/1752